MONEY AND CAPITAL MARKETS

SECOND EDITION

MONEY AND CAPITAL MARKETS

Pricing, Yields and Analysis

Second Edition

Michael Sherris

Routledge
Taylor & Francis Group

LONDON AND NEW YORK

First published 1996 by Allen & Unwin

Published 2020 by Routledge
2 Park Square, Milton Park, Abingdon, Oxon OX14 4RN
605 Third Avenue, New York, NY 10017

Routledge is an imprint of the Taylor & Francis Group, an informa business

National Library of Australia
Cataloguing-in-Publication
entry:

Sherris, Michael.

Money and capital markets.

2nd ed.
Bibliography.
Includes index.
ISBN 1 86448 159 5.

1. Securities. 2. Money market. 3. Financial
instruments Australia. 4. Money market-Australia. I.
Title.

332.0994

Set in 10/12 pt Times by DOCUPRO, Sydney

ISBN-13: 9781864481594 (pbk)

To my parents, Des and Ruth,
and to my wife, Mary

Contents

Preface to the Second Edition

Financial markets around the world have undergone major changes over the last decade. Deregulation and internationalisation have increased the complexity and competitiveness of financial markets. In this environment, money and capital market professionals require a sound understanding of the principles underlying the pricing and analysis of a wide range of financial transactions. This book aims to assist in that understanding.

Most mathematics of finance texts only provide the basic techniques required to analyse financial transactions and do not apply the mathematical techniques to financial market transactions. Other texts specifically directed to financial market transactions are often too technical and specialise in the coverage of particular transactions such as fixed interest securities, futures, swaps or options.

This book has been designed to provide a comprehensive basis for the analysis of financial transactions in money and capital markets. A wide range of examples are provided to illustrate the techniques and their application. Most of the book is written at an introductory level so that readers with limited knowledge of the mathematics of finance can work through the book and gain a better understanding of the fundamental basis for price and yield calculations and the analysis of financial transactions.

The first four chapters cover the price and yield calculations for short and long-term interest bearing securities. Chapter 1 develops the pricing formulae for short-term securities such as bills of exchange, commercial paper and short-term government securities. Chapter 2 develops the yield formulae for short-term securities and the techniques required to analyse transactions involving short-term securities to allow for sale prior to maturity, funding costs, transaction costs and taxation. Chapters 1 and 2 use the principles of simple interest and simple discount which are the basis for pricing and yield calculations for short-term securities. Chapter 3 covers the pricing of long-term securities including Treasury bonds.

These calculations are based on the principles of compound interest which are developed in this chapter. Chapter 4 covers yield calculations and techniques for the analysis of transactions involving long-term securities. The analytical techniques covered include yield analysis for variable interest rate securities such as floating rate notes, reinvestment analysis, sale prior to maturity or holding period analysis, allowing for transaction costs and a detailed coverage of the effect of Australian tax on security transactions. Chapter 4 concludes with an analysis of bond switches (or bond swaps) using the techniques covered in the chapter.

Chapter 5 is more mathematical than the other chapters, requiring a basic knowledge of differential calculus. The chapter covers the measures used to assess the interest rate risk of fixed income securities. The formulae for duration and convexity are derived and illustrated with examples. The use of duration and convexity measures for assessing price risk forms the basis of the chapter.

Chapters 6 to 9 cover the pricing of derivative securities which have become such an important part of modern financial markets. Chapter 6 covers forwards and futures, including the theoretical basis for their pricing. Chapter 7 covers the range of swap transactions available in financial markets—from bill swaps to cross currency and interest rate swaps. Chapter 8 covers options and develops the basic ideas underlying option valuation. Chapter 9 covers the techniques required for the valuation of interest rate derivatives which have become of increasing importance in recent years. The coverage in chapters 8 and 9 requires an introductory knowledge of statistics including the binomial and normal probability distributions.

A bibliography and further references are provided for readers interested in obtaining a broader coverage of the material in this book.

The book has been written primarily for Australian markets, although the underlying principles and techniques apply to these securities in whatever country they are traded. Where appropriate, international differences are mentioned in the text.

The book can be used as an undergraduate text for finance, business or actuarial students and as background reading for Masters courses covering the financial markets. Masters of Business Administration and Finance and Business students should find the book a useful reference. Graduates without financial training who are working in the money and capital markets should benefit from the book as well.

The second edition has involved an updating of all the examples in the text. Chapter 5 has been completely rewritten and Chapter 9 on 'Interest rate derivatives' is new.

Many of the calculations in the book can be performed using a spreadsheet or by writing simple computer programs. Most can be calculated using a financial calculator. It is not the aim of the book to teach readers to use a financial calculator or a computer spreadsheet, but readers will find sufficient details provided for them to reproduce the examples using a spreadsheet—particularly in chapters 5, 8 and 9.

The author welcomes comments and suggestions for improvement of the text. Comments can be sent by e-mail to msherris@efs.mq.edu.au

Acknowledgments

The preparation of the first edition of this book benefited from many people and institutions both directly and indirectly. The basis for the early chapters of the book was various seminar notes that were prepared by the author and used over a number of years for the Treasury Dealing Course, the Capital Markets Course and the Mathematics of Wholesale Financial Transactions Seminars of the Centre for Studies in Money, Banking and Finance (Macquarie University) and the Centre for Applied Finance (University of Technology Sydney). I would like to thank Tom Valentine for support during this time. The later chapters were written while the author was Molson Visiting Professor of Financial Economics and Investment at the University of Waterloo, Ontario, Canada. I would like to thank Phelim Boyle, Rob Brown and Harry Panjer for the invitation to visit Waterloo during Winter term in 1989.

The second edition was prepared just prior to and during Christmas 1995. Chapter 9 has been adapted from course notes prepared by the author for the Macquarie unit ACST200 Mathematics of Finance. I would like to thank Andrew Leung for assistance with the second edition and for checking many of the examples.

Michael Sherris
Sydney, Australia
January 1996

1 Price calculations for short-term securities

Simple interest

Price and yield calculations in the short-term money market are based on simple interest. Simple interest is not called simple interest because it is easy! Simple interest is called simple because the calculation of interest is a simple one which does not involve calculating interest on interest (i.e. compounding of interest). For simple interest the amount of interest is based only on the initial investment without allowing for interest on interest. Simple interest is also referred to as 'flat' interest.

Accumulation at simple interest

For any investment earning interest it is necessary to determine interest earnings which will be added to the principal or present value of the investment in order to determine the future value. The amount of simple interest is calculated as:

$$\text{Simple interest} = \text{Principal} \times \frac{\text{Interest rate \% p.a.}}{100} \times \text{Term}$$

or in symbols:

■ *Equation 1.1*

$$I = P \times \frac{r}{100} \times t$$

The term of the investment is always in years and fractions of a year in this calculation.

Example 1.1

A company makes a $100 000 deposit for 6 months at 8.5% p.a. How much interest will the company earn?

Solution

$$\text{Interest} = 100\,000 \times \frac{8.5}{100} \times \frac{1}{2}$$

$$= \$4250$$

Deposits are usually made for a specified number of days. In this case the number of days is expressed as a fraction of a year. This is because the interest rate is expressed as a percentage *per annum*. If the period over which the deposit is made is less than a year then with simple interest a year's interest is pro-rated on a proportional basis.

In Australia, the convention adopted in calculating fractions of a year is to assume that there are 365 days in every year. Another common convention is to assume a 360 day year—this is used in the US and in Euromarkets. For the time being calculations will be based on a 365 day year. Allowing for days, the simple interest equation becomes:

$$\text{Simple interest} = \text{Principal} \times \frac{\text{Interest rate (\% p.a.)}}{100} \times \frac{\text{Days}}{365}$$

or in symbols:

■ *Equation 1.2*

$$I = P \times \frac{r}{100} \times \frac{n}{365}$$

where *n* is the number of days the principal is invested.

Example 1.2

A bank accepts a $500 000 deposit to mature in 255 days and will pay 9.55% p.a. on the deposit. How much interest will it pay?

Solution

$$\text{Interest} = 500\,000 \times \frac{9.55}{100} \times \frac{255}{365}$$

$$= \$33\,359.59$$

When interest is paid in a single amount, it is normally calculated as simple interest. The calculation of simple interest can also apply for a period longer than one year.

Example 1.3

A bank accepts deposits for terms up to 5 years and pays interest on maturity. How much interest would it pay on a deposit of $50 000 for a term of 2 years and 55 days if the interest rate is 10.5% p.a. simple?

Solution

$$\text{Interest} = 50\ 000 \times \frac{10.5}{100} \times \left(2 + \frac{55}{365}\right)$$

$$= \$11\ 291.10$$

After the amount of simple interest has been calculated, the future value or maturity amount of the investment can be found by adding the present value (or principal) to the interest so that:

$$\text{Future value} = \text{Present value} + \text{Interest}$$
$$= \text{Principal} + \text{Interest}$$

The expression for simple interest which was given earlier is then substituted into the above equation to obtain:

$$\text{Future value} = \text{Principal} + \left(\text{Principal} \times \text{Interest rate} \times \frac{\text{Days}}{365}\right)$$

or in symbols:

■ *Equation 1.3*

$$S = P + \left(P \times \frac{r}{100} \times \frac{n}{365}\right)$$

$$= P \times \left(1 + \frac{r}{100} \times \frac{n}{365}\right)$$

Equation 1.3 gives a relationship for simple interest calculations between the future value (S), the present value (P), the interest rate (r) and the term in days (n). If any three of these are known then the unknown can be determined with a little algebra.

Example 1.4

What is the future or maturity value of $100 000 invested at 12.5% for 250 days?

Solution

$$\text{Future value} = 100\ 000 \left(1 + \frac{12.5}{100} \times \frac{250}{365}\right)$$

$$= \$108\ 561.64$$

Present value (or discounted value) at simple interest

With simple interest the future value can be determined from equation 1.3 by multiplying the present value (or principal) by the simple interest factor

$\left(1 + \dfrac{r}{100} \times \dfrac{n}{365}\right)$. This factor is simply the future value of $1 invested at simple interest at rate $r\%$ p.a. for a period of n days.

Often we know the future value of an investment (e.g. the maturity value of a bill) but require to calculate the present value (or price) of the investment. In these cases, equation 1.3 is used to find P, or the present value:

$$\text{Present value} = \frac{\text{Future value}}{\left(1 + \dfrac{r}{100} \times \dfrac{n}{365}\right)}$$

or in symbols:

■ *Equation 1.4*

$$P = \frac{S}{\left(1 + \dfrac{r}{100} \times \dfrac{n}{365}\right)}$$

Example 1.5

Find the present value of $100 000 payable in 184 days' time at 9.5% p.a.

Solution

$$\text{Present value} = \frac{100\,000}{\left(1 + \dfrac{9.5}{100} \times \dfrac{184}{365}\right)}$$

Remember that multiplication must be done before additions or subtractions, so the denominator becomes:

$$1 + \left(\frac{9.5}{100} \times \frac{184}{365}\right)$$

Using a scientific calculator, the calculation of the present value can be performed in several different ways. Three possibilities are:

1. Using the memory function, store the numerator (100 000) in memory. Calculate the denominator, then divide by the recalled memory. This procedure gives (denominator divided by numerator) so use the reciprocal button 1/x to reverse the process to (numerator divided by denominator).
2. Calculate the denominator first. Take its reciprocal and then multiply by the numerator.
3. Calculate the denominator and store it in memory. Then calculate (numerator divided by recalled memory). If your calculator does not automatically perform the multiplication before the division, then calculate the denominator as follows:

$$(0.095 \times 184 \div 365) + 1$$

Whichever of the above methods is chosen, the calculation has the following result:

Present value = $95 429.83

This example demonstrates that if $95 429.83 is invested now at 9.5% p.a. for 184 days then the maturity amount will be $100 000. That is, $95 429.83 accumulates to $100 000 because $4570.17 simple interest is earned over the period. The interest amount can also be checked by using equation 1.2.

Equation 1.4 is often rewritten by multiplying top and bottom of the right-hand side by 100 and also by 365. This gives:

$$P = \frac{S}{\left(1 + \dfrac{r}{100} \times \dfrac{n}{365}\right)} \times \frac{100 \times 365}{100 \times 365}$$

$$= \frac{S \times 36\,500}{\left(1 + \dfrac{rn}{36\,500}\right) \times 36\,500}$$

or

■ *Equation 1.5*

$$P = \frac{36\,500 \times S}{36\,500 + r \times n}$$

Equation 1.5 is often referred to as the standard bill formula used in the Australian market. However, equation 1.4 should be preferred because its terms are more logical and should be more readily understood. The equation 1.5 format might confuse the uninitiated as a few steps of algebra are required to put it into a logical format. It also involves the calculation of larger numbers than for equation 1.4 and can therefore be subject to rounding errors. Its only advantage is that it can be typed more easily than equation 1.4!

Example 1.6

Use both equations 1.4 and 1.5 to find the principal of a term deposit earning 8.5% p.a. for 167 days which has a maturity payment of $103 889.04.

Solution

(a) Using equation 1.4

$$\text{Present value} = \frac{103\ 889.04}{\left(1 + \frac{8.50}{100} \times \frac{167}{365}\right)}$$

$$= \frac{103\ 889.04}{(1.0388904)}$$

$$= \$100\ 000$$

(b) Using equation 1.5

$$\text{Present value} = \frac{36\ 500 \times 103\ 889.04}{36\ 500 + 8.5 \times 167}$$

$$= \$100\ 000$$

Both equations give the same answer, as expected.

Simple discount

Some instruments and some short-term money markets use the concept of simple discount to price securities. For example, discount rates are used to determine the price of short-term securities in the US and the UK commercial paper and bankers' acceptances markets. This is different to simple interest. With simple interest we determined future values by adding interest amounts to present values. Present values were determined by dividing future values by a factor equal to 1 plus (the interest rate times the period). (Remember that multiplications are done before additions.) Simple discount starts with the future value and determines the present value by subtracting a discount amount. The idea of a discount is the same as when you purchase some goods with a payment due at a future date (say, 3 months). The seller will usually offer a discount off the cost for payment now. The discount is usually expressed as a percentage of the cost.

Figure 1.1 summarises the difference between simple interest and simple discount.

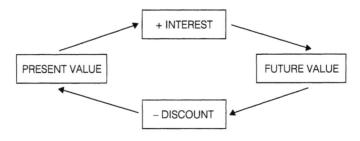

Figure 1.1

In financial markets, the discount is expressed as a % p.a. rate and is applied to the future (or maturity) value to determine the discount amount. The present value is simply the future value less the discount. The amount of discount is determined as:

$$\text{Discount amount} = \text{Future value} \times \frac{\text{Discount rate (\% p.a.)}}{100} \times \frac{\text{Days}}{365}$$

or in symbols:

■ *Equation 1.6*

$$D = S \times \frac{d}{100} \times \frac{n}{365}$$

The present value is then:

$$\text{Present value} = \text{Future value} - \text{Discount amount}$$

or in symbols:

$$P = S - \left(1 \times \frac{d}{100} \times \frac{n}{365}\right)$$

or

■ *Equation 1.7*

$$P = S \times \left(1 - \frac{d}{100} \times \frac{n}{365}\right)$$

Example 1.7

A customer owes a supplier $190 000 due in 45 days' time. The supplier offers the customer a discount of 10% p.a. for payment now. How much is the discount and what is the cash amount that can be paid in settlement of the customer's debt?

Solution

$$\text{Discount amount} = \$190\ 000 \times \frac{10}{100} \times \frac{45}{365}$$
$$= \$2\ 342.47$$

$$\text{Cash amount} = \text{Future payment} - \text{Discount amount}$$
$$= 190\ 000 - 2342.47$$
$$= \$187\ 657.53$$

The Reserve Bank of Australia uses simple discount when it calculates the price of a rediscounted Treasury note. The formula is:

$$P = 100 \times \left(1 - \frac{d}{100} \times \frac{n}{365}\right)$$

where d is the simple discount rate, and n is the number of days to maturity.

Example 1.8

Find the price of a Treasury note with 35 days to maturity at a 12% p.a. simple discount.

Solution

$$\text{Price} = 100 \times \left[1 - 0.12 \times \left(\frac{35}{365}\right)\right]$$

$$= \$98.84932 \text{ (to 5 decimal places)}$$

Relationship between simple interest and simple discount

Both simple interest and simple discount formulae are used to determine present values from future values. They are thus 2 different ways of expressing the same relationship. Given this, for any simple interest rate there must be an equivalent discount rate and for any discount rate there must be an equivalent interest rate. We can derive these relationships by equating the interest amount to the discount amount given by equations 1.2 and 1.6 so that:

$$\text{Interest amount} = \text{Discount amount}$$

or in symbols:

$$P \times \frac{r}{100} \times \frac{n}{365} = S \times \frac{d}{100} \times \frac{n}{365}$$

Start by assuming that the interest rate is known and we wish to determine the equivalent discount rate. In this case we know from equation 1.3 that:

$$S = P \times \left(1 + \frac{r}{100} \times \frac{n}{365}\right)$$

Substituting this in the above equation gives:

$$P \times \frac{r}{100} \times \frac{n}{365} = P \times \left(1 + \frac{r}{100} \times \frac{n}{365}\right) \times \frac{d}{100} \times \frac{n}{365}$$

Then divide both sides by:

$$P \times \left(1 + \frac{r}{100} \times \frac{n}{365}\right)$$

and multiply by 36 500/n to obtain:

■ *Equation 1.8*

$$d = \frac{r}{\left(1 + \frac{r}{100} \times \frac{n}{365}\right)}$$

Notice that in equation 1.8 the discount rate is the *present value* of the interest rate (compare with equation 1.4). Thus the discount rate will be lower than its equivalent interest rate and the difference is a function of the number of days over which the yield rate/discount rate applies.

If we know the discount rate and wish to determine the equivalent yield rate then, without doing the algebra, the result is:

■ *Equation 1.9*

$$r = \frac{d}{\left(1 - \frac{d}{100} \times \frac{n}{365}\right)}$$

In this case the yield or interest rate is the future value of the discount rate (compare with equation 1.7). Dividing by the discount factor $(1 - d/100 \times n/365)$ gives the future value at the discount rate since doing this is the reverse of the calculation used to obtain the present value with a discount rate.

To illustrate this relationship, table 1.1 was derived using equation 1.9. Notice from this table how the difference between the equivalent interest rate and the discount rate increases with the number of days over which the calculation is performed and this difference increases significantly with higher discount rates.

Table 1.1 Equivalent simple interest rates for given discount rates

| Term (days) | Discount rate (% p.a.) | | |
	10%	15%	20%
30	10.083	15.187	20.334
60	10.167	15.379	20.680
90	10.253	15.576	21.037
120	10.340	15.778	21.408
180	10.519	16.198	22.188
270	10.799	16.872	23.473
365	11.111	17.647	25.000
730	12.500	21.429	33.333

365 and 360 day years

US and Euromoney markets quote yields on a 360 day year basis. The term used for pricing short-term securities in these markets is based on the actual number of days divided by 360. Hence, to calculate a present value or future value using a 360 day year assumption, we calculate the fraction of a year as:

$$\frac{\text{Days}}{360}$$

Note that if a deposit is made for a period of a year, which contains 365 days, the interest amount using a 360 day year would be:

$$\frac{r}{100} \times \frac{365}{360}$$

We can convert a 360 day rate into an equivalent 365 day rate as follows:

$$365 \text{ day equivalent} = 365/360 \times 360 \text{ day rate}$$

The 365 day formulae can then be used with the 365 day rate.

It is very important to understand that using a 360 day year assumption is just a *convention* used in the calculation of prices and yields. The markets and countries using this convention have the same calendar as everybody else. It has no significance, apart from its effect on the resulting dollar values obtained using the assumption.

Example 1.9

A deposit for $100 000 is made for a period of 160 days at a rate of 8.5% p.a. Interest is calculated on a 360 day basis. Calculate the maturity value of the deposit. Determine the 365 day equivalent rate and calculate the maturity value using the 365 day year convention.

Solution

Using equation 1.3 with a 360 day year convention gives:

$$\text{Maturity value} = 100\ 000 \times \left(1 + \frac{8.5}{100} \times \frac{160}{360}\right)$$

$$= \$103\ 777.78$$

The 365 day equivalent rate is:

$$365 \text{ day equivalent rate} = \frac{365}{360} \times 8.5$$

$$= 8.61806\% \text{ p.a.}$$

The maturity value using the 365 day equivalent rate is:

$$\text{Maturity value} = 100\ 000 \times \left(1 + \frac{8.61806}{100} \times \frac{160}{365}\right)$$

$$= \$103\,777.78$$

Hence we get the same answer, provided the convention adopted for both the rate used and the number of days is consistent.

Bills, promissory notes and short-term government securities

By convention, the method that is used in financial markets to calculate the price of short-term securities is to calculate the present value of the maturity payment using simple interest or simple discount. In Australia, short-term securities such as bills of exchange, promissory notes, Treasury notes and short-term government bonds (with less than 6 months to maturity) are priced using simple interest and a 365 day year convention. These securities pay a single sum on their maturity date with no intermediate interest payments. Their maturity is less than 1 year and generally less than 6 months.

Example 1.10

A bill with a face value of $500 000 and term to maturity of 180 days is sold at a yield of 8% p.a. What are the proceeds of the sale?

Solution

The proceeds are the present value of the $500 000 at 8% p.a. simple interest for 180 days:

$$\text{Proceeds} = \frac{500\,000}{\left(1 + \frac{8}{100} \times \frac{180}{365}\right)}$$

$$= \$481\,022.67$$

The Reserve Bank of Australia uses the following formula for pricing Treasury notes:

$$P = \frac{100}{\left(1 + \frac{f}{365}\, i\right)}$$

where P is the price per hundred dollars of face value (payable on the maturity date of the note), f is the number of days to maturity and i is the simple p.a. yield per dollar (not per cent). This is simply the formula to calculate the present value of a future sum using simple interest.

Example 1.11

Find the price of a 180 day Treasury note at 7.35% p.a.

Solution

$$Price = \frac{100}{\left(1 + \frac{180}{365} \times 0.0735\right)}$$

$$= \$96.50213 \text{ (to 5 decimal places)}$$

A similar approach is adopted by the Reserve Bank of Australia (RBA) when valuing Treasury bonds within 6 months of their maturity. In this case, provided the bond has not gone ex-interest, the single final payment consists of the face value plus the last interest coupon payment. Hence the price is:

■ *Equation 1.10*

$$Price = \frac{100 + g}{\left(1 + \frac{f}{365} \times i\right)}$$

where *g* represents the final interest (coupon) payment, which is equal to half the annual coupon rate times the face value of the bond ($100 is the face value in this formula).

Example 1.12

Find the price of a 12% Treasury bond with 125 days to maturity to yield 8.5% p.a. to maturity.

Solution

Since Australian Treasury bonds pay half-yearly interest, the final interest payment, *g* per $100 face value, is

$$(1/2) \times (12/100) \times 100 = \$6.00$$

Therefore:

$$Price = \frac{100 + 6}{\left(1 + \frac{125}{365} \times 0.085\right)}$$

$$= \$103.00166 \text{ (to 5 decimal places)}$$

Since January 1993 Australian Treasury bonds have gone ex-interest 7 days prior to a coupon payment. If a short-term Treasury bond has less than 7 days to maturity then the price is the present value of the face value only, since the purchaser does not receive the last interest payment on an ex-interest security.

In the US short-term securities such as commercial paper and bills of exchange are priced using a discount rate and a 360 day convention. In the UK a discount basis is also used for these securities but with the use of a 365 day convention. Promissory notes are referred to as commercial paper in these markets. In the US Treasury notes are long-term securities equivalent to the Australian Treasury bond. The short-term US security equivalent to the Australian Treasury note is the US Treasury bill.

Example 1.13

A US company issues \$100 million face value commercial paper with 270 days to maturity at 7.5% p.a. (a discount rate for these securities). What are the proceeds of the issue?

Solution

The proceeds of the issue will be the present value of the maturity payment so that, from equation 1.7:

$$\text{Proceeds} = 100 \times \left(1 - \frac{7.5}{100} \times \frac{270}{360}\right)$$

$$= \text{US\$94.375 million}$$

US Treasury bills are also quoted in terms of a bond-equivalent yield. For securities with less than 6 months to maturity the bond-equivalent yield is the simple yield rate on a 365 day basis equivalent to the discount rate used to price the Treasury bill. The simple yield on a 360 day basis is often referred to as the money market yield since for other interest bearing securities, rates are quoted as simple yields on a 360 day basis in the US. The Treasury bill discount rate is often referred to as the yield rate even though it is a discount rate.

If the discount rate is $d\%$ p.a. and the Treasury bill has n days to maturity then the bond-equivalent yield (for maturities of less than 6 months) is given by:

■ *Equation 1.11*

$$\text{Bond-equivalent yield} = \frac{365}{360} \times \frac{d}{\left(1 - \frac{d}{100} \times \frac{n}{360}\right)}$$

Example 1.14

A 50 day US Treasury bill is priced to yield 7.25% p.a. (discount rate). Calculate the bond-equivalent yield on this Treasury bill.

Solution

$$\text{Bond-equivalent yield} = \frac{365}{360} \times \frac{7.25}{\left(1 - \frac{7.25}{100} \times \frac{50}{360}\right)}$$

$$= 7.42546\% \text{ p.a.}$$

For Treasury bills with more than 6 months to maturity the bond-equivalent yield is calculated slightly differently to allow for the (semi-annual) compounding of interest (see chapter 3). Since compound interest has yet to be covered the method for doing this is not covered here.

Certificates of deposit

Banks issue certificates of deposit (CDs) to depositors as evidence of the existence of a deposit at the bank with a specified maturity date and interest rate. These certificates are often negotiable (NCDs) and are traded in financial markets. There are 2 forms of CD issued by banks. The most common form in Australia is similar to a bill where a single payment equal to the face value of the bill is paid on maturity. The second form, which is more common in the US, is where interest is added to the principal, at a rate fixed at issue of the CD, so that the maturity value equals the sum of the face value and the fixed interest amount then due. The fixed interest rate payable on maturity of a previously issued CD is different to the market interest rate used to calculate its price which will vary over the life of the CD as market rates vary.

Example 1.15

Find the price of a $100 000 face value 180 day at issue 12% p.a. interest-bearing certificate of deposit which now has 95 days to maturity to yield 13.71% p.a.

Solution

First calculate the maturity value of the CD using equation 1.3:

$$\text{Maturity value} = 100\ 000 \left(1 + \frac{12}{100} \times \frac{180}{365}\right)$$

$$= \$105\ 917.81$$

Calculate the price using equation 1.4:

$$\text{Price} = \frac{105\ 917.81}{\left(1 + \frac{13.71}{100} \times \frac{95}{365}\right)}$$

$$= \$102\ 268.51$$

2 Yield calculations for short-term securities

Calculation of yields

The analysis of money market transactions often involves the calculation of the rate of interest (or yield) earned by a particular investment. For short-term securities this is done using equation 1.2 as follows:

$$\text{Interest} = \text{Principal} \times \frac{r}{100} \times \frac{n}{365}$$

so that:

$$\frac{\text{Interest}}{\text{Principal}} = \frac{r}{100} \times \frac{n}{365}$$

and:

■ *Equation 2.1*

$$r = 100 \times \frac{365}{n} \times \frac{\text{Interest}}{\text{Principal}}$$

or for a 360 day convention:

■ *Equation 2.2*

$$r = 100 \times \frac{360}{n} \times \frac{\text{Interest}}{\text{Principal}}$$

This expression for the rate of interest can be explained as follows. The interest amount divided by the principal gives the return per dollar invested over the full term of the investment. If this is divided by n, the term of the investment, then the result is the return per dollar per day. Multiplying by 365 (or by 360 if a 360 day convention is used) gives the simple per

15

annum return. Finally, multiplying by 100 gives the per hundred dollar or per cent return.

Example 2.1

A deposit of $100 000 with a maturity of 174 days has a maturity value of $104 052.05. What rate of return or yield will be earned on the deposit?

Solution

$$\text{Interest amount} = 104\,052.05 - 100\,000$$

$$= 4052.05$$

$$\text{Interest rate or yield} = 100 \times \frac{365}{174} \times \frac{4052.05}{100\,000}$$

$$= 8.5\% \text{ p.a.}$$

The above example was based on a single investment. However, in practice, it is common for short-term securities to be 'rolled over' so that there is a compounding effect. The yield earned on the overall investment will then depend on the interest rate at which maturing amounts are reinvested.

The compounding of interest will be considered in more detail in chapters 3 and 4. The compounding effects of rolling over short-term securities can be expressed as a simple p.a. yield which applies to the full term of the rolled over investment. This simple p.a. yield is sometimes referred to as an effective annualised return. Note that it is a simple interest rate which results from the compounding together of a number of simple interest rates and it is not a compound yield rate. It assumes interest is paid in one sum on the final maturity date.

Example 2.2

Calculate the effective annualised return for a $100 000 investment which earned:

- 6.5% p.a. for 90 days, then
- 7.5% p.a. for 60 days, then
- 6.2% p.a. for 45 days.

Solution

The value of the investment after 90 days is:

$$100\,000 \left(1 + \frac{90}{365} \times \frac{6.5}{100} \right)$$

After a further 60 days it becomes:

$$100\,000\left(1+\frac{90}{365}\times\frac{6.5}{100}\right)\left(1+\frac{60}{365}\times\frac{7.5}{100}\right)$$

Finally, after the full 195 days, the value is:

$$\text{Value} = 100\,000\left(1+\frac{90}{365}\times\frac{6.5}{100}\right)\left(1+\frac{60}{365}\times\frac{7.5}{100}\right)\left(1+\frac{45}{365}\times\frac{6.2}{100}\right)$$

$$= \$103\,641.58$$

or a return of 3.642% after 195 days.

$$\text{Annualised return} = 3.642\times\frac{365}{195}$$

$$= 6.816\%$$

Holding period calculations

In practice securities in a money market portfolio will be traded prior to their maturity date. In this event the yield earned on the security will not be equal to the yield to maturity at which it was purchased because of changes in market interest rates. For a security that is sold prior to its maturity date the actual return will be more or less than the original purchase yield. This return is referred to as the holding period return.

Example 2.3

A bill with a face value of $100 000 and 90 days to maturity is purchased to yield 8.4% p.a. After 40 days has elapsed the bill is sold at a yield of 8.3%. What is the rate of return earned over the period by the original purchaser? (Assume a 365 day year.)

Solution

In order to calculate the yield over the 40 days the bill is held we need to determine the purchase price (the present value) and the sale proceeds (the future value). The difference between these is the interest earned on the investment over the holding period. It is equivalent to making a deposit of the purchase price and receiving a maturity value of the sale proceeds after 40 days.

Using equation 1.4 we have:

$$\text{Purchase price} = \frac{100\,000}{\left(1+\frac{8.4}{100}\times\frac{90}{365}\right)}$$

$$= \$97\,970.80$$

$$\text{Sale proceeds} = \frac{100\,000}{\left(1+\frac{8.3}{100}\times\frac{50}{365}\right)}$$

$$= \$98\,875.80$$

The effect of this transaction is that the original purchaser has invested $97 970.80 over 40 days and received $98 889.19. The interest earned is 98 875.80 – 97 970.80 = $905.00

Using equation 2.1, the interest rate, yield or rate of return over the holding period is:

$$r = 100 \times \frac{365}{40} \times \frac{905.00}{97\,970.80}$$

$$= 8.43\% \text{ p.a.}$$

Note how in this example the purchaser has earned roughly the same rate of return as the original purchase yield over the 40 days that the bill was held. In order to do this the yield on the bill had to fall to 8.3% p.a. at sale.

Example 2.4

A treasury note with a face value of $500 000 and a maturity of 85 days is purchased to yield 8.45% p.a. After 10 days it is rediscounted at the Reserve Bank at a discount rate of 9.0% p.a. What rate of return is earned over the 10 days it is held?

Solution

The purchase price of the note is:

$$\frac{500\,000}{\left(1 + \frac{8.45}{100} \times \frac{85}{365}\right)} = \$490\,350.84$$

The amount received on rediscount, using equation 1.7, is:

$$500\,000 \times \left(1 - \frac{9.0}{100} \times \frac{75}{365}\right) = \$490\,753.42$$

The rate of return over 10 days, using equation 2.1, is:

$$100 \times \frac{365}{10} \times \frac{(490\,753.42 - 490\,350.84)}{490\,350.84}$$

$$= 3.0\% \text{ p.a.}$$

Riding the yield curve

A strategy that is often used to improve the return on a short-term investment is referred to as 'riding the yield curve'. It involves the purchase of a longer-term security and holding the security until it has a shorter maturity and a lower sale yield than the original purchase yield. The security is then sold and the return obtained should exceed that which could have been obtained if a security with a maturity equal to the holding period had been purchased outright. This strategy requires the yield curve (for the securities involved) to have a normal shape with longer-term yields higher than shorter-term yields. It also relies on the shape and level of the yield curve remaining stable over the holding period. Riding the yield curve analysis is a direct application of holding period calculations.

In doing this analysis it is important to recognise that the bid rate is the interest rate at which a buyer will bid to purchase securities and the offer rate is the interest rate at which a seller will offer to sell securities in the market. In order to transact in the market, a seller of a security will have to sell at the market bid rate and a buyer of a security will have to buy at the market offer rate, since for every buyer of a security there needs to be a seller (and vice versa) and the market sets the rates at which transactions take place.

Example 2.5

The returns in table 2.1 are available on bank bills for varying maturities:

Table 2.1   Bank bid yields

Maturity	Yield (% p.a.)	
	Bid	Offer
30 days	7.50	7.25
60 days	8.00	7.75
90 days	9.00	8.75

An investor is interested in investing approximately $500 000 for 30 days. Assuming that market yields remain unchanged over the 30 day period, determine if 'riding the yield curve' can improve the returns available for the investor.

Solution

The investor has a number of strategies available to obtain a 30 day investment. These are analysed in turn. (*Note*: investors are assumed to buy at quoted offer rates and it is assumed that these rates do not change over the relevant holding period.)

(a) Invest in a 30 day bill: the return will be 7.25% p.a. since this is the offer from sellers in the market for 30 day bills.
(b) Purchase a 60 day bill, hold it for 30 days and then sell it as a 30 day bill in 30 days' time:

$$\text{Cost of \$500 000 60 day bill} = \frac{500\,000}{\left(1 + \frac{7.75}{100} \times \frac{60}{365}\right)}$$

$$= \$493\,710.27$$

In 30 days' time:

$$\text{Sale proceeds from 30 day bill} = \frac{500\,000}{\left(1 + \frac{7.50}{100} \times \frac{30}{365}\right)}$$

$$= \$496\,936.69$$

since the security is sold to the market in 30 days' time at the bid or buy rate in the market of 7.5% p.a. for a 30 day security.

The 30 day return, or holding period return, from this strategy would be:

$$100 \times \frac{365}{30} \times \frac{(496\,936.69 - 493\,710.27)}{493\,710.27} = 7.95\% \text{ p.a.}$$

(c) Purchase a 90 day bill, hold it for 30 days and then sell it as a 60 day bill in 30 days' time:

$$\text{Cost of } \$500\,000 \text{ 90 day bill} = \frac{500\,000}{\left(1 + \frac{8.75}{100} \times \frac{90}{365}\right)}$$

$$= \$489\,440.16$$

In 30 days' time:

$$\text{Sale proceeds from 60 day bill} = \frac{500\,000}{\left(1 + \frac{8.00}{100} \times \frac{60}{365}\right)}$$

$$= \$493\,510.01$$

since the security is sold to the market in 30 days' time at the bid or buy rate in the market of 8.0% p.a. for a 60 day security.

The 30 day return, or holding period return, from this strategy would be:

$$100 \times \frac{365}{30} \times \frac{(493\,510.01 - 489\,440.16)}{489\,440.16} = 10.12\% \text{ p.a.}$$

From these calculations it can be seen that if there were no change in market yields then the best strategy would be to purchase a 90 day bill and ride the yield curve for 30 days. Riding the yield curve involves the risk that yields will move adversely. This risk is greatest for longer-term securities. Although the holding of the longest security appears to provide the highest return, it also involves the highest level of risk. To offset this risk it would be possible to fix the sale yields using forward or futures contracts which would remove this risk. Interest rate risk and the use of forwards and futures are covered in later chapters.

Break-even analysis and funding costs

Break-even analysis is used to assess the yield or price of a transaction so that it will 'break even' with some other transaction or cash flows. The most important application of break-even analysis is in allowing for funding and other costs in money market calculations. Purchasing money market securities provides a return on funds invested which will have to be sufficient to cover the costs involved if a profit is to be made. The most important cost is typically the funding costs. Holding period calculations can be performed to determine the future sale yield (or price) for a security if it is to cover the funding costs over the period the security is held.

Example 2.6

An investment bank can purchase $500 000 face value 90 day bank bills to yield 7.75% p.a. to maturity. Funding costs for 30 day funds are 7.75% p.a. At what yield will the bank have to sell the 90 day bills in 30 days' time to break even on the funding costs?

Solution

The bank will need to fund the purchase cost of the bills (not their face value). The purchase cost is:

$$\frac{500\ 000}{\left(1 + \frac{7.75}{100} \times \frac{90}{365}\right)} = \$490\ 624.37$$

Funding costs on this for 30 days at 7.75% p.a. amount to:

$$490\ 624.37 \times \frac{7.75}{100} \times \frac{30}{365} = \$3125.21$$

In order to break even on the funding costs the bank needs to sell the bills in 30 days, when they have 60 days to maturity, for proceeds of:

$$\$490\ 624.37 + \$3125.21 = \$493\ 749.58$$

The break-even sale yield is therefore:

$$100 \times \frac{365}{60} \times \frac{(500\ 000 - 493\ 749.58)}{493\ 749.58} = 7.70\%\ \text{p.a.}$$

since this is the sale yield for a $500 000 face value bill with 60 days to maturity that will provide proceeds of $493 749.58 which will be sufficient to repay the original funding ($490 624.37) and the funding cost for 30 days ($3125.21).

Notice in this example that, although the purchase yield and the funding costs were both 7.75% p.a., the bills had to be sold at a lower yield than 7.75% p.a. in order to break even. This is because the funding cost is a 30 day simple interest rate and the purchase yield is a 90 day simple interest rate. If the funding is rolled over to the maturity of the bill then the funding cost will *compound* to a higher rate than 7.75% for the 90 day period. The funding cost, on an equivalent basis to the purchase yield, is higher than the 30 day simple rate. This highlights the fact that it is not valid to compare simple interest rates which apply for different periods, since an allowance for the effect of compound interest must be made.

Transaction costs

The effect of transaction costs needs to be allowed for in calculations of yields on both short-term and long-term financial instruments. The allowance is made by including these costs in the cash flows and then calculating a yield on these adjusted cash flows. Transaction costs are treated as negative cash flows and reduce the proceeds available from a borrowing.

Costs incurred on the purchase of a security, or up-front costs, will in general be some combination of a flat amount and a percentage of the face value of the instrument. For bill facilities the costs may include flat charges in the form of establishment fees and mortgage registration costs, as well as charges related to the face value in the form of facility fees and activation fees.

If the flat charges are C and the costs related to the face value are $k\%$ p.a. then for a bill with a face value of F and n days to maturity at issue the total fees charged will be:

$$\text{Fees} = C + [(k/100) \times F \times (n/365)]$$

If the market yield is $r\%$ then the proceeds (P) on the bill before allowing for charges will be:

$$P = \frac{F}{[1 + (r/100) \times (n/365)]}$$

and the net proceeds after charges will be:

$$P - \text{Fees}$$

The yield on the bill, expressed as a per cent per annum, allowing for transaction costs, is then calculated using the net proceeds and equation 2.1 (or 2.2) to give:

$$100 \times \frac{365}{n} \times \frac{(F - \text{Net proceeds})}{\text{Net proceeds}}$$

Example 2.7

A bill facility is provided to ABC Pty Ltd under which a $500 000 bill with a maturity of 120 days is issued. The bill is issued at a yield of 7.5%. Transaction costs include a flat charge of $400, a facility fee of 0.5% p.a., payable half-yearly in advance, and an activation fee of 1.5% p.a. Calculate the cost of borrowing with this bill facility after allowing for transaction costs.

Solution

The proceeds from issuing the bill before transaction costs will be:

$$P = \frac{500\,000}{1 + (7.5/100) \times (120/365)} = \$487\,967.91$$

The flat charge is $400.
The facility fee is:

$$(0.5/100) \times 500\,000 \times (1/2) = \$1250$$

The activation fee is:

$$(1.5/100) \times 500\,000 \times (120/365) = \$2465.75$$

Transaction costs amount to a total of $4115.75 (= $400 + $1250 + $2465.75).
The net amount provided under the bill is:

Proceeds − Transaction costs = 487 967.91 − 4115.75 = $483 852.16

The yield is then calculated using this net proceeds to determine the cost of borrowing adjusted for transaction costs, which gives:

$$r = 100 \times \frac{365}{120} \times \frac{500\,000 - 483\,852.16}{483\,852.16}$$

$$= 10.15\% \text{ p.a.}$$

Effect of tax

Most investors pay tax on their security returns. Tax is usually paid in some form on interest and capital gains. For short-term securities that pay their face value on maturity it is difficult to distinguish interest returns from capital gains. Total returns representing the difference between the purchase cost and the maturity value or sale proceeds are usually subject to tax as income for short-term securities.

In order to assess the effect of tax on a security's return an after-tax yield is calculated. This is the yield on the security after adjusting the cash flows for any tax payments. Tax payments are treated as negative cash flows in a similar manner to the treatment of transaction costs. It is also possible for the tax adjustment to be a positive amount if rebates or tax losses can be offset against other taxable income. In practice tax is paid at a different time to the date of interest returns or capital gains or losses since tax payments are made at prespecified dates.

The taxation rules are complex and often change so that in practice it is best to consult a tax adviser for professional tax advice. In fact there are proposals to alter the tax rules for financial instruments at the time of writing. The taxation rules differ depending on the type of institution and the financial instrument. For short-term securities, interest payments are taxed on an accruals basis, which apportions the interest to the financial years in which it was earned on a straight line basis. Realised gains or losses are treated as income and not as capital gains or losses. Interest can be prepaid and is deductible as a tax expense immediately. Discount

Table 2.2 Classification of Australian taxpayers

Likely tax ($)	Type of taxpayer
0–7999	Small
8000–300 000	Medium
300 000+	Large

securities are taxed on the amount of the discount in a similar manner to the taxation of interest.

In Australia corporate or company tax is paid in instalments which are usually based on the previous financial year's taxable income. An adjustment is made to these payments when the current year's taxable income is known so that total tax payments for the current year are correct. This is usually referred to as the make-up payment.

Up until 1990 company tax for the financial year ending 30 June XX had been assessed on approximately 30 April XX + 1 since it took around 9 months for a company to prepare its tax accounts and for the Tax Office to issue an assessment. Instalments of company tax would be paid during the financial year ending 30 June XX + 2 equal to 25% (one quarter) of the assessed company tax for the financial year ending 30 June XX. These would be paid on or about 15 August XX + 1, 15 November XX + 1, and 15 February XX + 2. When the company assessment for the financial year ending 30 June XX + 1 was made on or around 30 April XX + 2 the instalments made during the year to date were deducted from the total tax due and a net payment equal to the difference was made. Tax payments are in effect deferred on income derived during a particular financial year. The 1989 Budget altered the company tax system so that the first instalment was due on 15 July and was 85% of the expected tax payment usually based on the previous year's taxable income. The make-up payment occurred on 15 March of the following year.

A new instalment system applies from the 1994–95 tax year for small and medium company tax payers and from the 1995–96 tax year for large company tax instalment payers. The instalment system not only applies to company tax payments but also to tax payments by investors such as superannuation funds. The difference is that the company tax rate is 36% and the superannuation fund tax rate is 15% (as at the end of 1995). Table 2.3 sets out some brief information about the instalment system from 1995–96. Taxpayers are classified according to the amount of tax they are likely to pay and the classification determines the instalment timing (see table 2.2).

Likely tax is based on the income tax assessed in the previous year or on an estimate made by the taxpayer. This book assumes that the former is the case.

The instalment dates are given in table 2.3.

Table 2.3   Australian tax instalment system

Type of taxpayer	Instalment date for tax year end 30 June XX	Instalment amount
Small	1 December XX	100% of tax assessed for current year
Medium	1 June XX	25% of likely tax (previous year's tax) for current year
	1 September XX	25% of likely tax for current year
	1 December XX	25% of likely tax for current year
	1 March XX + 1	Tax assessed for current year minus previous instalments (usually 75% of previous year's tax)
Large	1 March XX	25% of likely tax (previous year's tax) for current year
	1 June XX	25% of likely tax for current year
	1 September XX	25% of likely tax for current year
	1 December XX	Tax assessed for current year minus previous instalments (usually 75% of previous year's tax)

Note: for the 1995–96 tax year large taxpayers are not required to make the first instalment as a transitional measure.

Example 2.8

An investor pays company tax at the rate of 36% of taxable income. For the financial year 30 June XX tax is assumed to be assessed as for a medium taxpayer with a final assessment on 1 March XX + 1. On 1 July XX the investor purchases a $500 000 face value 180 day bank bill at a yield of 7.25% p.a. which is held to maturity. Determine the after-tax cash flows on the investment allowing for instalments of company tax.

Solution

The purchase cost of the bank bill is:

$$\frac{500\,000}{1 + (7.25/100) \times (180/365)} = \$482\,740.38$$

so that taxable income for the financial year ending 30 June XX + 1 will be increased by $500 000 − 482 740.38 or $17 259.62 as a result of the purchase.

Tax will be paid on 1 March XX + 2 of 36% of this amount or $6213.46. Because instalments of tax for the financial year ending 30 June XX + 2 will be based on the tax assessed on 1 March XX + 2 there will be an increase in tax instalments of 1/4 × $6213.46 or $1553.37 on 1 June XX + 2, 1 September XX + 2 and 1 December XX + 2. When the tax is assessed for the financial year ending 30 June XX + 2 on 1 March XX + 3 then credit will be given for the 3 instalments of $1553.37 so that, in effect, a reduction of tax on 1 March XX + 3 of $3 \times \$1553.37$ or $\$4660.11$ will occur.

The after-tax cash flows on the investment are given in table 2.4.

Table 2.4   After-tax cash flows for example 2.8

Date	Cash flow	Description
1 July XX	−482 740.38	Purchase cost
28 December XX	+500 000.00	Maturity payment
1 March XX + 2	−6 213.46	Tax assessed
1 June XX + 2	−1 553.37	Instalment for XX + 2
1 September XX + 2	−1 553.37	Instalment for XX + 2
1 December XX + 2	−1 553.37	Instalment for XX + 2
1 March XX + 3	+4 660.11	Credit for tax instalments

In order to calculate the after-tax yield on this transaction it makes more sense to use the principles of compound interest which are the basis for the pricing of longer-term financial instruments, covered in chapters 3 and 4.

3 Pricing of long-term securities

Compound interest

Chapter 1 discussed the pricing of short-term securities. Simple interest is used for pricing these securities where interest is calculated as a single amount and then added to the principal or initial investment. In chapter 2 a transaction was considered where the maturity proceeds of a short-term investment were rolled over or reinvested from one security to another. In this situation interest is earned on the interest received from the previous investment as well as on the initial principal. This is compound interest. Long-term fixed interest securities are referred to as bonds. In the UK these securities are also referred to as stocks. Compound interest is the convention used for pricing and yield calculations for long-term fixed interest securities.

Accumulation with compound interest

The convention that is adopted for compound interest calculations is that the interest rate for the subsequent investments (referred to as the reinvestment rate) is assumed to be the same as for the first investment. Although this is the assumption for pricing purposes, analysis need not assume this to be the case and varying reinvestment rates can easily be incorporated in the calculations. Varying reinvestment rates are covered in chapter 4.

Example 3.1

An investment of $100 000 is made at 10% p.a. compound for a 3 year term. What is the maturity value of the investment?

Solution

The maturity value can be determined by calculating the accumulated value of the investment at the end of each year.

At the end of year 1, value = $100\,000 \times (1 + 0.1)$

= $110\,000

At the end of year 2, value = $110\,000 \times (1 + 0.1)$

= $121\,000

= $100\,000 \times (1 + 0.1)^2$

At the end of year 3, value = $121\,000 \times (1 + 0.1)$

= $133\,100

= $100\,000 \times (1 + 0.1)^3$

If simple interest had been used, the maturity value after 3 years would have been:

$100\,000 \times (1 + 0.1 \times 3)$ or $130\,000

The general equation for accumulation at compound interest is:

$$\text{Accumulated value (or Future value)} = \text{Initial value (or Present value)} \times (1 + i/100)^n$$

where i is the per cent interest rate per period, and n is the time in periods, which may include a fractional period.

In symbols:

■ *Equation 3.1*

$$S = P \times (1 + i/100)^n$$

Example 3.2

Find the value of a $100\,000 investment earning 7.35% p.a. in:
(a) 3 years;
(b) 4 years and 6 months;
(c) 7 years and 233 days.

Solution

(a) Value in 3 years = $100\,000\,(1.0735)^3 = \$123\,710.38$
      This calculation is easily computed on a calculator using the y^x key which raises y to the power of x, or in this case 1.0735 to the power of 3.
(b) Value in 4 years and 6 months = $100\,000\,(1.0735)^{4.5} = \$137\,597.08$
(c) Value in 7 years and 233 days = $100\,000\,(1.0735)^{7\,233/365}$
      = $171\,900.45
      In this calculation work out 233/365 (0.638356), add 7 and store the result in memory. Then calculate 1.0735 to the power of 'memory recall' and multiply by 100 000.

Present values with compound interest

To accumulate with compound interest for n years at rate $i\%$ p.a. the initial investment is multiplied by the compound interest accumulation factor $(1 + i/100)^n$. Present values are calculated by reversing this procedure which involves the division of future values by the compound interest accumulation factor so that:

$$\text{Present value} = \frac{\text{Future value}}{\left(1 + \dfrac{i}{100}\right)^n}$$

or in symbols:

■ *Equation 3.2*

$$P = \frac{S}{\left(1 + \dfrac{i}{100}\right)^n}$$

A common practice is to let the one period present value factor be denoted by $v = \dfrac{1}{1 + \dfrac{i}{100}}$. The present value factor for n periods is then the one period factor raised to the power n. Using the v notation gives:

$$\text{Present value} = \text{Future value} \times v^n$$

or:

■ *Equation 3.3*

$$P = S \times v^n$$

Now:

$$v = \frac{1}{1 + \dfrac{i}{100}}$$

which can be written as:

$$v = \left(1 + \frac{i}{100}\right)^{-1}$$

(remembering that an expression in the denominator which is raised to any power can be rewritten as the expression raised to the same power but with a negative sign, so that $1/x = x^{-1}$, $1/x^2 = x^{-2}$ and so on). This means that:

$$v^n = \left(1 + \frac{i}{100}\right)^{-n}$$

and equation 3.3 can thus be written as:

■ *Equation 3.4*

$$P = S \times \left(1 + \frac{i}{100}\right)^{-n}$$

Equations 3.2, 3.3 and 3.4 are all identical ways of expressing the present value formula for compound interest.

Example 3.3

Find the present value of $100 000 due in 3 years and 153 days at a compound yield of 6.19% p.a.

Solution

$$\text{Present value} = 100\,000\,(1.0619)^{-3\,153/365}$$

$$= \$81\,435.82$$

The convention adopted to value payments received from long-term securities is to use present values with compound interest. The convention used to quote compound interest rates is outlined next before considering the valuation of long-term securities.

Nominal and effective rates

Compound interest yields are quoted in terms of nominal per cent p.a. yields. This means that the effective p.a. interest rate depends on the frequency with which interest is assumed to compound during each year. For nominal rates the number of times interest is assumed to compound during a year is divided into the nominal p.a. rate to get the per fractional period interest rate. For example, if interest compounds quarterly then the nominal p.a. rate is divided by four to get the quarterly interest rate. To compare interest rates which have different (assumed) compounding frequencies it is necessary to convert them to a common basis. This is usually done by converting them to effective p.a. rates which are interest rates that assume interest is paid (or compounds) only once a year and is paid at the end of the year (in arrears).

If the nominal rate is $r\%$ p.a. and interest is paid m times per year then the per period interest rate is:

$$i = \frac{r}{m}$$

The effective p.a. rate is determined by compounding \$1 with interest over the m periods in a year at $r\%$ nominal. After 1 period the \$1 plus interest is $(1 + i/100)$ and, with compounding, after m periods it becomes $(1 + i/100)^m$ at the end of the year. When the original principal is subtracted we are left with the effective interest amount per dollar invested equivalent to $r\%$ nominal p.a. or $i\%$ per period. Multiplying this amount by 100 gives the effective interest rate as a per cent.

Thus the effective interest rate is j given by:

■ *Equation 3.5*

$$j = 100 \times \left[\left(1 + \frac{i}{100} \right)^m - 1 \right]$$

where $i = r/m$.

Example 3.4

An investment which pays quarterly interest is quoted as yielding 7.5% p.a. and an investment which pays semi-annual interest is quoted as yielding 7.75% p.a. Which investment provides the highest effective yield?

Solution

The 7.5% p.a. paid quarterly is the same as 7.5/4 = 1.875% per quarter. Compounded over 4 quarters this gives, for every dollar invested:

$$\left(1 + \frac{1.875}{100} \right)^4 = (1.01875)^4 = \$1.077136$$

Subtracting the \$1 invested gives \$0.077136 in interest or an effective p.a. interest rate of:

$$100 \times 0.077136 = 7.72\% \text{ p.a.}$$

The 7.75% p.a. paid semi-annually is the same as 7.75/2 = 3.875% per half year. Compounded over 2 half-years this gives, for every \$1 invested:

$$\left(1 + \frac{3.875}{100} \right)^2 = 1.079002$$

or an effective interest rate of 7.90% p.a.

Thus 7.75% p.a. semi-annually compounding provides a higher effective return than 7.5% p.a. quarterly compounding.

For long-term interest-paying securities, the convention used in financial markets is to quote nominal yields with interest compounding at the same frequency as the coupon interest payments.

Zero coupon bonds

Zero coupon bonds are securities that pay only one sum at a future date as they have no interest payments during the term of the security. They are like a long-term Treasury note or commercial bill. In the past, securities were often held as 'bearer' securities and interest was paid on presentation of a 'coupon' that entitled the holder to the interest payment. This is the reason for the use of the term 'coupon' for interest payments. These days ownership of securities is recorded as inscribed stock and interest is usually paid electronically or by cheque. Zero coupon bonds are often quoted on a semi-annual nominal per cent p.a. yield basis when priced, because this enables their yield to be compared with that quoted on government securities which typically have semi-annual interest (coupon) payments. Their price is calculated by present valuing the face value at compound interest.

Example 3.5

A zero coupon bond maturing in 2 years' time has a face value of $100 000. What is the price of this bond to yield 9% p.a. (semi-annual)?

Solution

The interest rate per semi-annual period is 9/2 = 4.5% since the 9% p.a. is a nominal rate. Over the 2 years there are 4 half-year periods. Hence, using equation 3.3:

$$\text{Price} = 100\ 000 \times v^4 \text{ at } 4.5\%$$

$$= 100\ 000 \times (1.045)^{-4}$$

$$= \$83\ 856.13$$

Annuities

The coupon payments of a bond are a series of identical payments at even intervals. Such a series of payments is referred to as an annuity. An annuity of coupon payments is equivalent to a series of zero coupon bonds each with a maturity value equal to the coupon payment and a time to maturity equal to the time of receipt of the coupon payment. The present value of each coupon can therefore be calculated using the compound interest present value formula and each of these values can be summed to determine the present value of all the coupon payments.

If each coupon payment is for an amount c and the first is payable in 1 period's time we have:

$$\text{Present value of 1st coupon} = c \times v$$
$$\text{Present value of 2nd coupon} = c \times v^2$$

and so on until:

$$\text{Present value of } n\text{th coupon} = c \times v^n$$

The value of the annuity is the sum of these values or:

$$\text{Value} = [c \times v] + [c \times v^2] + \ldots + [c \times v^n]$$
$$= c \times [v + v^2 + \ldots + v^n]$$

which can also be written, using summation notation, as:

$$c \sum_{i=1}^{n} v^i$$

This formula is simplified by recognising that it is the sum of a geometric progression. Thus if the value is equal to A then:

$$A = c \times [v + v^2 + \ldots + v^n]$$

Multiplying both sides by v gives:

$$v \times A = c \times [v^2 + v^3 \ldots + v^{n+1}]$$

Subtracting the second expression from the first expression gives:

$$A - v \times A = c \times [v - v^{n+1}]$$

or:

$$A(1 - v) = c \times v \times [1 - v^n]$$

Dividing both sides by $(1 - v)$ gives:

$$A = c \times \frac{v}{(1 - v)} \times [1 - v^n]$$

Consider $\dfrac{v}{(1 - v)}$.

Dividing top and bottom by v gives $\dfrac{1}{(1/v - 1)}$.

The inverse of the discount factor is the accumulation factor so that $\dfrac{1}{v} = 1 + \dfrac{i}{100}$. Substituting this into $\dfrac{1}{(1/v - 1)}$ and simplifying gives the result $\dfrac{1}{\dfrac{i}{100}}$. Therefore:

$$A = c \times \frac{1}{\dfrac{i}{100}} \times [1 - v^n]$$

or:

■ **Equation 3.6**

$$\text{Value} = c \times \left[\frac{1 - v^n}{\dfrac{i}{100}} \right]$$

The value of an annuity is usually written as $a_{\overline{n}|}$ which denotes the present value of an annuity of \$1 per period at an interest of $i\%$ per period paid over n periods with the first payment due in 1 period's time. The formula for $a_{\overline{n}|}$ is

■ **Equation 3.7**

$$a_{\overline{n}|} = \frac{[1 - v^n]}{\dfrac{i}{100}}$$

Example 3.6

Coupon payments of \$5000 per half year are paid on a bond over 2 years. What is the value of this annuity of coupon payments to provide a yield of 9% p.a. (semi-annual)?

Solution

Using equation 3.6:

$$\text{Value} = 5000 \times \frac{[1 - v^4]}{\dfrac{i}{100}}$$

where $i = 9/2\% = 4.5\%$ and $v = (1 + i/100)^{-1} = (1.045)^{-1} = 0.9569378$

Thus:

$$\text{Value} = 5000 \times \frac{[1 - (0.9569378)^4]}{0.045}$$

$$= \$17\,937.63$$

Treasury bonds

Treasury bonds are quoted in the market in terms of a yield to maturity and the compounding frequency is the same as the frequency of payment of the coupon. For Australian Government bonds this is semi-annual. The yields to maturity on Australian Government securities are quoted by traders in the government bond market. These are rates at which the dealers are prepared to buy and sell these securities for fixed amounts. Dealers quote 'bid' and 'ask' yields to maturity since they will buy bonds at a price lower than that at which they are prepared to sell bonds. Yields to maturity on actual transactions in the government bond market are reported by bond dealers to the Reserve Bank of Australia (RBA). Not all government securities trade every day, although quoted yields to maturity are available all the time that the bond market is open. These yields to maturity are used to price these bonds.

Bonds pay regular coupons, or interest payments, and the face value on maturity. The word 'coupon' refers to the interest paid on the bond. The amount of the coupon is based on the original interest rate on the loan, the frequency with which the coupon is payable in a year and the face value of the loan. Securities that are issued as bearer securities have 'coupons' attached to the ownership certificate, with the amount of the coupon to be paid and the date of payment indicated. The interest is paid on presentation of the coupon to the paying agent of the borrower. In Australia bearer securities are no longer issued by the government. Ownership is 'registered' in a security register and owners of the bonds are paid interest on the coupon due date by cheque or through the banking payment system.

In Australia it should be noted that Australian Commonwealth Government bonds pay interest coupons every half year. Australian Commonwealth Government bonds pay coupons on the 15th of the relevant month. For instance the 7% April 2000 Commonwealth Government bond pays interest of half the coupon or 3.5% on 15 April and 15 October of each year until maturity and pays the face value plus the final coupon of 3.5% on the maturity date of 15 April 2000.

In many countries treasury bonds, including the Australian Government Treasury bond, provide payments to investors in 2 forms:

1. regular interest payments, paid semi-annually, and equal to half the coupon interest rate multiplied by the face value; and
2. the final capital repayment equal to the face value, sometimes referred to as a 'bullet' or 'balloon' repayment.

These can be valued respectively as:

1. an annuity of the interest payments (coupons), and
2. a zero coupon bond equal to the face value.

Notice that the final coupon is paid on the same day as the face value so that the maturity payment consists of the face value plus a coupon.

Example 3.7

Find the price per hundred dollars of face value of a 10% Treasury bond redeemed at par in 8 years' time to yield 9% p.a. (semi-annual).

Solution

Each semi-annual interest payment is $5 per $100 face value and there are 16 half years to maturity.

$$\text{Price} = 5a_{\overline{16}} + 100v^{16} \text{ at } 4.5\%$$

$$5a_{\overline{16}} = 5\frac{[1 - v^n]}{\dfrac{i}{100}} \text{ at } 4.5\%$$

$$= 5\frac{[1 - (1.045)^{-1})^{16}]}{0.045}$$

$$= 5 \times 11.234015$$

$$= 56.170075$$

$$100v^{16} = 100 \times (1.045^{-1})^{16}$$

$$= 100 \times (1.045)^{-16}$$

$$= 49.446932$$

$$\text{Price} = 56.170075 + 49.446932$$

$$= 105.617 \text{ per } \$100 \text{ face value (to 3 decimal places)}$$

Example 3.7 valued a Treasury bond with a full interest period before the next interest coupon payment. In practice bonds are bought or sold with only a part period remaining until the next interest payment. In these cases the procedure used is to value the bond at the next interest payment, allowing in full for the interest payment then due, and then to discount this for the appropriate number of days in the part period from the calculation date to the next interest payment date. This period is also referred to as the broken period.

Example 3.8

A 10% Treasury bond pays semi-annual interest on 15 April and 15 October and is to be redeemed at par on 15 October in 6 years' time. Find the price to yield 8.5% p.a. (semi-annual) on 30 June.

Solution

First calculate the price on the next interest payment date, 15 October. The price on 15 October of the current year immediately after the interest payment due on that date will be:

$$5\,a_{\overline{12}} + 100v^{12} \text{ at } 4.25\%$$

To allow for the interest payment due on 15 October add a coupon payment to this, so that the price becomes:

$$5\,(1 + a_{\overline{12}}) + 100v^{12} \text{ at } 4.25\%$$

Now discount this price back to 30 June so that the price becomes:

$$\{5(1 + a_{1\overline{2}|}) + 100v^{12}\}v^{107/183} \text{ at } 4.25\%$$

assuming that there are 107 days from 30 June to 15 October and 183 days from 15 April to 15 October for the broken period.

$$[5(1 + 9.250395) + 100 \times 0.606858] \times 0.975958$$

$$= 109.246539 \ (109.247 \text{ to } 3 \text{ decimal places})$$

Reserve Bank of Australia Treasury bond formula

The formula used by the RBA to value Treasury bonds is expressed as:

■ *Equation 3.8*

$$P = v^{f/d}\left[(c + ga_{\overline{n}|}) + 100v^n\right]$$

where:

- c is the next coupon payment,
- g is the regular semi-annual coupon payment,
- f is the number of days until the next interest payment, and
- d is the number of days in the current half year.

This is identical to the formula that was used in example 3.8.

Since January 1993, Australian Commonwealth Government bonds have gone ex-interest 7 days prior to the interest payment date. This means that the holder of the bond on that date will receive the next coupon even if it is sold after that date and before the next coupon date. The buyer of an ex-interest bond does not receive the next coupon due. For an ex-interest Treasury bond the next coupon (c) is zero and this value for c is used in the pricing formula for ex-interest bonds. If the bond is not ex-interest then the next coupon is a regular coupon payment so that $c = g$. For new issues of Treasury bonds the first coupon payment may not be a full coupon payment so that the appropriate value for c needs to be determined and used in pricing the bond.

Other securities with a frequency of coupon payments other than semi-annual are priced using the annuity and zero coupon formulae developed earlier, as demonstrated in the next example.

Example 3.9

A semigovernment security pays quarterly coupons of 12% p.a., has a face value of $500 000 and matures in 4 years' time. Treasury bonds for the same maturity yield 7.5% p.a. (semi-annual). What price would have to be paid for the semigovernment security in order to yield 1% p.a. (semi-annual) more than the same maturity Treasury bond?

Solution

The quarterly coupon is:

$$\frac{0.12}{4} \times 500\,000 = 15\,000$$

The price for the bond will be:

$$15\,000 a_{\overline{16}|} + 500\,000 v^{16} \text{ at } i$$

where i is the quarterly rate equivalent to 8.5% p.a. (semi-annual). Now 8.5% p.a. (semi-annual) is 4.25% per half year. If i is to be equivalent to this, then it has to compound each quarter over a half year to equal this rate, so that:

$$\left(1 + \frac{i}{100}\right)^2 = 1.0425$$

Taking the square root of each side gives:

$$1 + \frac{i}{100} = (1.0425)^{\frac{1}{2}}$$

Therefore:

$$i = 100 \times [(1.0425)^{\frac{1}{2}} - 1]$$

$$= 2.103\% \text{ (per quarter) to 3 decimal places}$$

Hence the yield required is 8.412% p.a. (quarterly compounding) to 3 decimal places.

Using this yield, but retaining all the decimal places in the calculator, to calculate the price gives:

$$a_{\overline{16}|} = \frac{1 - v^{16}}{i/100} \text{ where } i = 2.103\%$$

and:

$$v = \frac{1}{1 + i/100} = \frac{1}{1.02103} = 0.979404$$

$$v^{16} = (0.979404)^{16} = 0.716789$$

so that $a_{\overline{16}|} = 13.467696$, and:

$$\text{Price} = 15\,000 \times 13.467696 + 500\,000 \times 0.716789$$

$$= 202\,015.44 + 358\,394.63$$

$$= 560\,410.07$$

Accrued interest

Accrued interest on bonds is calculated for accounting and tax purposes using a simple apportionment of the coupon payment based on the number of days in the coupon period to the date of calculation. The price calculated using the bond formula is the present value of all the payments on the bond which includes both capital and accrued interest components. To calculate the capital component of a bond the accrued interest is determined on a pro-rata basis and subtracted from the bond price.

The accrued interest is the amount that a buyer would deduct from cash coupon receipts in order to determine taxable income if the buyer is taxed on an accruals basis. This is the basis that currently applies for most taxpayers in Australia. The easiest method of calculating accrued interest is to use the formula $NC - f/d\, C$ where NC is the actual amount of the next coupon to be received. This formula is quite general since it allows for the case where the bond is ex-interest. For ex-interest bonds the next coupon NC is zero and the accrued interest is negative.

Example 3.10

Calculate the accrued interest and capital price of the Treasury bond in example 3.8.

The bond has a 10% coupon and is priced on 30 June with interest payments on 15 April and 15 October. The number of days in the current interest period is 183 and the number of days accrued interest is from 30 June to 15 October which is 107 days.

Solution

$$\text{Accrued interest} = 5 - \frac{107}{183} \times 5$$

$$= \$2.077 \text{ per } \$100 \text{ face value}$$

$$\text{Capital price} = \text{Total price} - \text{Accrued interest}$$

$$= 109.247 - 2.077$$

$$= \$107.170$$

It is a convention in the Australian bond markets to quote prices of Treasury bonds to 3 decimal places for the price per $100 face value. Settlement payments are then based on these rounded prices.

Overseas markets

Overseas markets use a variety of conventions for price and yield quotations. In the US bond market, government securities with less than 10 years to maturity are called Treasury notes. US government securities with longer terms than this are called Treasury bonds. Treasury notes and bonds are quoted in dollars and 32nds of a dollar per $100 face value in the US market. Thus a price of 92.15 for a US Treasury security is equal to 92 and 15/32nds or 92.46875.

Indexed bonds

Governments as well as private companies issue indexed bonds in a number of different forms. These bonds are either capital or interest indexed. An interest indexed bond pays the face value of the bond on maturity in the same way as for a conventional bond, as well as varying interest payments during the life of the bond on the face value at a rate equal to an inflation rate, usually the change in the Consumer Price Index (CPI) or equivalent, plus a specified margin. As the inflation rate changes, so does the interest payment on the bond. The margin is designed to provide a 'real rate of return' over and above inflation. Such indexed securities are assessed using the techniques for floating rate securities covered in chapter 4.

Capital indexed bonds pay an indexed capital value on the maturity date equal to the indexed value of their nominal face value. This indexed maturity value increases at the rate of indexation (the rate of change of the CPI for Australian Treasury Indexed Bonds). The coupon interest payments are at a fixed rate times the current indexed capital value. The coupon rate is usually a low rate equal to the 'real', or inflation adjusted, interest rate. In order to price capital indexed securities these varying future coupons and maturity payment must be valued. The method commonly used to do this is to assume that future percentage changes in the index used will be constant.

The coupon payment in t periods per $100 of nominal (not indexed) face value will then have:

$$\text{Present value} = \text{Indexed coupon amount} \times \text{Present value factor}$$
$$= [c \times 100 \times (1 + I)^t] \times v^t$$
$$= [c \times 100 \times (1 + I)^t] \div (1 + i)^t$$

where:

- $v = 1/(1 + i)$,
- i is the per period interest rate,
- c is the per period coupon rate,

and:

- I is the assumed constant per period rate of indexation.

All of these rates—i, c and I—are per dollar rates and not per cent rates.

The value of the indexed coupon can also be obtained by determining a 'real' yield or interest rate at which these cash flows can be present valued. If a rate R is determined such that:

$$\frac{(1 + I)}{(1 + i)} = \frac{1}{(1 + R)}$$

so that:

■ *Equation 3.9*

$$R = \frac{(1+i)}{(1+I)} - 1$$

then R is referred to as the 'real' rate of interest for the indexed bond. This is used to obtain the present value of the coupon in t periods time as:

$$\text{Present value} = c \times 100 \times \frac{1}{(1+R)^t}$$

$$= c \times 100 \times v^t$$

where v is now calculated at rate R. This is identical in value to that which is obtained from the formula previously derived in terms of I and i given by:

$$[c \times 100 \times (1+I)^t] \div (1+i)^t$$

The present value of the coupon payments on an indexed bond can be calculated using this alternative method if the real rate of interest is available, since the same formula as for a conventional bond is used except that the annuity formula is calculated at the 'real' yield. The value of the coupons will be:

$$c \times 100 \times a_{\overline{n}|} \text{ at an interest rate of } R$$

where n is the number of periods to maturity.

The indexed nominal value of the bond payable on maturity in n periods will have present value:

$$100 \times (1+I)^n \times v^n \text{ at the nominal rate } i$$

$$= 100 \times [(1+I)/(1+i)]^n$$

$$= 100 \times v^n \text{ at the 'real' rate } R$$

The price of a capital indexed bond can be calculated in the same way as for a conventional bond using the real yield. If this yield is not known then it can be estimated using the rate of inflation expected to apply over the life of the security (I), the interest rate for nominal securities with the same maturity (i) and equation 3.9.

Example 3.11

A capital indexed bond with a $100 000 nominal value will mature in 10 years. It pays quarterly coupons of 4% p.a. of the indexed nominal value. Assuming that the rate of indexation is expected to average 5% p.a. (quarterly compounding) and the nominal yield rate required is 9% p.a. (quarterly compounding), calculate the price of the capital indexed bond.

Solution

The price of the bond can be calculated using the conventional bond formula at an interest rate per quarter (the 'real' yield) given by:

$$R = 100 \times \left[\frac{(1 + 9/400)}{(1 + 5/400)} - 1 \right]$$

$$= 0.987654\%$$

This gives a price of:

$$(4/400) \times 100\,000 \times a_{\overline{40}|} + 100\,000 \times v^{40} \text{ at rate } 0.987654\%$$

$$= 1000 \times \left(\frac{1 - 0.674945}{0.00987654} \right) + 100\,000 \times 0.674945$$

$$= 32\,911.78 + 67\,494.54$$

$$= \$100\,406.32$$

In practice, the conventional bond formula using a real yield cannot be used to price indexed bonds without some modification. First, the current indexed value of the nominal face value is usually not known on the day that any coupon is paid, since the latest value of the index will not be available. An earlier value of the index has to be used to determine the latest indexed value. Second, indexed bonds are purchased and sold between coupon dates and the indexed bond formula requires a different modification to allow for the broken period to that used in the conventional bond formula. The Reserve Bank of Australia Treasury Indexed Bond pricing formula allows for these factors. The formula for the price of Treasury Indexed Bonds is set out in an October 1992 Reserve Bank press release that altered the formula in the original prospectus. The current RBA formula used for pricing capital index linked bonds is:

■ *Equation 3.10*

$$v^{f/d} \left[g(x + a_{\overline{n}|}) + 100v^n \right] \frac{K_t(1 + p/100)^{-f/d}}{100}$$

where:

- $a_{\overline{n}|}$ and v^n are calculated at rate R,
- R is the real rate of interest,
- p is the average percentage change in the CPI over the 2 quarters ending in the quarter which is 2 quarters prior to the quarter in which the next

interest payment falls (used to adjust the nominal face value in the current quarter),

- c is the value of the next coupon which is zero if the bond is ex-interest,
- g is the fixed coupon rate per quarter,
- K_t is the indexed value of the nominal face value on the next coupon date based on the current quarter's change in the index of $p\%$, so that $K_t = K_{t-1} \times (1 + p/100)$,
- f is the number of days from the value date to the next coupon date,
- d is the number of days in the current quarter.

Note that K_t is rounded to 2 decimal places per 100 and that Commonwealth Treasury Indexed Bonds go ex-interest 7 days prior to the coupon date.

The valuation or pricing of indexed bonds follows directly from that used for conventional bonds, the main difference being the use of the 'real' yield or rate of interest and the incorporation of an indexed capital value.

Indexed annuities

In Australia in recent years there has been a growth in various types of indexed securities, including indexed annuities. Indexed annuities and indexed annuity bonds are 2 forms of indexed annuity that have annuity payments similar to standard annuities, except that the amount of the annuity payment is indexed to an inflation index. These 2 types of indexed annuity differ for tax purposes with the indexed annuity taxed on the whole payment with a pro-rata deduction for the purchase price of the annuity. The indexed annuity bond is taxed by dividing the payments into principal and interest and taxing the interest plus the increase in each payment due to inflation. Indexed annuities typically have quarterly payments.

The valuation formula used for indexed annuities is:

■ *Equation 3.11*

$$\left(\frac{v}{q}\right)^{f/d} B_{T-1}\, q\, (Z + a_{\overline{n}|})$$

where:

- $B_{T-1} = B_0 \dfrac{CPI_{T-1}}{CPI_0}$
- CPI_0 is the value of the CPI index for the calendar quarter prior to issue,

- CPI_{T-1} is the highest CPI index from time 0 to the calendar quarter preceding the $T-1$ annuity payment,
- B_0 is the base annuity payment usually rounded to 6 decimal places per 100,
- B_{T-1} is the annuity payment at time $T-1$,
- q is the per period inflation indexation factor $= \dfrac{CPI_j}{CPI_{j-1}}$,
- $v = \dfrac{1}{1+i}$ and $a_{\overline{n}}$ is calculated at i where i is the real yield divided by 4 for quarterly payments,
- n is the number of full quarters from the next annuity payment to maturity,
- f is the number of days from settlement to the next annuity payment date,
- d is the number of days in the full quarter ending on the next annuity payment date,
- $Z=1$ if the purchaser is to receive the next annuity payment and $Z=0$ if the purchaser is not to receive the next payment (ex-interest).

If the next annuity payment is known then the formula is:

$$\left(\frac{v}{q}\right)^{f/d} B_T (Z + a_{\overline{n}})$$

and if the value is being calculated on an annuity payment date then the formula is:

$$B_T\, a_{\overline{n}}$$

Example 3.12

Calculate the value on 1 May 1996 at a real yield of 4.5% p.a. of an indexed annuity that matures 15 August 2020 and has quarterly payments on 15 February, 15 May, 15 August and 15 November of each year. Assume that the next payment will be received by the purchaser and will be equal to 2.060418 per 100 and that $q = 1.000932$.

Solution

In this case $v = [1/(1 + 0.045/4] = 0.9888751$, $q = 1.000932$, $f = 14$ and $d = 90$ so that the value, using equation 3.11, is:

$$0.9981166 \times 2.060418 \times (1 + a_{\overline{97}}) \text{ at } 1.125\% = 123.100013$$

4 Yield calculations for long-term securities

Chapter 3 considered the calculation of prices of long-term securities for a given yield to maturity. Because long-term securities are often quoted in terms of their yield to maturity, the calculation of prices is needed in order to carry out and settle transactions. Some securities, such as floating rate notes, are quoted in terms of a price and it will be of interest to determine the yield on the security. In other cases the cash flows of a security or long-term transaction will be known and the yield on the cash flows will be required in order to assess the transaction.

Holding period calculations for long-term securities require the determination of a yield on a set of cash flows using compound interest formulae. Similarly, in order to assess the effect of tax and transaction costs on a security, a yield is calculated on the cash flows of the security after including tax effects and transaction costs in the cash flows.

To calculate these yields for longer-term securities it is necessary to use a trial and error procedure since it is not possible to write down a simple equation with the yield on only one side of the equation. These securities will involve returns in the form of interest payments and in the form of capital gains or losses. The yield calculated will reflect both of these forms of return. Financial calculators, such as the HP12C, and spreadsheets use a trial and error process to determine yields. This process is programmed into the calculator or spreadsheet function.

There are a number of steps involved in these trial and error methods. The first is to get a starting value. An approximate value for a per period yield given a security that involves a net investment of P, net returns of C per period and a net maturity payment of M in n periods' time is given by:

■ *Equation 4.1*

$$i = \frac{C + (M - P)/n}{(M + P)/2}$$

In this formula C is the interest return per period, $(M - P)$ is the capital profit respread over the n periods to get a per period capital return, and $(M + P)/2$ is an approximation to the average amount on which the return is earned. The investment and returns are adjusted for any factors that are going to be allowed for in the yield calculation—such as taxes and costs.

This approximate yield is then used to calculate the discounted value of the returns of C per period and M on the maturity date. If this value is equal to P, then the approximate yield equals the yield on the investment. Usually the value will differ from P. In this case another value for the yield is determined and the discounted value of the Cs and M recalculated. This other yield is determined by adding or subtracting from the approximate yield an amount of, say, 0.5%. If the discounted value is less than P, the amount is subtracted and if it is greater than P, the amount is added. The results of these 2 calculations are then used to determine a better approximation to the yield required using some form of interpolation. Programmed calculators and spreadsheet functions carry out this interpolation many times to obtain an accurate yield. If the calculations are performed manually then it may only be practical to perform 1 or 2 interpolations.

Linear interpolation

The simplest form of interpolation when 2 approximate yields are available is linear interpolation. This fits a straight line through the 2 points given by the yield and discounted value of the Cs and M and uses this straight line to determine the value for the yield which corresponds to P. If the first approximate yield used is i_0, the value obtained for the discounted value of the Cs and M using this yield is P_0, the second approximate yield is i_1, and the discounted value at this yield is P_1, then the interpolated value corresponding to the discounted value P, given by fitting a straight line through these points, is determined from the equation:

$$\frac{i - i_0}{i_1 - i_0} = \frac{P - P_0}{P_1 - P_0}$$

■ *Equation 4.2*

$$i = i_0 + (i_1 - i_0) \times \frac{P - P_0}{P_1 - P_0}$$

Example 4.1

A long-term security pays half-yearly interest coupons of 6% (12% p.a.) and on maturity in 6 years pays the face value of $100% (i.e. $100 per $100 of face value). The current price of the security is $90%. Calculate an approximate yield for this security. Improve the approximation using linear interpolation.

Solution

Using equation 4.1, the approximate yield is given by:

$$i = \frac{6 + (100 - 90)/12}{(100 + 90)/2}$$

since $C = 6$, $M = 100$, $P = 90$ and $n = 12$ periods, which gives:

$$i = 0.07193 \text{ or } 7.193\% \text{ per half year}$$

This answer is improved using linear interpolation by first calculating the discounted value of the returns at this approximate yield. This is given by:

$$6a_{\overline{12}|} + 100(1 + i)^{-12} \text{ where } i = 0.07193$$

$$= 6 \times 7.861628 + 100 \times 0.434513$$

$$= 90.62108$$

This value is higher than 90 so the next step is to use a higher yield for the second value. Because the answer is so close to the price of 90 an addition of 0.25% should be sufficient. The discounted value of the returns at the new $i = 0.07193 + 0.0025$ or 0.07443 is:

$$6 \times 7.758501 + 100 \times 0.422535$$

$$= 88.80448$$

The 2 sets of values for linear interpolation are (0.07193, 90.62108) and (0.07443, 88.80448) so that a more accurate yield is given by using equation 4.2:

$$i = 0.07193 + \left[(0.07443 - 0.07193) \times \frac{(90 - 90.62108)}{(88.80448 - 90.62108)} \right]$$

$$= 0.07193 + 0.0025 \times \frac{-0.62108}{-1.81660}$$

$$= 0.072785 \text{ or } 7.2785\% \text{ per half year}$$

To test the accuracy of this second answer calculate the discounted value of the returns at this yield to get:

$$6 \times 7.826123 + 100 \times 0.430376 = 89.99430$$

which is very close to the 90 required. Financial calculators and spreadsheet functions carry out interpolation a number of times until the answer is within a preprogrammed accuracy. They also typically use better methods of interpolation than linear interpolation.

In the above calculations rounding differences occur between the answer obtained from the intermediate steps shown and the final answer actually given. The final answer is determined using all the decimal places available in the calculator for all intermediate steps. Intermediate steps are shown as determined by the calculator but are rounded in the text for convenience. Final answers have been rounded to 5 decimal places. Final answers may also be rounded because of market conventions. For example, prices for Treasury bonds in Australia are determined as prices per $100 face value and rounded to 3 decimal places in the bond market. (This was mentioned in chapter 3.)

Net present value and internal rate of return

Financial calculators and spreadsheets have built-in functions for determining the yield on any given stream of payments. These functions calculate the internal rate of return or *IRR* of a specified set of cash flows. They also have a function to evaluate the net present value or *NPV* of a set of cash flows at a specified yield. The net present value is the sum of the present values of each of the cash flows where outgoings, such as the initial investment and costs, are treated as negative cash flows and incomings, such as interest and capital payments, are treated as positive cash flows.

The internal rate of return is the yield (or interest rate) that will give a zero net present value (*NPV*) for the payment stream. Hence the *IRR* equates the present value of the negative flows to the present value of the positive flows on an investment, since their net value will be zero if these 2 are equal. Each of the payments does not need to be equal, as in the case of a coupon paying bond, for these calculations. This internal rate of return calculation involves trial and error calculations in an identical fashion to that outlined above. The calculations are carried out by determining the present values of the cash flows individually at an approximate yield rate and improving this approximation using some form of interpolation between successive values.

Example 4.2

Calculate the internal rate of return (*IRR*) on a security that has an initial cost of $100 000 and returns $3500 each quarter for 2 years as well as paying $1000 at the end of each year for 2 years and $100 000 on maturity in 2 years.

Solution

The *IRR* is the yield that gives a zero net present value. The net present value (*NPV*) is:

$$-100\,000 + 3500a_{\overline{8}|} + 1000 \times (v^4 + v^8) + 100\,000v^8$$

at rate i, the quarterly rate.

This *NPV* can be determined using a financial calculator, such as the HP12C, by entering the cash flows of $-100\,000$, 3500 (3 times), 4500, 3500 (3 times), and 104 500 and using the *IRR* function to obtain the quarterly rate. Doing this the answer is 3.736417% per quarter or 14.945668% p.a. (payable quarterly).

Alternatively, a trial and error procedure can be used. An approximate yield is given by:

$$i = \frac{3750 + (100\,000 - 100\,000)/8}{(100\,000 + 100\,000)/2}$$

$$= 3750/100\,000$$

$$= 0.0375$$

where the 3750 is the average interest return determined as:

$$(3500 \times 8 + 1000 \times 2)/8$$

At 3.75% the *NPV* is:

$NPV = -100\,000 + 3500 \times 6.802795 + 1000 \times (0.863073 + 0.744895)$

$\qquad + 100\,000 \times 0.744895$

$\qquad = -100\,000 + 23\,809.78 + 1607.97 + 74\,489.52$

$\qquad = -92.73$

A lower yield will be required since the *NPV* is below the target value of zero. A rate of 3.5% will be used to get a second value for interpolation since the net present value at 3.75% is quite close to zero. The *NPV* becomes:

$NPV = -100\,000 + 3500 \times 6.873955 + 1000 \times (0.871442 + 0.759412)$

$\qquad + 100\,000 \times 0.7594116$

$\qquad = -100\,000 + 24\,058.84 + 1630.85 + 75\,941.16$

$\qquad = 1630.85$

These 2 values are then used for interpolation to improve the answer to get:

$$\frac{i - 0.035}{0.0375 - 0.035} = \frac{0 - 1630.85}{-92.73 - 1630.85}$$

or:

$$i = 0.035 + 0.0025 \times (-1630.85/-1723.58)$$

$$= 0.037365 \text{ or } 3.7365\% \text{ per quarter } (14.9462\% \text{ p.a.})$$

This yield is the same as the *IRR* calculated using the HP12C to 3 decimal places.

Floating rate securities

Floating rate securities pay interest as a margin over a variable or floating rate. Interest indexed securities pay an interest margin over an inflation index. Other securities pay a margin over a floating interest rate. An important floating rate security is the floating rate note (FRN).

Floating rate notes (FRNs) have a fixed maturity date like other longer-term securities but also have a coupon rate which is a fixed margin over a specified short-term interest rate. The coupon is reset usually on a semi-annual or quarterly basis using the then current short-term interest rate plus the margin to determine the interest payment at the next coupon date. The coupon reset date is also referred to as the coupon rollover date. Eurodollar floating rate notes generally use LIBOR (the London Interbank Offer Rate for Eurodeposits), or sometimes the average of the LIBID (the London Interbank Bid Rate) and LIBOR rates (referred to as the mid rate), as the floating rate. Margins are typically of the order of 0.125% to 0.25%. Euromarket securities use a 360 day year for pricing and the determination of coupon amounts. Other floating rates used include Bank Accepted Bill rates and other Commercial paper rates.

Some FRNs have features such as minimum coupon levels, sinking fund and call provisions, or the option to convert to fixed rate bonds. These features are ignored here. Methods of allowing for call and conversion features are based on the techniques covered in chapter 8, since these are option features which require an option pricing model to value their effect on the security price.

FRNs and Eurobonds are traded on a percentage price basis, with a spread between bid and ask prices usually of the order of 0.25% in the price. Prices are usually quoted as 'flat' prices which exclude accrued interest. Settlement is then for the principal amount times the price plus the accrued interest.

A number of methods can be used to assess the relative value of FRNs. A simple method is the current yield method, which is:

$$\text{Current yield} = \frac{\text{Current coupon}}{\text{Price}}$$

This method makes no allowance for any premium/discount on purchase and ignores the effect of accrued interest. If an FRN is purchased at a price above its face value then it is purchased at a premium and, if purchased at a price below its face value, then it is purchased at a discount. For these reasons it does not give a reliable guide to the relative value of FRNs.

Methods that provide a more accurate assessment of value calculate an effective margin allowing for:

1. the fixed margin in the coupon,

2. the respreading of the discount/premium to maturity,
3. an adjustment for interest on the discount/premium, and
4. the 'carry' or 'funding gain' for purchase/sale between coupon dates.

Some banks/brokers use methods that make approximate allowances for these factors and these give inaccurate results. A common approximation is to respread the discount/premium by dividing by the number of periods to maturity. This implies a straight line writing up (down) or amortisation of the discount/premium. This results in an overstatement of the effective margin for discount FRNs and an understatement for premium FRNs. The amortisation should be on a compound interest basis. A more accurate allowance can be made by assuming an average rate over the term for the floating rate used to set the coupon. This average rate is then used to determine expected coupon payments. The values of these coupon payments are then equated to the purchase price to obtain a yield to maturity. The average rate used to determine the coupons is then deducted from the yield to maturity to obtain an effective margin. In what follows the floating rate used will be assumed to be LIBOR and a 360 day convention will be adopted which is usually the case for a Eurodollar FRN. The accurate formula will be to determine R, such that:

$$(P_p + A) = \frac{\dfrac{C_c \times D_1}{360}}{\left[1 + \dfrac{R}{100} \times \dfrac{D_s}{360}\right]} + \frac{\dfrac{C_2 \times D_2}{360}}{\left[1 + \dfrac{R}{100} \times \dfrac{D_s}{360}\right]\left[1 + \dfrac{R}{100} \times \dfrac{D_2}{360}\right]} + \ldots$$

$$+ \frac{100 + \dfrac{C_n \times D_n}{360}}{\left[1 + \dfrac{R}{100} \times \dfrac{D_s}{360}\right]\left[1 + \dfrac{R}{100} \times \dfrac{D_2}{360}\right] \times \ldots \times \left[1 + \dfrac{R}{100} \times \dfrac{D_n}{360}\right]}$$

The effective margin is then given by $R - R_a$ where:

- P_p is the flat purchase price,
- A is accrued interest,
- C_c is the current coupon rate (p.a.) payable at the next reset date,
- R_a is the assumed average LIBOR over the life of the FRN,
- C_i is the coupon rate in the ith period equal to $R_a + S$,
- S is the coupon spread over LIBOR,
- D_i is the number of days in the coupon period,
- D_s is the number of days from calculation date to the next coupon date,
- R is the *IRR* on the cash flows which have been estimated using the average LIBOR. This is determined using the iterative techniques covered previously or by using a preprogrammed financial calculator or spreadsheet function.

If it is assumed that coupon periods after the first are at equal intervals, even though the exact number of days between coupon payments may not be exactly the same, then an accurate approximation to the effective margin is given by the formula:

■ *Equation 4.3*

$$R - R_a = \frac{\left[S + \dfrac{(100 - P_a) \times f}{s_{\overline{n}|}} + \dfrac{(100 - P_a) \times R_a}{100} \right]}{P_a} \times 100$$

where:

- f is the frequency of coupon payments (2 for semi-annual),
- $s_{\overline{n}|}$ is the accumulated value of 1 per period over n periods and is equal to:

■ *Equation 4.4*

$$s_{\overline{n}|} = \frac{\left[1 + \dfrac{R_a}{100 \times f} \right]^n - 1}{\dfrac{R_a}{100 \times f}}$$

- and P_a is the flat purchase/sale price adjusted for the 'carry' or 'net funding gain' and is equal to:

■ *Equation 4.5*

$$P_a = P_p - \left[1C_c - \frac{R_s \times (P_p + A)}{100} \right] \times \frac{D_s}{360}$$

where R_s is equal to the funding rate from the settlement date to the next coupon date.

To understand the 'carry' adjustment which is used to determine P_a, consider the following 2 transactions. First, borrow the total cost of the FRN equal to $(P_p + A)$ from the date of purchase to the next coupon date. On the coupon date an amount equal to this borrowing plus interest, or:

$$(P_p + A) \left(1 + \frac{R_s}{100} \times \frac{D_s}{360} \right)$$

will have to be repaid. Second, use the borrowed funds to purchase the FRN for $(P_p + A)$ and hold the security to the next coupon date. The FRN will then be worth P_a, the price applying immediately after receipt of the coupon plus the next coupon of $\dfrac{D_c}{360} \times C_c$, where D_c is the number of days in the current coupon period. The 'carry' is allowed for by requiring the values of these 2 transactions as at the next coupon date to be equal, so that:

$$(P_p + A)\left(1 + \frac{R_s}{100} \times \frac{D_s}{360}\right) = P_a + \left(\frac{D_c}{360} \times C_c\right)$$

or solving for P_a:

$$P_a = (P_p + A)\left(1 + \frac{R_s}{100} \times \frac{D_s}{360}\right) - \left(\frac{D_c}{360} \times C_c\right)$$

$$= (P_p + A) + \left[(P_p + A) \times \left(\frac{R_s}{100} \times \frac{D_s}{360}\right)\right] - \left(\frac{D_c}{360} \times C_c\right)$$

The accrued interest A is equal to:

$$\frac{(D_c - D_s)}{360} \times C_c = \left(\frac{D_c}{360} \times C_c\right) - \left(\frac{D_s}{360} \times C_c\right)$$

Substituting this expression for A in the first part of the expression for P_a above gives:

$$P_a = P_p + \left(\frac{D_c}{360} \times C_c\right) - \left(\frac{D_s}{360} \times C_c\right) + (P_p + A)\left(\frac{R_s}{100} \times \frac{D_s}{360}\right) - \left(\frac{D_c}{360} \times C_c\right)$$

$$= P_p - \left(\frac{D_s}{360} \times C_c\right) + (P_p + A)\left(\frac{R_s}{100} \times \frac{D_s}{360}\right)$$

$$= P_p - \left[C_c - \frac{R_s}{100}(P_p + A)\right] \times \frac{D_s}{360}$$

which is the same as equation 4.5.

The terms in the top line of equation 4.3 represent the margin, the respreading of the discount/premium and the interest on the discount/premium respectively. These are added together, divided by the adjusted price and multiplied by 100 to get the effective margin on the FRN as a per cent. This effective margin is the return or yield that will be earned on the FRN on a basis that can be compared with other FRN returns. The effective margin is a method for use in the selection of the best value FRNs. The higher the effective margin the better the return. These effective margins cannot be compared directly with fixed rate security yields.

Example 4.3

A Eurodollar FRN that is quoted at a price of 98.50 for settlement on 7 July of the current year with maturity on 21 April in 7 years' time has a spread over LIBOR of 0.25%. Coupons are payable semi-annually and the current coupon is 9.5625% p.a. Calculate an effective margin on this FRN assuming that R_s is 7.2% and R_a is 7%.

Solution

Before carrying out the calculations it is necessary to determine the accrued interest and the adjusted price. The number of days from 21 April to 7 July is 76 on a 360 day basis.

$$\text{Accrued interest}= 9.5625 \times \frac{76}{360} = 2.01875$$

The number of days from settlement to the next coupon date (21 October) is 104 on a 360 day basis (180 – 76). The 'carry' or 'net funding gain' is:

$$\left[9.5625 - \frac{7.2}{100} \times (98.5 + 2.01875)\right] \frac{104}{360} = 0.6717$$

Hence, the adjusted price is:

$$98.50 - (0.6717) = 97.8283$$

Considering each component of yield in turn, the effective margin is calculated as:
Margin from spread:

$$S = 0.25$$

Respreading of discount:
There are 13 coupons so we need $s_{\overline{13}|}$ which, using equation 4.4, is:

$$\frac{\left[1 + \frac{7}{100 \times 2}\right]^{13} - 1}{\frac{7}{100 \times 2}} = \frac{0.563956}{0.035} = 16.11303$$

The respread of the discount is then:

$$\frac{(100 - 97.8283) \times 2}{16.11303} = 0.26956$$

The interest on the discount is:

$$(100 - 97.8283) \times (7/100) = 0.1520$$

The effective margin, using equation 4.3, is then:

$$\frac{(0.25 + 0.2696 + 0.1520)}{97.8283} \times 100 = 0.6865$$

Australian Treasury Interest Indexed bonds are similar to FRNs in that the coupon payment varies in line with the rate of change in the CPI. Other interest indexed bonds are similar since the coupon payment is a specified margin over the rate of change of a specified index. The 'real' return on these securities can be assessed using the effective margin formula for FRNs in order to adjust the margin for any premium/discount in the purchase price and to allow for purchase/sale between interest payment dates.

Reinvestment assumptions and holding period analysis

The yield to maturity (*IRR*) calculation for long-term securities implicitly assumes that the coupon or interest payments can be reinvested when they are received at this yield to maturity. The calculation is also based on the assumption that the security is held to the maturity date. In practice these assumptions will not hold since future yields will change and coupons will inevitably be reinvested at a different interest rate to the yield to maturity. Very often a security will be sold prior to its maturity date to meet a liability or to take advantage of a trading opportunity.

A realistic estimate of the return on the security is required for analysis. This needs to allow for other assumptions about future yields at which coupons can be reinvested, or at which securities are sold, in the calculation of yields and requires a modification to the yield calculations. To allow for reinvestment at yields other than the yield to maturity, a reinvestment yield or terminal rate of return calculation is used. This yield incorporates assumptions about future reinvestment rates by accumulating the interest coupons at the assumed future reinvestment rates to the maturity date of the security. The accumulated value of coupons and maturity value is then treated as a zero coupon bond maturing on that date and a yield to maturity of the zero coupon bond calculated. This yield is also referred to as the total realised compound yield since it aims to represent the actual return realised on the investment under the reinvestment assumptions used.

Example 4.4

A bond with semi-annual coupons of 12% p.a. and maturing in 2 years' time is bought at a yield to maturity of 8% p.a. Determine the reinvestment yield on this bond, allowing for reinvestment of coupons at 7% p.a.

Solution

The cost of the bond, per $100 face value, at a 8% yield to maturity is given by:

$$6a_{\overline{4}|} + 100v^4 \text{ at } 4\% = 107.259790$$

The accumulated value of the coupons at 3.5% per half year will be:

$$6 \times \{(1.035)^3 + (1.035)^2 + (1.035)^1 + 1\}$$

$$= 6 \times \{1.108718 + 1.071225 + 1.035 + 1\}$$

$$= 6 \times 4.214943$$

$$= 25.289657$$

The accumulated value of the coupons allowing for reinvestment of $25.289657 along with the maturity value of $100 is then treated as being received as a single sum on the maturity date. The reinvestment yield is found by solving for the interest rate that will accumulate the cost of the bond to an amount equal to this sum. If the reinvestment yield is denoted by $r\%$ per half year, then it is determined by solving the equation:

$$107.259790 \times (1 + r/100)^4 = 125.289657$$

so that, after dividing both sides by the cost and taking the 4th root of both sides, r is given by:

$$\left(1 + \frac{r}{100}\right) = \left[\frac{125.289657}{107.259790}\right]^{\frac{1}{4}} = 1.039608$$

so that r equals 3.961% per half year or 7.92% p.a. with semi-annual compounding.

In general, the accumulated value of n coupons as at the date of the last coupon, including this last coupon, at an interest rate of $r\%$ per period is denoted by $s_{\overline{n}|}$. The formula for $s_{\overline{n}|}$ is:

■ *Equation 4.6*

$$s_{\overline{n}|} = \frac{\left(1 + \dfrac{r}{100}\right)^n - 1}{\dfrac{r}{100}}$$

The accumulated value of the coupons is better determined using this formula instead of adding up the individual future values. For long-term securities this formula makes the calculations easier. Thus, for the example, the accumulated value of the coupons would have been determined as:

$$6s_{\overline{4}|} \text{ at } 3.5\% = 6 \times \{(1.035)^4 - 1\}/0.035$$

$$= 6 \times \{1.147523 - 1\}/0.035$$

$$= 6 \times 4.214943$$

$$= 25.289657$$

A large component of the total return on long-term securities is in the form of reinvestment income or interest on interest. For a fixed maturity date, higher coupon bonds have a larger proportion of their return provided through interest on interest than lower coupon bonds. Zero coupon bonds have no reinvestment problems and the yield to maturity is not affected by reinvestment assumptions. The yield actually realised on higher coupon longer-term securities will be sensitive to the reinvestment rates available at the time of receipt of coupon income. In practice it is important to assess the sensitivity of the total return to changes in reinvestment rates. This is how interest rate risk is often assessed. Chapter 5 covers interest rate risk measures.

If we assume that the security is sold prior to maturity, then the price at which it is sold will be determined by the market yields at the time of sale. If yields have fallen from the time of purchase then the market value at sale will exceed the purchase cost, and a higher yield than the yield to maturity will be earned over the period the security was held. In order to calculate a yield over the period from purchase to the date of assumed sale, it is necessary to base the calculation on an assumed sale yield. Calculations that are based on an assumed sale are referred to as *holding period returns* as they represent the return earned over the holding period of the investment from purchase to sale. Another term used to describe these calculations is *horizon analysis*.

Example 4.5

A 10 year bond with an annual coupon of 10% is bought at a yield to maturity of 9%. Calculate the holding period yield if the bond is assumed to be sold in 3 years at a yield of 8%.

Solution

The purchase cost of the bond is:

$$10a_{\overline{10}|} + 100v^{10} \text{ at 9\% per \$100 face value}$$

$$= 10 \times 6.417658 + 100 \times 0.422411$$

$$= 106.417658$$

The sale proceeds in 3 years' time will be:

$$10a_{\overline{7}|} + 100v^{7} \text{ at 8\%}$$

$$= 10 \times 5.206370 + 100 \times 0583490$$

$$= 110.412740$$

The holding period yield is given by equating the purchase cost with the value of the coupons received over the 3 years that the bond is held plus the sale proceeds, as follows:

$$106.417658 = 10a_{\overline{3}|} + 110.412740v^{3}$$

This equation can be solved using the iterative techniques covered in this chapter or more simply by using a programmed financial calculator or a spreadsheet *IRR* function. The holding period yield calculated using the HP12C financial functions is 10.525% p.a. This can be checked by calculating the right-hand side of the above equation at this yield to get:

$$10 \times 2.464029 + 110.412740 \times 0.740652 = 106.417658$$

as expected.

Total realised compound yields are usually calculated using both reinvestment assumptions and assumed sale yields for a given holding period.

Transaction costs

When a company or a bank raises funds using long-term securities, such as Eurobonds, transaction costs will have to be met. These include flat costs such as printing of bonds, trustee and paying agent fees as well as costs related to the face value of the issue such as listing fees, underwriting commissions and management fees. An issuer of these securities needs to allow for these costs in calculating the effective yield or borrowing cost of the issue. This is done by adjusting the cash flows, mainly the initial proceeds since most of the costs are charged up-front, and calculating the internal rate of return or yield on the adjusted cash flows.

Example 4.6

A Eurobond issue for A$100 million is made at par with an annual coupon of 12% and a maturity of 10 years. Initial costs are $10 000 plus a listing fee of 0.25% of the face value, underwriting commission of 2.5% of the face value and management fees of 0.5% of the face value. Determine the effective interest cost of the bond, allowing for the up-front costs.

Solution

Costs amount to $10 000 plus 3.25% of the face value, a total of $3.26 million. Hence the net proceeds of the issue will amount to $96.74 million. To calculate the effective interest cost the yield, which equates the value of the coupons and maturity proceeds to the net proceeds, is determined. This is given by:

$$96.74 = 12a_{\overline{10}|} + 100v^{10}$$

The solution to this can be determined using a trial and error procedure or by using an *IRR* function on a financial calculator or spreadsheet. Using the financial functions on the HP12C gives a yield of 12.59% p.a. Hence transaction costs add 0.59% to the cost of this borrowing.

A similar technique is used to allow for recurrent transaction costs. For Eurobonds, recurrent costs will include paying agent fees, listing fees and an administration charge. These can be added to the interest payments on the borrowing and a yield calculated using the altered cash flows to determine the cost of borrowing allowing for these other costs.

Example 4.7

The Eurobond issue in example 4.6 also involves recurrent transaction costs of $5000 plus 0.25% p.a. of the face value payable on the same date as each coupon. Determine the effective p.a. cost of the bond allowing for all transaction costs.

Solution

The recurrent costs amount to $255 000 or $0.255 million. The effective p.a. cost is the yield which equates the net proceeds (reduced by up-front costs) with the total outgoings of coupons and recurrent costs. This equation is:

$$96.74 = 12.255a_{\overline{10}|} + 100v^{10}$$

This equation gives a yield of 12.85% p.a. so that recurrent costs add $12.85 - 12.59 = 0.26\%$ p.a. to the cost of this borrowing.

Effect of tax

The costs of borrowing funds and the returns earned on a long-term security will be directly affected by taxation. In order to assess transactions in these securities we need to allow for tax. The tax effect varies with the taxpayer. Non-tax-paying investors need not concern themselves with tax effects directly, since their returns will just be the gross return on the security. For many companies the imputation system of company tax in Australia will mean that any tax paid by the company will be credited to shareholder investors so that allowing for tax is not as important as it is for countries without an imputation system of company tax. Institutional investors such as superannuation funds and life insurance companies who benefit from imputation credits under the Australian company tax system need to consider the effect of tax on total returns. For individual investors the effect of tax will be important in assessing the relative worth of different securities, especially where the timing of tax payments differs from one security to another. For some assets the effect of tax will also differ depending on whether the tax is paid in the form of tax on interest income or on capital profits/losses on redemption or sale.

It is not the aim of this book to cover the rules for the determination of tax on specific transactions for specific institutions but rather to illustrate general principles so that specific cases can be handled by a suitable application of these principles. In practice it is important to obtain tax advice in order to assess the effect that tax will have on any borrowing or investment transaction where the rules that will apply are not clear or the transaction is not standard. Tax rules are constantly changing and it is important to allow for the current tax rules in any analysis.

Tax effects can influence the cost of borrowing since interest costs are deductible and the earlier these tax deductions can be claimed, the lower the effective after-tax cost of borrowing. Tax effects are also important in assessing returns from investments and the deferral of tax payments will be beneficial in this case. After-tax yields are important in any investment or trading strategy using long-term securities, since it is the after-tax yield which gives the true return to the investor. It must always be remembered that, for tax-paying investors, the government is a joint venture partner in any investment (except in the event of major losses) and this has to be allowed for in the calculations.

Before considering the allowance for tax in security transactions, a simple borrowing example will be used to illustrate the principles.

Example 4.8

An individual borrower pays tax at the rate of 47% of taxable income, has a 30 June financial year and pays tax for the financial year 30 June XX on 15 April XX + 1. On 29 June XX this borrower raises $500 000 for 90 days to invest in the equity market. Determine the after-tax cost of borrowing, as a simple interest rate for a 90 day investment, assuming:

(a) interest is paid in arrears at 14% p.a., and
(b) interest is prepaid in advance (and is deductible for tax purposes on this basis) at 13.5328% p.a., the discount rate equivalent to 14% p.a. in arrears.

Note that, ignoring tax, interest prepaid in advance has the same effect as issuing a discount security so that the interest rate for interest prepaid in advance, equivalent to any interest in arrears rate, will be the equivalent discount rate.

Solution

(a) For $500 000 the interest cost will be:

$$500\ 000 \times \frac{14}{100} \times \frac{90}{365} = \$17\ 260.27$$

which will be claimed as a tax deduction in the tax year ending 30 June XX + 1. The tax reduction will be:

$$0.47 \times \$17\ 260.27 = \$8112.33$$

and this will reduce the tax payable on 15 April XX + 1.
The effective after-tax borrowing cost is given by $r\%$ p.a. where:

$$500\,000 = \frac{517\,260.27}{\left[1 + \dfrac{r}{100} \times \dfrac{90}{365}\right]} - \frac{8112.33}{\left[1 + \dfrac{r}{100} \times \dfrac{90}{365}\right]^{\frac{656}{90}}}$$

since there are 656 days from 29 June XX to 15 April XX + 2, ignoring leap years. In this case the *IRR* routine on a financial calculator cannot be used because of the uneven time period between cash flows, so that we need to use trial and error to solve for *r*. This is readily done on a spreadsheet. As a first estimate we could use the simple rule of thumb:

$$\text{After-tax rate} \approx \text{Before-tax rate}$$

$$\text{After-tax rate} \approx (1 - \text{Tax rate}) \times \text{Before-tax rate}$$

This estimate is based on the assumption that tax is paid on the same date as the interest or coupon payment date and that the security is priced at par. This gives an after-tax rate of $(1 - 0.47) \times 14 = 7.42\%$.

The right-hand side of the equation for the after-tax borrowing costs at 7.42% is 500 858.48.

A higher yield is required. At 8.4% the right-hand side equals 499 777.66. Linear interpolation gives a new estimate of the yield of 8.198%. The right-hand side at 8.198% is 500 000.17 so that the after-tax borrowing cost is 8.198%.

(b) The interest cost paid in advance will be:

$$500\,000 \times \frac{13.5328}{100} \times \frac{90}{365} = \$16\,684.28$$

which will be claimed as a tax deduction in the tax year ending 30 June XX. The tax deduction will be:

$$0.47 \times 16\,684.28 = \$7841.61$$

which will reduce the tax payable on 15 April XX + 1.

The effective after-tax borrowing cost is given by *r*% p.a. from the equation:

$$483\,315.72 = \frac{500\,000}{\left[1 + \dfrac{r}{100} \times \dfrac{90}{365}\right]} - \frac{7841.61}{\left[1 + \dfrac{r}{100} \times \dfrac{90}{365}\right]^{\frac{291}{90}}}$$

where the net proceeds of 483 315.72 is equal to the total amount borrowed of 500 000 less the interest prepaid of 16 684.28.

Once again it is necessary to use trial and error to solve for *r*. At 7.42% the right-hand side equals 483 621.28. A higher rate is required so try 8%. At 8% the right-hand side equals 482 966.13. Interpolation gives 7.691%. The right-hand side equals 483 314.95 at this rate.

By claiming the interest cost in advance the borrower has reduced the after-tax cost of borrowing from 8.198% to 7.691% or by about 0.5% p.a. after tax. This is equivalent to about 1% p.a. on a gross or before-tax basis using the rule of thumb for converting from before to after-tax rates. The lender can share in some of these tax benefits by increasing the rate charged if interest is prepaid in advance on 29 June by anywhere up to 1% p.a.

An accurate allowance for tax will determine a yield based on the after-tax cash flows. These differ for a purchase and a sale since when a security is sold a gain or loss is realised, whereas when a security is purchased the premium or discount will be realised as a loss or gain on maturity or on sale prior to maturity under tax rules in Australia for fixed interest securities at the time of writing. There are proposals to alter the taxation treatment of fixed interest securities to bring taxable income into account on a daily compounding rate of return basis. Under current tax rules the cash flows to be brought into account in an after-tax yield calculation are:

1. for a purchase:
    (a) consideration paid for the security;
    (b) interest returns on the security;
    (c) tax payments on interest on the payment or instalment dates for tax;
    (d) redemption proceeds on maturity (or sale proceeds if the security is assumed to be sold prior to maturity);
    (e) tax payments or deductions on any taxable gains or losses at redemption (or sale).
2. for a sale:
    (a) sale proceeds;
    (b) increases or reductions in tax resulting from taxable gains or losses on sale, on the dates of the actual tax payment or instalments;
    (c) returns given up in the way of interest;
    (d) reductions in tax representing the tax payments on the interest payments given up on the sale;
    (e) redemption proceeds which would otherwise have been received on the maturity date, given up on the sale;
    (f) increases or reductions in tax which would have occurred through a gain or loss on redemption or maturity.

The timing of tax payments can be allowed for using a number of different assumptions. Approximate allowance for tax may be sufficient in practice. This approximate allowance could be based on the assumption that tax is paid on the same day as the receipt of interest or profit, so that the net amount only is assumed to be received on the payment date.

An accurate allowance for tax would be based on the actual tax instalments paid which would be determined from the taxable income arising in each financial year from the transaction. Tax instalment dates for company tax payers in Australia, including institutional investors such as superannuation funds, were given in chapter 2.

Example 4.9

A $100 000 face value 10% bond paying semi-annual interest on 15 July and 15 January matures on 15 July in 3 years' time. The bond is purchased on 15 July at a redemption yield of 8.5%. The purchaser is an Australian superannuation fund which pays tax at 15% on taxable income and has a financial year ending 30 June. Taxable income for bonds includes coupon income and gains and losses on redemption are taxed as income.

Calculate the after-tax yield that the fund will earn on the following assumptions:

(a) tax payments are made on the same date as the coupons and gains or losses;
(b) tax payments for the financial year ended 30 June XX are paid on 1 March XX + 1; and
(c) tax instalments are paid based on the previous year's tax of 25% on 1 June XX, 1 September XX, 1 December XX and tax is assessed for the current year on 1 March XX + 1.

For cases (b) and (c) assume that tax on coupons is paid on a straight line accruals basis so that the coupon cash receipts are apportioned to financial years based on the proportion of the coupon period that falls within the financial year.

Solution

(a) The purchase cost on 15 July is:

$$5000a_{\overline{6}|} + 100\,000v^6 \text{ at } 4.25\% = 103\,899.81$$

The after-tax yield is given by equating purchase cost with the after-tax returns. Tax is assumed to reduce the coupons by 15% or $0.15 \times 5000 = 750$. On maturity the purchaser incurs a loss of 3899.81 since the bond was purchased for 103 899.81 and is redeemed for 100 000. This loss gives rise to a tax benefit of $0.15 \times 3899.81 = 584.97$. It is assumed that the fund has sufficient taxable income from other investments to absorb the tax loss on maturity.

The after-tax yield is given by the yield that solves the following equation:

$$103\,899.81 = 5000a_{\overline{6}|} + 100\,000v^6 - 750a_{\overline{6}|} + 584.97v^6$$

$$= 4250a_{\overline{6}|} + 100\,584.97v^6$$

An *IRR* function on a financial calculator or spreadsheet is used to determine the yield that equates the right-hand side of this equation to the cost. Using the HP12C gives 3.605% per half year or 7.21% p.a. Notice that the rule of thumb approximation would give an after-tax yield of $(1 - 0.15) \times 8.5 = 7.225\%$ p.a.

(b) To adjust for tax in this case the taxable income arising from the purchase needs to be determined based on the accrual of coupon income and the tax loss on maturity. Table 4.1 shows the taxable income and the tax payable for each tax year:

Table 4.1

Tax year ended 30 June	Taxable income (accruals, $)	Tax payable on 1 March of following year ($)
XX	Nil	Nil
XX + 1	$(11.5/12) \times 10\,000 = 9583.33$	1437.50
XX + 2	10 000	1500
XX + 3	10 000	1500
XX + 4	$(1.5/12) \times 10\,000 - 3899.81$	−397.47

The after-tax yield obtained by the purchaser is given by the following equation:

$$103\,899.81 = 5000a_{\overline{5}|} + 100\,000v^6 - 1437.50v^{(19.5/6)}$$

$$- 1500v^{(31.5/6)} - 1500v^{(43.5/6)} + 397.47v^{(55.5/6)}$$

since there are 19.5 months from 15 July XX to 1 March XX + 2 when the first tax payment is assumed to be made, which is (19.5/6) half years, and each tax payment after that is 12 months later again.

This equation must be solved by trial and error. Using the 3.6% answer determined in (a), the right-hand side of this equation is:

$$5000 \times 5.311094 + 100\,000 \times 0.808801 - 1437.5 \times 0.891417$$

$$- 1500 \times 0.830541 - 1500 \times 0.773823 + 397.47 \times 0.720978$$

$$= 104\,034.14$$

Using a higher yield of 4% gives a value for the right-hand side of:

$$5000 \times 5.242137 + 100\,000 \times 0.790315 - 1437.5 \times 0.880322$$

$$- 1500 \times 0.813907 - 1500 \times 0.752503 + 397.47 \times 0.695731$$

$$= 101\,903.59$$

Linear interpolation gives a yield of 3.625%. The right-hand side at this yield is 103 899.35 so that the after-tax yield is 7.25% p.a.

The calculations involved in allowing for tax are complex and best performed by a computer. These days many computer-based packages calculate after-tax yields for tax-paying investors as part of the standard output. The yield obtained here manually by trial and error can be quickly calculated using a spreadsheet and the trial and error built in solver function that all spreadsheets contain.

(c) Allowing for the instalment dates is a little more complex since each tax payment will result in instalment effects in the following financial year. In (b) it was assumed that tax for the year 30 June XX was paid on 1 March XX + 1. This is still the case with the instalment system except that the tax paid on 1 March XX + 1 will give rise to instalments of 0.25 of this tax on 1 June XX + 1, 1 September XX + 1, 1 December XX + 1 and these instalments will be credited when tax is assessed on 1 March XX + 2. Thus each tax payment must be multiplied by the factor:

$$\{1 + 0.25v^{(3/6)} + 0.25v^{(6/6)} + 0.25v^{(9/6)} - 0.75v^{(12/6)}\}$$

to allow for the instalments.

The equation for determining the after-tax yield in this case will be:

$$103\,899.81 = 5000a_{\overline{6}|} + 100\,000v^6 + \{-1437.50v^{(19.5/6)}$$

$$-1500v^{(31.5/6)} - 1500v^{(43.5/6)} + 397.47v^{(55.5/6)}\}$$

$$\times \{1 + 0.25v^{(3/6)} + 0.25v^{(6/6)} + 0.25v^{(9/6)} - 0.75v^{(12/6)}\}$$

Using the yield of 7.25% p.a., or 3.625% per half year, determined in (b), the right-hand side of this equation is:

$$5000 \times 5.306743 + 100\,000 \times 0.807631 + \{-3397.42\} \times \{1.025395\}$$

$$= 103\,813.07$$

At 3.6% the right-hand side equals:

$$5000 \times 5.311094 + 100\,000 \times 0.808801 + \{-3401.39\} \times \{1.025232\}$$

$$= 103\,948.32$$

Linear interpolation gives a yield of 3.61% or 7.22% p.a.
In this example with a low 15% tax rate the rule of thumb works remarkably well.

Calculating after-tax give-up yields on sale transactions is slightly more complicated than for purchases, since allowance has to be made for any tax loss or gain realised on the sale and also for the gain or loss on maturity that would have otherwise occurred on maturity. Thus a sale will bring forward a gain or loss that would have been realised on maturity to the date of sale.

Example 4.10

Assume the superannuation fund in example 4.9 sells the bond after holding it for 6 months on 15 January at a yield to maturity of 9% p.a. Calculate the after-tax give-up yield on sale assuming that tax for the financial year ended 30 June XX is paid on 1 March XX + 1 and that it has sufficient taxable income to absorb the tax loss on sale.

Solution

The sale proceeds will be:

$$5000a_{\overline{5}|} + 100\,000v^5 \text{ at } 4.5\% = 102\,194.99$$

so that a tax loss of:

$$103\,899.81 - 102\,194.99 = 1704.82$$

will occur on sale. The effect on taxable income of the sale is given in table 4.2:

Table 4.2   Tax calculations for example 4.10

Tax year ended 30 June	Taxable income (accruals, $)	Tax payable on 1 March of following year ($)
XX	Nil	Nil
XX + 1	$-(5.5/12) \times 10\,000 - 1704.82 = -6288.15$	−943.22
XX + 2	−10 000	−1500
XX + 3	−10 000	−1500
XX + 4	$-(1.5/12) \times 10\,000 + 3899.81 = 2649.81$	+397.47

The after-tax give-up yield is determined from the equation:

$$102\,194.99 = 5000a_{\overline{5}|} + 100\,000v^5 - 943.22\,v^{(13.5/6)} - 1500v^{(25.5/6)}$$

$$- 1500v^{(37.5/6)} + 397.47v^{(49.5/6)}$$

As an initial yield use the rule of thumb to determine the after-tax yield as $(1 - 0.15) \times 9 = 7.65\%$ or 3.825% per half year. The right-hand side of the equation at 3.825% is:

$$5000 \times 4.473793 + 100\,000 \times 0.828877 - 943.22 \times 0.919011$$

$$- 1500 \times 0.852544 - 1500 \times 0.790884 + 397.47 \times 0.733684$$

$$= 102\,216.35$$

The right-hand side at 3.85% is 102 103.87. Linear interpolation gives an improved estimate of the sale give-up yield of 3.83% or 7.66% p.a. At this yield the right-hand side equals 102 193.84.

The rule of thumb works quite well for the tax rate of 15%. For higher tax rates the timing of tax instalments and the size of the realised gains and losses has a more significant effect on the after-tax yield and the rule of thumb does not work as well.

Bond switch (swap) analysis

Returns on long-term securities can be improved by trading these securities. A trade that involves the simultaneous sale of 1 bond and the purchase of another bond is referred to as a switch or a swap. They generally rely on the switch or swap being reversed at a future date in order to capitalise any profits from the transaction. Once a profit has been made on a switch, the sooner it is reversed the higher will be the potential gain from the switch.

There are a number of different ways in which switches can improve yields. The source of additional return is reflected in the commonly adopted terms used to describe the different types of switch. The types of switch are:

The anomaly switch or substitution swap   This transaction involves taking advantage of an arbitrage opportunity between bonds that, for all practical purposes, are identical except for their yields to maturity. The lower yielding bond is sold and, simultaneously, the higher yielding bond is purchased. The net effect is a higher return. The yields used to assess these switches should be after-tax yields. In some cases these switches are motivated by tax effects, in which case they are referred to as tax loss switches. In a tax loss switch a bond with a tax loss is sold, to realise the loss, and the proceeds reinvested in a similar, if not identical, security. This transaction brings forward the tax loss and enhances the return at the expense of the taxation authorities. Pure anomaly switches, with no tax effects, can be reversed when the yields move back into line and the higher yield will be capitalised as profit. True anomalies will eventually move back into line through arbitrage transactions as other traders in the market realise the profit potential involved and try to trade. Supply and demand pressures move the yields back into line. Genuine anomalies do not last long in actively traded financial markets.

The intermarket spread switch or swap   Long-term securities with identical terms to maturity will often provide different yields to maturity because of the differences in credit risk of the issuer or differences in liquidity in the market. Federal Government bonds are lower yielding than semigovernment bonds, which are lower yielding than company debentures for these reasons. These differences in yields are referred to as intermarket spreads. Intermarket spread switches attempt to take advantage of anomalies in these spreads. An intermarket spread switch involves the sale of a bond (say, a Treasury bond) and the simultaneous purchase of another similar bond (say, a semigovernment bond). The choice of bond to be sold depends on whether the intermarket spread is expected to reduce or increase. If spreads are expected to reduce then the higher yielding security should be bought and the lower yielding security sold. When the spread narrows as expected, the switch is reversed and a profit taken. The reverse technique is used if spreads are expected to increase.

The policy switch or rate anticipation swap   This type of switch involves taking a view on interest rate movements and switching into a security that is expected to have a large price rise. When yields move as expected, the switch is reversed and a profit taken. An example would be if rates were expected to fall by a constant percentage across all maturities. In those circumstances long-term securities will provide the highest price rise so that short-term securities would be switched into longer-term securities. If rates do fall then the switch is reversed and the profit capitalised. If the rates do not move as anticipated then no additional return will be made. Rate anticipation switches, by their very nature, involve interest rate risk since a position is being taken on future interest rate movements. Chapter 5 will show how interest rate risk can be quantified for fixed interest securities.

The best technique to use in the analysis of bond switches is to compare the yield given up on the sale (after tax) with the yield obtained on the purchase. These yields would either be to the maturity date or on the assumption that the switch is reversed at a future date. Reversal of the switch would take place when the anomaly that gave rise to the switch has disappeared or when the yield change that was expected has occurred. The difference in the sale yield (which is given up) and the purchase yield (which is obtained) is the benefit of the switch. These calculations are complex, especially when allowance is made for tax effects and the reversal of the switch, and are best suited for analysis by an appropriate computer program.

Example 4.11

Anomaly switch An investor with a large portfolio of bonds estimates market yields each day with a trading model and tracks the difference between the estimated yield and the actual market yield on bonds traded in the market. The investor holds 10 year maturity 10% bonds (with semi-annual coupons) which are trading at 0.1% p.a. above the estimated yield for this bond. A 10 year 10.5% bond is trading at 0.2% p.a. above the estimated yield for this bond. The investor is considering the following switch:

Sell: 10 year 10% bond at 8.5% p.a.

Buy: 10 year 10.5% bond at 8.4% p.a.

Assess this switch assuming that the 10% bond yield falls by 0.1% at the end of 6 months and the 10.5% bond yield falls by 0.2% at the end of 6 months. Ignore tax.

Solution

To assess the switch it is necessary to calculate the yield given up over the next 6 months on the sold security allowing for the reversal. This is determined as follows:

Sale proceeds $= 5a_{\overline{20}|} + 100v^{20}$ at $8.5 + 2\%$ $(= 4.25\%)$

$$= 5 \times 13.294366 + 100 \times 0.434990$$

$$= 109.970774 \text{ per } \$100 \text{ face value}$$

Purchase cost in 6 months $= 5a_{\overline{19}|} + 100v^{19}$ at $8.4 + 2\%$ $(= 4.2\%)$

$$= 5 \times 12.913600 + 100 \times 0.457629$$

$$= 110.330880$$

The proceeds from the sale are equated to the coupon of $5 given up on the sale and the purchase cost required to repurchase the bond to determine the give-up yield over the next 6 months. This is given by i in the following equation:

$$109.970774 = (110.330880 + 5) / (1 + i/100)$$

Solving for i gives:

$$i = 100 \times \left(\frac{115.330880}{109.970774} - 1 \right)$$

$= 4.874\%$ per half year (9.748% p.a. with semi-annual compounding). This has to be compared with the yield obtained on the purchase, allowing for the reversal of the switch calculated as follows:

Purchase cost $= 5.25a_{\overline{20}|} + 100v^{20}$ at $8.4 + 2$ $(= 4.2\%)$

$$= 5.25 \times 13.352783 + 100 \times 0.439183$$

$$= 114.020423 \text{ per } \$100 \text{ face value}$$

Sale proceeds in 6 months $= 5.25a_{\overline{19}|} + 100v^{19}$ at $8.2 + 2\%$ $(= 4.1\%)$

$$= 5.25 \times 13.023076 + 100 \times 0.466054$$

$$= 114.976537$$

The yield obtained on the purchased bond over the 6 months from initiating the switch to reversal is given by i in the following equation:

$$114.020423 = (114.976537 + 5.25) / (1 + i/100)$$

so that:

$$i = 100 \times \left(\frac{120.226537}{114.020423} - 1 \right)$$

$$= 5.443\% \text{ or } 10.886\% \text{ p.a.}$$

Hence the switch is worth doing since the yield given up over the next 6 months on the sale of 9.748% is less than that obtained on the purchase of 10.886%, assuming that the anomaly is reversed.

Another method of assessing the switch is to determine the incremental cash flows that arise from the switch. In order for the switch to be worth doing, these incremental cash flows should provide a positive return. If the incremental return is negative then the switch will not be worth doing. The cash flows are given in table 4.3.

Table 4.3   Cash flows for example 4.11

	Present	6 months	1 year	9 years and 6 months	10 years
Original bond	−109.970774	+5	+5	+5	+105
Switch					
Sale	+109.970774	−5	−5	−5	−105
Purchase	−114.020423	+5.25	+5.25	+5.25	+105.25
Switch reversal					
Purchase		−110.330880	+5	+5	+105
Sale		+114.976537	−5.25	−5.25	−105.25
Net cash flows	−114.020423	9.895657	5	5	105

These net additional cash flows arising from the switch have an *IRR* of 4.296% per half year or 8.59% p.a. Since this is higher than the 8.5% p.a. yield to maturity on the original security, the switch is worth doing. These calculations assume that the switch will be reversed in 6 months.

Switches can be used to bring forward tax losses that would otherwise occur on redemption. The taxation treatment of bonds in Australia at the time of writing brings to account gains and losses as income for tax purposes when they are realised. There are proposals to bring these to account on a compound return basis. Many other countries have tax rules similar to the current Australian tax rules for bonds. For many investors, including individuals and some institutional investors such as superannuation funds, under these tax rules it is beneficial to realise losses if these can be offset against taxable income. This is carried out using a bond switch.

Example 4.12

Tax loss switch An investor holds a $500 000 face value 10 year 6.75% bond which has a cost for tax purposes of $495 000. The investor has taxable income against which any losses on bond sales can be offset. The investor is considering the following switch:
Sell: $500 000 face value 10 year 6.75% bond at 8.5% p.a.
Buy: $500 000 face value 10 year 7.5% bond at 8.5% p.a.
Assuming that tax effects occur on the date of the associated cash flow, that the tax rate is 15% and that the switch will not be reversed at a future date, calculate the yields given up and obtained in this switch.

Solution

The sale proceeds of the switch will be:

$$500\ 000 \times (3.375a_{\overline{20}|} + 100v^{20})/100 \text{ at } 4.25\% = \$441\ 837.15$$

The tax loss on the sale is the difference between the cost for tax purposes and the sale proceeds of $495\,000 - 441\,837.15 = 53\,162.85$ which gives rise to a tax benefit of $0.15 \times 53\,162.85 = 7974.43$. If the bond was held to maturity a taxable gain of $500\,000 - 495\,000 = 5000$ would have been realised, giving rise to a tax payment of $0.15 \times 5000 = 750$.

The after-tax give-up yield on the sale is given by i, determined from equating the proceeds to the tax benefit on sale and the after-tax cash flows given up, including the tax payments as negative cash flows:

$$\$441\,837.15 = -7974.43 + 16\,875\,(1 - 0.15)a_{\overline{20}} + 500\,000v^{20} - 750v^{20}$$

or:

$$449\,811.58 = 14\,343.75a_{\overline{20}} + 499\,250v^{20} \text{ at } i\%$$

for which $i = 3.575\%$ per half year or 7.15% p.a. This can readily be calculated using the HP12C financial functions or using a spreadsheet.

The after-tax purchase yield on the 7.5% bond is given by equating the purchase cost of:

$$500\,000 \times (3.75a_{\overline{20}} + 100v^{20})/100 \text{ at } 4.25\%$$

$$= 500\,000 \times 93.352817/100$$

$$= \$466\,764.09$$

to the after-tax receipts, including the tax payable on the taxable gain on redemption, with value:

$$18\,750\,(1 - 0.15)a_{\overline{20}} + 500\,000v^{20} - 0.15\,(500\,000 - 466\,764.09)v^{20}$$

$$= 15\,937.50a_{\overline{20}} + 495\,014.62v^{20}$$

which gives a yield of 3.626% per half year or 7.251% p.a.

The net gain in yield on the switch is $7.251 - 7.15 = 0.101\%$ p.a. after tax.

This switch could also be assessed by considering the after-tax cash flows on the original bond along with the effects of the switch. These are given in table 4.4.

Table 4.4   Cash flows for example 4.12

	Present	6 months	1 year	9 years and 6 months	10 years
Original bond	−441 837.15	14 343.75	14 343.75	14 343.75	499 250
Switch Sale	+449 811.58	−14 343.75	−14 343.75	−14 343.75	−499 250
Purchase	−466 764.09	15 937.50	15 937.50	15 937.50	495 014.61
Net cash flows	−458 789.66	15 937.50	15 937.50	15 937.50	495 014.61

The after-tax yield on the net cash flows is given by the yield obtained from the equation:

$$458\ 789.66 = 15\ 937.5050a_{\overline{20}} + 479\ 077.11v^{20}$$

since the last cash flow of 495 014.61 effectively contains an after-tax coupon payment of 15 937.50 plus a capital amount of 479 077.11.

The after-tax yield is 3.628% per half year or 7.256% p.a. after tax.

The after-tax yield on the original bond is given by the yield on the after-tax cash flows from the first line of table 4.4. This is determined from the equation:

$$441\ 837.15 = 14\ 343.75a_{\overline{20}} + 484\ 906.25v^{20}$$

The yield is 7.176% p.a. so that the switch provides an increase of $7.256 - 7.176 = 0.106\%$ p.a. in after-tax yield. This result is consistent with the previous result.

Book value switches

Book value switches are switches that use the book value prices of the securities that are being bought and sold for settlement. Any net difference between the book and market values is allowed for by an adjustment to the face value of the security which is purchased. A motivation for book value switches is to avoid showing a realised loss (or profit) on the security in the accounting results of the seller. This might be desirable for presentation purposes if, for example, realising a loss on sale of a security were considered to be a sign of poor investment management. Book value switches could be used to switch out of low coupon bonds into higher coupon bonds without showing an accounting loss on the sale. For tax purposes the loss on the sale of the low coupon bonds would reduce taxable income since an actual loss would be realised on the sale.

Example 4.13

A bank is holding $500 000 face value 10 year 6.75% bonds currently yielding 8.5% p.a. (semi-annual compounding) in the market which were purchased at par. It wishes to replace these bonds, without realising an accounting loss, with 10 year 10% bonds, which currently yield 8.5% p.a. It decides to do a book value switch with a merchant bank where it will sell the 6.75% bonds at par and purchase the 10% bonds also at par. Analyse the switch.

Solution

The market price of the 6.75% bonds is:

$$16\ 875.75a_{\overline{20}} + 500\ 000v^{20}\ \text{at } 4.25\%$$

$$= 441\ 847.12$$

(Australian market conventions for Treasury bonds round bond prices per $100 face value to 3 decimal places, so that if this were a Treasury bond, the market value would be 500 000 × 88.369/100 = 441 845.00.)

The market price of the 10% bonds is:

$$25\ 000a_{\overline{20}} + 500\ 000v^{20} \text{ at } 4.25\%$$

$$= 549\ 853.87$$

(Using Treasury bond market conventions and rounding the price per $100 face value to 3 decimal places gives 500 000 × 109.971/100 = 549 855.00.)

The switch, based on market yields, should involve a net payment of 549 853.87 − 441 847.12 = $108 006.75 (or $108 010.00 based on market conventions) if $500 000 face value of bonds are bought and sold. If the face value of the bonds that are bought is adjusted to have a market value equal to the market value of the bonds to be sold, then the switch will require no net payment. The face value required is (88.369/109.971) × 500 000 = 401 783. The price used for the purchase in the switch per $100 face value is then (500 000/401 783) × 100 = $124.445 and for the sale the price per $100 is par. Using this face value and price for the purchase will ensure that the market value of the securities bought and sold is the same (441 847.12). Notice that the yield to maturity on the sale at par will be 6.75% p.a. and the yield to maturity on the purchase will be based on the switch price of $124.445 which is 6.62% p.a. These yields are not the same as the market yields for the sale and purchase.

The analysis of switches considered above ignores the change in interest rate risk resulting from the switch. The securities which are bought and sold are assumed to have similar risk. An assessment of these changes in risk should be made using the duration and convexity measures covered in chapter 5. Although the returns from a switch may be increased, this may be at the expense of an additional risk of capital loss. This will be especially so for policy or rate anticipation switches.

5 Interest rate risk analysis

Interest rate risk is an important factor in analysing any security or transaction whose return depends on interest rates. This risk is the risk that interest rates move up unexpectedly and an unexpected capital loss is incurred or that interest rates fall unexpectedly and maturing investments have to be reinvested at unexpectedly low reinvestment rates. This risk is quantified using a variety of measures of the effect of interest rate changes on the value of fixed interest securities. These interest rate risk measures originated in the concept of the average time to receipt of the cash flows of the security, which has been referred to using different terminology including 'Macaulay duration', 'average period', 'weighted average time period' and the 'mean term of the value of the cash flows'. Nearly all participants in financial markets use the term 'duration'. The longer the duration of the security, the more sensitive the security value is to interest rate changes.

The duration of a fixed interest security is related to the sensitivity of the value of the cash flows to small changes in interest rates, as given by the first derivative of the security value with respect to the interest rate. The negative of the value of this derivative as a proportion of the value of the cash flows is most often referred to as 'modified duration' or 'effective duration'. It is also referred to as bond price volatility.

Although duration can be used as a measure of how much prices of fixed interest securities will change for a given change in interest rates, it only provides a first order approximation since price changes will be functions of the higher derivatives as long as the relationship between prices and interest rates is not linear. The second derivative is used to calculate a measure of price changes referred to as convexity. This second derivative is related to the 'spread' of the values of a set of cash flows about their duration, which is often referred to as M^2 in the finance industry.

Duration

The duration of a set of cash flows is calculated as the weighted average term of the cash flows of a security, including both coupon receipts and maturity payment, where the weights used are the present values of the cash flows. Duration for any set of cash flows can be calculated using the formula:

■ *Equation 5.1*

$$D = \frac{\sum_{t=0}^{t=n} t C_t v^t}{\sum_{t=0}^{t=n} C_t v^t}$$

where:

- C_t is the cash flow occurring at time t (in years and fractions of a year),
- $v = \dfrac{1}{\left(1 + \dfrac{i}{100}\right)}$ is the discount factor,

- and i is the per annum effective yield on the cash flows which is obtained by converting the nominal yield to an effective p.a. yield.

This formula is usually referred to as the *Macaulay duration* after F. R. Macaulay, who first used the term 'duration' in 1938. It is a weighted average time to receipt of the cash flows using the weights $C_t v^t$ which are the present values of each of the cash flows. The total of the weights is the total value, or price, of the cash flows.

Formulae can be developed for the duration of many fixed interest securities. The duration can also be calculated using a spreadsheet or simple computer program.

Example 5.1

The cash flows from an investment and the interest rates to be used to value the cash flows are given in Table 5.1.

Table 5.1 Interest rates and cash flows for example 5.1

Time (years)	Interest rate (% p.a.)	Net cash flow ($)
1	5.50	500 000
2	5.75	400 000
3	6.00	300 000
4	6.25	200 000
5	6.50	100 000

Calculate the duration of the cash flows.

Solution

The solution is set out in tabular form in table 5.2 (this is the appropriate format for using a spreadsheet). Column (5) is the present value of the individual cash flows and the sum of this column is the total present value of the cash flows. Column (6) is the weighted value of the cash flows using the time in years as the weight.

Table 5.2   Duration calculation for example 5.1

Time (yrs) (1)	i_t (2)	C_t (3)	v^t (4)	$(5) = (3) \times (4)$	$(6) = (1) \times (5)$
1	5.50	500 000	0.947867	473 933.65	473 933.65
2	5.75	400 000	0.894209	357 683.77	715 367.55
3	6.00	300 000	0.839619	251 885.78	755 657.35
4	6.25	200 000	0.784665	156 932.99	627 731.95
5	6.50	100 000	0.729881	72 988.08	364 940.42
Total				1 313 424.28	2 937 630.92

The duration of the cash flows is then the ratio of the total of column (6) to the total of column (5) or 2 937 630.92/1 313 424.28 = 2.237 years.

For fixed interest securities the yield to maturity is often used to determine the weights in the duration formula. If the yield to maturity is used, then the duration of securities with different maturity dates will be calculated inconsistently since cash flows that occur on the same date will be valued using different yields to maturity. To avoid this problem a zero coupon yield curve that is consistent with the yields to maturity is derived and the zero coupon yields used in the duration calculations. The method of deriving the zero coupon yields from the yields to maturity is covered in chapter 6. In this chapter yields to maturity are used for calculating duration and other interest rate risk measures.

Treasury bonds pay semi-annual coupons. Some fixed interest rate securities pay quarterly coupons. These securities are priced using nominal yields to maturity with a compounding frequency the same as the coupon frequency. To calculate the duration of these securities the time period used in equation 5.1 should always be in years, since duration is usually measured in years. The present value factor can, however, be based on the nominal yield to maturity. If the nominal p.a. yield to maturity is denoted by $j\%$ p.a., with compounding p times per year, and the effective p.a. yield equivalent to this is $i\%$ p.a., then:

$$\left(1 + \frac{i}{100}\right) = \left(1 + \frac{j}{p \times 100}\right)^p$$

The present value factor in equation 5.1 can be written in terms of j, instead of i, by substituting this formula for v and using:

$$v^t = \left(1 + \frac{i}{100}\right)^{-t} = \left[\left(1 + \frac{j}{p \times 100}\right)^p\right]^{-t} = \left(1 + \frac{j}{p \times 100}\right)^{-pt}$$

Example 5.2

A 10% coupon bond pays interest semi-annually and matures in 3 years' time. The yield to maturity of the bond is 8% (semi-annual compounding). Calculate the (Macaulay) duration of the bond.

Solution

The duration is readily calculated by evaluating individual terms in the duration equation 5.1 as given in table 5.3.

Table 5.3   Duration calculation for example 5.2

Time (t) (years)	Cash flows (C_t)	$v^t = (1.04)^{-2t}$	(2) × (3)	(4) × (1)
0.5	5	0.961538	4.807692	2.403846
1.0	5	0.924556	4.622781	4.622781
1.5	5	0.888996	4.444982	6.667473
2.0	5	0.854804	4.274021	8.548042
2.5	5	0.821927	4.109636	10.27409
3.0	105	0.790315	82.98303	248.9491
Total			105.2421	281.4653

The duration in years is 281.4653/105.2421= 2.674 years.

The duration of fixed interest securities often needs to be evaluated between coupon dates. This is readily handled using the tabular approach.

Example 5.3

Consider the 10% coupon bond paying interest semi-annually of example 5.2. Assume that the bond will mature in 2.75 years' time so that it is halfway through a coupon period. The yield to maturity of the bond is still 8% (semi-annual compounding). Calculate the (Macaulay) duration of the bond. Compare this with the duration calculated in example 5.2.

Solution

Table 5.4 sets out the calculations in tabular form.

Table 5.4   Duration calculations for example 5.3

Time (t) (years)	Cash flows (C$_t$)	$v^t = (1.04)^{-2t}$	(2) × (3)	(4) × (1)
0.25	5	0.980581	4.90290	1.22573
0.75	5	0.942866	4.71433	3.53575
1.25	5	0.906602	4.53301	5.66626
1.75	5	0.871733	4.35866	7.62766
2.25	5	0.838204	4.19102	9.42980
2.75	105	0.805966	84.62641	232.7226
Total			107.3263	260.2078

The duration is equal to 260.2078/107.3263= 2.424 years. The difference between this duration and that in example 5.2 is 2.674 – 2.424 = 0.25 years. This is exactly equal to the reduction in time from the date of calculation of the duration in example 5.2. The duration decreases in a straight line in proportion to the time elapsed between coupon dates. This result has been shown to hold in this example. It can be shown to hold in general but the algebra involved is tedious and is left to the more dedicated reader.

A formula for the duration of a coupon-paying bond can be derived and can be used in place of the tabular approach used in the examples so far. Consider a bond paying a regular annual coupon of C p.a. with a face value of F. In this case the numerator in equation 5.1 is given by $S + nFv^n$ where:

$$S = \sum_{t=0}^{t=n} tC_t v^t = C\sum_{t=0}^{t=n} tv^t = C\{v + 2v^2 + 3v^3 + \ldots + nv^n\}$$

Multiply both sides of this expression by v to get:

$$vS = C\{v^2 + 2v^3 + 3v^4 + \ldots nv^{n+1}\}$$

Subtract this expression from the first to get:

$$S - vS = C\{v + v^2 + v^3 + \ldots + v^n - nv^{n+1}\} = C\{a_{\overline{n}} - nv^{n+1}\}$$

so that:

$$S = \frac{C\{a_{\overline{n}} - nv^{n+1}\}}{1 - v} = \frac{C\left\{\left(1 + \dfrac{i}{100}\right)a_{\overline{n}} - nv^n\right\}}{\dfrac{i}{100}}$$

since:

$$\frac{1}{1 - v} = \frac{\left(1 + \dfrac{i}{100}\right)}{\dfrac{i}{100}}$$

The denominator in equation 5.1 is:

$$\sum_{t=0}^{t=n} C_t v^t = C\{v + v^2 + v^3 + \ldots + v^n\} + Fv^n = Ca_{\overline{n}|} + Fv^n$$

which is the bond price. Equation 5.1 can now be rewritten for an annual coupon-paying bond as:

■ **Equation 5.2**

$$\frac{C\left\{\left(1 + \dfrac{i}{100}\right)a_{\overline{n}|} - nv^n\right\}}{\dfrac{i}{100}} + nFv^n \over Ca_{\overline{n}|} + Fv^n$$

This formula can be adapted to allow for coupons being paid more frequently than annually and to allow for the calculation to be made between coupon dates. In practice it is usually just as easy to calculate the individual terms in equation 5.1 using a spreadsheet or computer program as it is to evaluate equation 5.2.

Usually duration increases with the term to maturity. However, for discount bonds—that is, where the yield to maturity exceeds the coupon rate, the duration can decrease for long maturities as the term to maturity increases. For par and premium bonds, duration increases with increases in the term to maturity. Higher coupon bonds have shorter duration than lower coupon bonds with the same maturity and same yield to maturity. The duration of a bond is greater at lower yields to maturity for any given bond. These features of duration are illustrated in tables 5.5 to 5.7 where calculations are for semi-annual coupon bonds. These tables cover discount, premium and par bonds. Discount bonds have prices below par (face value) since their yield to maturity is higher than the coupon rate. Premium bonds have prices above par since their yield to maturity is below their coupon rate. Par bonds have coupon rates equal to their yield to maturity.

From tables 5.6 and 5.7 it can be seen that for the discount bonds (the 5% coupon bond in table 5.6 and both the 5% and 10% coupon bonds in table 5.7), the duration increases at first and then declines at longer maturities. After first increasing, the duration for these bonds declines but does not fall below a limiting value. The other bonds' duration increases to a limiting value. The limiting value for bond duration does not depend upon the coupon rate of the bond, only upon the yield to maturity and is given by:

Table 5.5 Bond duration (years) yield to maturity 5% p.a.

Term (yrs)	Coupon (% p.a.)		
	5	10	15
2	1.928	1.868	1.818
5	4.485	4.156	3.926
10	7.989	7.107	6.610
20	12.865	11.233	10.509
30	15.841	14.025	13.312
40	17.656	15.992	15.380

Table 5.6 Bond duration (years) yield to maturity 10% p.a.

Term (yrs)	Coupon (% p.a.)		
	5	10	15
2	1.924	1.862	1.809
5	4.414	4.054	3.810
10	7.489	6.543	6.046
20	10.376	9.009	8.462
30	10.957	9.938	9.573
40	10.876	10.288	10.087

Table 5.7 Bond duration (years) yield to maturity 15% p.a.

Term (yrs)	Coupon (% p.a.)		
	5	10	15
2	1.920	1.855	1.800
5	4.335	3.945	3.689
10	6.927	5.956	5.480
20	8.090	7.126	6.769
30	7.656	7.222	7.073
40	7.345	7.195	7.145

$$\frac{1}{p}\left[1 + \frac{1}{\dfrac{j}{p \times 100}}\right]$$

where j is the % p.a. yield to maturity (compounding p times per year) for the bond. The bonds in table 5.5 with yield to maturity of 5% (semi-annual compounding) have a limiting value for duration of:

$$\frac{1}{2}\left[1 + \frac{1}{\dfrac{5}{200}}\right] = 20.5 \text{ years}$$

The limiting values for the bonds in tables 5.6 and 5.7 are 10.5 years and 7.1667 years, respectively.

Modified duration

The (Macaulay) duration of a fixed interest security is related to the interest rate risk of the security as measured by the sensitivity of the security value to changes in interest rates. Fixed interest securities change in value as the interest rates used to value them change. The value of these securities also changes as time passes even if the interest rate does not change. Different fixed interest rate securities will suffer different changes in capital value as a result of interest rate changes. The larger the potential change in capital value of a fixed interest security arising from a change in interest rates, the riskier the fixed interest security. Thus the sensitivity of a set of cash flows to changes in interest rates is important since it is an indicator of the level of interest rate risk of the cash flows.

The term 'modified duration' is used in financial markets to refer to the proportionate change in value of a set of cash flows resulting from a small change in the yield to maturity. The change in value of the security is measured using the differential of the security value with respect to the interest rate. The modified duration is defined as $\dfrac{-P'(i)}{P(i)}$ where $P(i)$ is the present value or price of the cash flows at interest rate i and $P'(i)$ is the first derivative of the value with respect to i.

Consider a set of cash flows valued at a yield to maturity of i p.a. with cash flow C_t occurring at time t. The value of the cash flows will be:

$$P(i) = \sum C_t v^t = \sum C_t (1 + i)^{-t}$$

and the derivative of the value with respect to i is:

$$P'(i) = \sum C_t [-t (1 + i)^{-(t + 1)}] = -(1 + i)^{-1} \sum t C_t (1 + i)^{-t}$$

$$= -v \sum t C_t (1 + i)^{-t} = -v \sum t C_t v^t$$

The modified duration is given by:

■ *Equation 5.3*

$$\frac{-P'(i)}{P(i)} = \frac{-\left\{ -v \sum t C_t v^t \right\}}{\sum C_t v^t} = vD$$

where D is the duration of the security.

In practice the derivative is usually approximated using the numerical approximation:

■ *Equation 5.4*

$$P'(i) \approx \frac{P(i+h) - P(i-h)}{2h}$$

where h is usually taken as 1 basis point or 0.01% p.a.

In practice the interest rate sensitivity is determined with respect to a movement in market yields which are quoted as nominal yields. Thus for Treasury bonds the movement in yield is in the semi-annual compounding yield to maturity. In this case the value is $P(j) = \sum C_t \left(1 + \frac{j}{p}\right)^{-pt}$, where j is the per dollar yield and the derivative is given by:

$$P'(j) = \sum C_t \left[-tp \left(1 + \frac{j}{p}\right)^{-tp-1}\right] \frac{1}{p} = -\sum t C_t \left(1 + \frac{j}{p}\right)^{-tp-1}$$

$$= -\left(1 + \frac{j}{p}\right)^{-1} \sum t C_t \left(1 + \frac{j}{p}\right)^{-tp}$$

In this case the modified duration is equal to the duration multiplied by the present value factor for a single compounding period for the yield j. Thus for semi-annual compounding yields the modified duration is the duration times the present value factor for half a year.

Example 5.4

A bond pays semi-annual coupons of 12% p.a. and matures in 2 years at par. It trades at a yield to maturity of 9.5% p.a.

Calculate the duration of the bond using a tabular approach. Determine the modified duration of the bond. Approximate the modified duration of the bond using the numerical approximation for the derivative and compare your answer with the accurate answer.

Solution

Table 5.8 provides the details for the duration calculation.

Table 5.8   Calculation of duration for example 5.4

Time (t) (yrs) (1)	Cash flow (2)	v^t (3)	(2) × (3)	(1) × (4)
0.5	6	0.954654	5.72792	2.86396
1.0	6	0.911364	5.46818	5.46818
1.5	6	0.870037	5.22022	7.83034
2.0	106	0.830585	88.04197	176.08393
Total			104.45830	192.24642

The duration is 192.24642/104.45830 = 1.840 years.

Modified duration is the duration multiplied by the present value factor for a half year in this case, so that modified duration is equal to 0.954654 × 1.840 = 1.757.

A numerical approximation is given by calculating the value of the bond at a yield of 9.51% p.a. to get 104.43995 and then at a yield of 9.49% p.a. to get 104.47666. The numerical approximation using equation 5.4 is then {[−(104.43995 − 104.47666) / (2 × 0.0001)]/104.45830} = 1.757.

Convexity

Modified duration is a measure of the interest rate sensitivity of a fixed interest security to small changes in yield to maturity. An estimate of the change in price resulting from any change in interest rates can be developed. To do this the price at yield to maturity i_1 can be expressed as a Taylor series in terms of the price evaluated at the current yield to maturity i_0 and the price derivatives as follows:

$$P(i_1) = P(i_0) + \frac{(i_1 - i_0)}{1!} P'(i_0) + \frac{(i_1 - i_0)^2}{2!} P''(i_0) + \ldots$$

If the price at i_0 is deducted from both sides, and then both sides are divided by the price, then:

$$\frac{P(i_1) - P(i_0)}{P(i_0)} = \frac{(i_1 - i_0)}{1!} \frac{P'(i_0)}{P(i_0)} + \frac{(i_1 - i_0)^2}{2!} \frac{P''(i_0)}{P(i_0)} + \ldots$$

As a first approximation to the proportionate price change for any change in interest rates, the first term on the right-hand side can be used to give:

■ *Equation 5.5*

$$\boxed{\frac{P(i_1) - P(i_0)}{P(i_0)} = \frac{(i_1 - i_0)}{1!} \frac{P'(i_0)}{P(i_0)} = -(i_1 - i_0) \, MD}$$

where MD is the modified duration of the security. Thus the proportionate price change can be estimated for any given yield change by taking the change in yield, in basis points, and multiplying this change by the modified duration of the security. If the yield change is taken as the change in the yield expressed as % p.a. then the resulting estimate will be the percentage change in the price, since the right-hand side yield change will be 100 times larger.

A more accurate approximation would be given by including the second term in the expansion. For this purpose a measure referred to as convexity is defined as:

$$C = \frac{P''(i_0)}{P(i_0)}$$

since this measures the amount of curvature or convexity in the price/yield relationship. The approximation to the proportionate change in the price is then given by:

■ *Equation 5.6*

$$\frac{P(i_1) - P(i_0)}{P(i_0)} = -(i_1 - i_0)\,MD + \frac{(i_1 - i_0)^2}{2}\,C$$

Convexity can be estimated numerically by approximating the second derivative with the formula:

■ *Equation 5.7*

$$P''(i) = \frac{P(i + h) - 2P(i) + P(i - h)}{h^2}$$

Otherwise it is necessary to twice differentiate the formula for the price directly. In the case of a zero coupon bond the formula for the second derivative is given by:

$$\frac{d^2 P(i)}{di^2} = \frac{d^2}{di^2}(1 + i)^{-t} = t(t + 1)(1 + i)^{-(t+2)} = v^2 t\,(t + 1)v^t$$

so that convexity of a zero coupon bond is given by:

$$t(t + 1)v^2$$

which is obtained by dividing the second derivative of the price of the zero coupon bond by the price v^t.

Notice that t would usually be in units of a year and if i is an effective per annum yield then the formulae above are correct. In practice t is in units of a year but the yield is often a semi-annual compounding yield as it is for Treasury bonds. It is simple to allow for semi-annual compounding rates or other compounding frequencies. Keeping t in years and using $i_{(2)}$ for the nominal (per dollar) semi-annual compounding rate, and using v to denote the discount factor for a full year, gives the following expression for the second derivative of the price:

$$\frac{d^2 P(i_{(2)})}{di^2{}_{(2)}} = \frac{d^2}{di^2{}_{(2)}}\left(1 + \frac{i_{(2)}}{2}\right)^{-2t} = t\left(t + \frac{1}{2}\right)\left(1 + \frac{i_{(2)}}{2}\right)^{-(2t+2)} = vt\left(t + \frac{1}{2}\right)v^t$$

where $v = \left(1 + \dfrac{i_{(2)}}{2}\right)^{-2}$ is the present value factor for a year.

Example 5.5

Calculate the convexity for the bond in example 5.4. Recall that this is a bond that pays semi-annual coupons of 12% p.a. and matures in 2 years at par. It trades at a yield to maturity of 9.5% p.a. Use the modified duration and convexity to approximate the change in price resulting from a +1% change in the yield to maturity from 9.5% p.a. to 10.5% p.a. Check your answer by determining the exact change.

Solution

Table 5.9 sets out the calculations for the convexity.

Table 5.9   Convexity calculation for example 5.5

Time (t) (yrs) (1)	Cash flow (2)	v^t (3)	(2) × (3)	(1) × {(1) + 0.5} × (4)
0.5	6	0.954654	5.72792	2.86396
1.0	6	0.911364	5.46818	8.20228
1.5	6	0.870037	5.22022	15.66067
2.0	106	0.830585	88.04197	440.20984
Total			104.45830	466.93675

Convexity is 0.911364 × (466.93675/104.45830) = 4.07387.

For a +1% change in yield, equation 5.6 gives a proportionate price change of:

$$- (0.105 - 0.095) \times 1.757 + 0.5 \times (0.105 - 0.095)^2 \times 4.07387 = -0.017366$$

and multiplying this by the price of 104.45830 gives the dollar change in the price of –1.814.

The actual price for a +1% yield change is 102.64409 so that the exact change in price is –1.814.

Spread or M^2 of cash flows

Another measure of interest rate risk that is often used in practice is referred to as M^2. This measure was called the 'spread' of the values of a set of cash flows about the duration by the British actuary Frank Redington in 1952. The M^2 of a set of cash flows can be described as a weighted variance of the time to receipt of the cash flows around the duration of the cash flows, the weights being the same as are used to calculate the duration. The formula for M^2 is:

■ *Equation 5.8*

$$M^2 = \sum_t (t - D)^2 w_t$$

where the weights are:

$$w_t = \frac{C_t v^t}{\sum\limits_{t} C_t v^t}$$

If 2 securities have the same duration then the one with the higher value for M^2 will have larger price changes for any given yield change.

Example 5.6

Calculate the M^2 of the bond in example 5.5.

Solution

The calculation of M^2 is most suited to using a spreadsheet or computer program. It can be done manually using a tabular approach and equation 5.8. The tabular approach for this example is set out in table 5.10.

Table 5.10 Calculation of M^2

Time (t) (years) (1)	Cash flow (C_t) (2)	v^t	(2) × (3)	$[(1) - D]^2 \times (4)$
0.5	6	0.954654	5.72792	10.29140
1.0	6	0.911364	5.46818	3.86215
1.5	6	0.870037	5.22022	0.60493
2.0	106	0.830585	88.04197	2.24225
Total			104.45830	17.00073

The M^2 is equal to 17.0073/104.45830 = 0.1628.

This calculation of convexity is often approximated using equation 5.7 with a change in the per cent yield used for h and then expressed as a per cent of the current price. Convexity can also be approximated using a change in the per dollar yield i and expressed per dollar of price rather than as a per cent of price. In this case the approximation to the second derivative will be $(100)^2$ or 10 000 times larger and the price used will also be divided by 100 to get per dollar convexity. The relationship between these 2 alternatives is:

Convexity per dollar price, for per dollar yield changes

$$= \frac{10\,000}{100} \times \text{Convexity as \% of price, for \% yield change}$$

$$= 100 \times \text{Convexity as \% of price, for \% yield change}$$

The units of convexity will depend on whether the calculation is based on per dollar or per cent values for the price and yield change. Similar comments apply to the duration measure but the 2 figures will not be any different, since the first derivative for per dollar price and per dollar yield changes will be 100 times larger and the resulting duration will also be divided by 100 to get a per dollar figure. These 2 adjustments cancel out for the duration. In practice it is important to determine the units that are used for convexity since both methods for determining convexity are used.

Duration and convexity for portfolios

When securities are held in portfolios the interest rate risk of the portfolio will reflect the modified duration and convexity of the individual securities contained in the portfolio. The modified duration and convexity for the portfolio can be used to approximate the change in the value of the portfolio that would occur if interest rates moved using equation 5.6. The duration and modified duration of a portfolio is the weighted average of the duration and modified duration of the individual securities using the prices of the securities as weights. Thus for a portfolio of n securities:

■ *Equation 5.9*

$$D_p = \frac{\sum\limits_{i=1}^{n} P_i D_i}{\sum\limits_{i=1}^{n} P_i}$$

where:

- D_p is the duration (or modified duration) of the portfolio,
- P_i is the price of the ith security, and
- D_i is the duration (or modified duration) of the ith security.

A similar formula applies for the convexity of the portfolio:

■ *Equation 5.10*

$$C_p = \frac{\sum\limits_{i=1}^{n} P_i C_i}{\sum\limits_{i=1}^{n} P_i}$$

Example 5.7

An investor holds a portfolio of 3 semi-annual coupon bonds each with face value $100 000. Details of the portfolio are given in table 5.11.

Table 5.11

Bond	Price	Yield	Duration	Convexity
14% 5 year bond	105.455	12.5	3.7937	0.1668% (16.68 per $)
13% 10 year bond	97.299	13.5	5.8098	0.4295% (42.95 per $)
15% 15 year bond	108.189	13.7	6.6313	0.6221% (62.21 per $)

Calculate the duration and convexity of the portfolio and determine the approximate change in portfolio value for a +0.1% change in market yields.

Solution

Using equation 5.9 gives:

Portfolio duration

$$= \frac{(105.455 \times 3.7937 + 97.299 \times 5.8098 + 108.189 \times 6.6313)}{(105.455 + 97.299 + 108.189)}$$

$$= 5.4119$$

Using equation 5.10 gives:

Portfolio convexity

$$= \frac{(105.455 \times 0.1668 + 97.299 \times 0.4295 + 108.189 \times 0.6221)}{(105.455 + 97.299 + 108.189)}$$

$$= 0.4074$$

To get the per cent change in the portfolio value it is necessary to use modified duration. The portfolio modified duration is a weighted average of the individual modified duration which is obtained by dividing the duration by $(1 + i/200)$ where i is the market yield for the security. Hence:

Modified duration

$$= \frac{(105.455 \times 3.5705 + 97.299 \times 5.4424 + 108.189 \times 6.2062)}{(105.455 + 97.299 + 108.189)}$$

$$= 5.0733$$

The per cent change in portfolio value for a +0.1% movement in all yields is estimated using equation 5.6 as:

$$0.1 \times -5.0737 \times \frac{1}{2} \times (0.1)^2 \times 0.4074 = -0.505293\%$$

The dollar change in portfolio value is:

$$-310\ 943 \times (0.505293/100) = -\$1571.17$$

which compares with the actual change which would occur of −$1570.76.

Managing interest rate risk

To manage interest rate risk it is necessary to match future receipts and payments or to ensure that the value of future receipts changes in a similar manner to the value of future payments when interest rates change. The duration of a security has the property that, if this is used as the holding period for horizon analysis, then the total realised compound return is unaffected by changes in interest rates which occur at the current date and remain in effect throughout the holding period. This occurs because the reinvestment gains or losses on coupon income are offset by the capital losses or gains on realisation of the security at the end of the holding period. Thus the return on the security from the current date to a time in the future equal to the duration of the security will not be affected by current interest rate changes.

From an interest rate risk point of view, holding a security is equivalent to holding a zero coupon bond with maturity equal to the duration of the security. Thus, if a liability payment has to be met in the future, then the interest rate risk in meeting this payment can be offset by holding a security with a duration equal to the maturity of the liability payment.

Example 5.8

A 12% p.a. semi-annual coupon bond matures in exactly 2 years' time and has a current yield to maturity of 9.5% p.a. Determine the total realised compound yield for a holding period equal to the duration of the security, assuming that interest rates rise by 1% and also assuming that interest rates fall by 1% immediately.

Solution

This bond is the same as that given in example 5.4. Its duration is 1.840 years. To calculate the total realised compound yield, the coupons are reinvested to the end of the holding period at the altered interest rate and the bond is assumed to be sold at that time at the altered yield.

The accumulated coupons over the duration of the security will be the value of the coupons reinvested for 1.840 years. The 3 coupons received in the first 1.5 years will accumulate to $6s_{\overline{3}|}$ at $i/2\%$ where i is the altered yield. Remember from equation 4.6 in chapter 4 that $s_{\overline{n}|}$ is the accumulated value of n payments each of $1 paid at equal intervals valued on the date of the nth payment. The accumulated value needs to be accumulated for a further $1.840 - 1.5 = 0.34$ years. Because a half-yearly time interval is being used, this is $(0.34/0.5)$ half years and the total accumulated value will then be:

$$6s_{\overline{3}|}(1 + i/100)^{(0.34/0.5)} \text{ at } i/2\%$$

For the rise in rates to 10.5% this equals:

$$6 \times 3.160256 \times 1.035407 = 19.632906$$

and for the fall to 8.5% this equals:

$$6 \times 3.129306 \times 1.028707 = 19.314837$$

The sale proceeds at the end of the holding period will be the present value of the future payments of the bond. After holding the bond for 1.84 years it will have 0.16 years to maturity and the future payments will be the face value plus the final coupon due on the bond. This amount of $106 has a present value of:

$$106v^{(0.16/0.5)} \text{ at } i/2\%$$

For the 1% interest rate rise this will be:

$$106 \times 0.983759 = 104.278504$$

and for the 1% interest rate fall it will be:

$$106 \times 0.986769 = 104.597553$$

Note that if the current market yield does not change, then the reinvested coupons would accumulate to $6 \times 3.144756 \times 1.032060 = 19.473454$ at the end of the holding period and the sale proceeds would have been $106 \times 0.985260 = 104.437526$.

The holding period total realised compound yields are given by equating the purchase price (104.45830) to the total returns, including accumulated coupons and sale proceeds at the end of the holding period. For the 1% rise the yield is given by solving:

$$104.45830 = (19.632906 + 104.278504) \, v^{(1.84/0.5)}$$

so that:

$$i = \left[\frac{123.91141}{104.45830}\right]^{(0.5/1.84)} - 1$$

$$= 0.0475 \text{ per half year}$$

or 9.5% p.a.

For the 1% fall the yield is given by:

$$104.45830 = (19.314837 + 104.597553) v^{(1.84/0.5)}$$

so that:

$$i = \left[\frac{123.912390}{104.45830}\right]^{0.5/1.84} - 1$$

$$= 0.047503 \text{ per half year}$$

or 9.5% p.a. also.

From this example it can be seen that, although the yield to maturity will not be earned if the security is held to the maturity date because coupons will not be reinvested at the yield to maturity, this yield will be earned over a holding period equal to the duration of the security regardless of the reinvestment rate for coupons. Note that if yields remained the same for any part of the holding period and were then assumed to change, then the reinvestment effects would not offset the capital gain/loss on realisation. This result will only hold for yield changes which are assumed to occur immediately and stay in effect throughout the holding period.

A technique that is used in interest rate risk management is referred to as immunisation. The British actuary Frank Redington used the term 'immunisation' to refer to the selection of investments to meet liabilities such that the value of the asset cash flows would always be sufficient to meet the value of the liability cash flows for small, immediate changes in interest rates. Redington implicitly made the assumptions that:

- all cash flows are fixed and not dependent on interest rates. This excludes any asset or liability where the timing or amount of the cash flows depends on the level of interest rates. Cash flows whose timing or amount depends on the level of interest rates are referred to as interest rate sensitive or interest rate contingent cash flows;
- all cash flows are valued using the same interest rate. This means that the yield curve is assumed to be flat across all maturities;
- cash flows are to be immunised against small changes in the force of interest and this change is the same for all yields to maturity. Thus the yield to maturity curve is assumed to move in a parallel fashion.

In order to be immunised the difference between the value of the asset cash flows and the value of the liability cash flows has to be positive, or at least not negative, if interest rates change. If this difference is denoted by $S(i)$ then:

$$S(i) = \sum_t (A_t) \, v^t - \sum_t (L_t) \, v^t = \sum_t (A_t - L_t) v^t$$

where i is the yield to maturity for time t, assumed to be independent of t, and A_t is the asset cash flow at time t and L_t is the liability cash flow at time t. If the yield changes from i to $i + \varepsilon$ then using the Taylor's series expansion:

$$S(i + \varepsilon) \approx S(i) + \varepsilon S'(i) + \frac{\varepsilon^2}{2} S''(i)$$

Thus if $S'(i) = 0$ and $S''(i) > 0$ then $S(i + \varepsilon) > S(i)$.

By carrying out the differentiation these conditions can be expressed as:

■ *Equation 5.11*

$$\sum_t tA_t v^t = \sum_t tL_t v^t$$

and:

■ *Equation 5.12*

$$\sum_t t^2 A_t v^t > \sum_t t^2 L_t v^t$$

If we set the value of the asset cash flows equal to the value of the liability cash flows initially then:

$$\sum_t A_t v^t = \sum_t L_t v^t$$

and dividing both sides of equations 5.11 and 5.12 by the value of the assets (or liabilities) produces the immunisation conditions that the durations should be set equal and the convexity of the assets should be greater than the convexity of the liabilities. If the duration of the assets (equal to the duration of the liabilities) is deducted from both sides of equation 5.12 then the condition is that the spread (or M^2) of the assets should exceed the spread (or M^2) of the liabilities.

In practice the conditions under which Redington immunisation will hold do not occur. Yield curves are very rarely flat and they do not move in parallel shifts. Other researchers have developed the conditions for immunisation by allowing for more general conditions. The conditions have been extended to the case of non-flat yield curves but with the assumption that yield curve shifts are parallel. Measures of immunisation with respect to changes in the interest rate at single maturities on the yield curve, with all the other yields to maturity remaining fixed, have been developed. These sensitivities with respect to changes in a single maturity interest rate are called partial durations. This approach enables the detection of particular maturities where the value of the net cash flows (assets less liabilities) is sensitive to interest rate movements. Duration measures the change in value with respect to changes in interest rates for all maturities and is the sum of these partial durations.

In practice interest rate movements do not move by fixed amounts. Interest rates change as government policy and financial and other news is taken into account by investors in setting their desired interest rate. These interest rate changes can be modelled using a random or stochastic model for interest rates rather than the fixed or deterministic model used in immunisation. Interest rate models are introduced in chapter 9. It should also be noted that short-term interest rates tend to be more variable than long-term interest rates. They are said to have a higher volatility than long-term rates where the term 'volatility' means the standard deviation of interest rates. Measures of immunisation do not take the amount of variability of interest rates into account.

Example 5.9

Assume that the interest rates in table 5.12 apply to zero coupon bonds in the market. A company has a liability cash flow of $20 000 in 1 year's time and another of $40 000 in 2 years' time. The company has been advised to invest its funds in a portfolio of the zero coupon bonds maturing in 0.5 years and 2.5 years to ensure the asset cash flows have a higher convexity or spread than the liability cash flows.

Table 5.12

Term to maturity (yrs)	Yield to maturity (% p.a. semi-annual)
0.5	6.1
1.0	6.2
1.5	6.3
2.0	6.4
2.5	6.5

(a) Calculate the value of the liability cash flows using the interest rates in table 5.12.
(b) Calculate the face value and present value of the zero coupon bonds that will have the same present value and duration as the liability cash flows.

Solution

(a) The liability value is:

$$PV(L) = \frac{20\ 000}{\left(1 + \dfrac{6.2}{200}\right)^2} + \frac{40\ 000}{\left(1 + \dfrac{6.4}{200}\right)^4}$$

$$= 54\ 080.15$$

(b) The duration of the liability is:

$$D(L) = \frac{\left[\dfrac{20\ 000}{\left(1 + \dfrac{6.2}{200}\right)^2} + \dfrac{40\ 000}{\left(1 + \dfrac{6.4}{200}\right)^4}\right]}{54\ 080.15}$$

$$= 1.652 \text{ years}$$

Assume that the investment will consist of x in face value of the zero coupon bond maturing in 0.5 years' time and y in face value of the zero coupon bond maturing in 2.5 years' time.

The present value of the assets is equated to that of the liabilities to get:

$$PVA = \frac{x}{\left(1 + \frac{6.1}{200}\right)} + \frac{y}{\left(1 + \frac{6.5}{200}\right)^5}$$

$$= 0.970403x + 0.852216y$$

$$= PV(L)$$

$$= 54\,080.15$$

so that:

$$0.970403x + 0.852216y = 54\,080.1522 \qquad (1)$$

The duration of the assets are equated to that of the liabilities to get:

$$D(A) = \frac{\left[\frac{0.5x}{\left(1 + \frac{6.1}{200}\right)} + \frac{2.5y}{\left(1 + \frac{6.5}{200}\right)^5}\right]}{0.970403x + 0.852216y}$$

$$= D(L)$$

$$= 1.652084$$

so that:

$$1.117985x - 0.722608y = 0 \qquad (2)$$

Solving (1) and (2) simultaneously gives $x = 23\,627.02$ and $y = 36\,554.61$.

The face value of the zero coupon bond maturing in 0.5 years' time is 23 627.02 and the present value is $22 927.72. The face value of the zero coupon bond maturing in 2.5 years' time is $36 554.61 and the present value is $31 152.43.

6 Forwards and futures

There are many different forwards and futures contracts, including exchange-traded contracts and over-the-counter contracts on interest rates, foreign exchange rates, equity prices, bond prices and commodities. The main exchange-traded contracts in Australia are the Sydney Futures Exchange (SFE) contracts.

The Share Price Index (SPI) contract is for an amount of 25 times the value of the All Ordinaries Index. It is settled in cash, based on the difference between the futures contract price and the Share Price Index on the settlement day. Trading terminates on the second last business day of the contract month and contracts are available for March, June, September and December up to 18 months ahead. Futures contracts are available in all major international markets. Futures contracts are available on a number of indices in the US, including the S&P 500. This contract trades on the Chicago Mercantile Exchange and is on 500 times the index. The contract is also cash-settled based on the opening price of the index the morning after the last trading day.

The 90 day Bank Accepted Bill (BAB) futures contract on the SFE is quoted as $(100 - i)$ where i is the yield to maturity. The value of the contract is the price of a 90 day bank bill at the quoted yield to maturity using a 365 day convention. Settlement is on the second Friday of the delivery month. The contract involves physical delivery of BABs with 85 to 95 days to maturity and face value of $500 000. The US equivalent is the Treasury bill contract which requires delivery of $1 million 90 day Treasury bills. This is quoted as $100 -$ Treasury bill cash price. Treasury bills in the US market are quoted using a discount rate on a 360 day basis.

The 3 and 10 year bond futures contracts on the SFE are based on a notional $100 000 face value 12% p.a. coupon bond. The price is quoted as $100 - y$ where y is the yield to maturity (semi-annual compounding).

The contract is non-deliverable and is cash-settled based on market quotes for bonds of similar maturity. Contract months are March, June, September and December up to 12 months ahead. The US contracts are the Treasury bond and Treasury note contracts for $100 000 face value. These contracts involve physical delivery and conversion factors are used to adjust the cash paid on delivery of the bond. Prices are quoted as flat prices net of accrued interest per $100 face value with the price in 32nds, so that a price of 92.16 is $92 and 16/32 of a dollar or $92.50.

Forwards and futures markets are very important parts of the money and capital markets. They allow market participants to fix future interest rates, exchange rates or security and commodity prices. In order to understand the pricing and analysis of forwards and futures contracts it is necessary to understand how forward interest rates, exchange rates and asset prices are determined.

Spot and forward interest rates

Bond prices are calculated by present valuing each of the coupons and the face value at the yield to maturity. The yield or interest rate used to value each of the cash flows does not change, even though the time to receipt of the cash flow changes. The yield to maturity does change as the maturity of the bond changes so that coupon payments on bonds with different maturities which are received on the same date are, in effect, present valued with a different interest rate.

If each future date were to have a separate interest rate to be used to value cash flows received on that date, then the coupons and maturity payment on bonds would each be present valued with different interest rates which depended on the time to receipt of the cash flow. These interest rates are referred to as 'spot rates'. Spot interest rates are the yields to maturity on zero coupon bonds for varying maturities.

The cash flows of a bond can also be valued by applying a different interest rate to each time period between cash flows, so that the interest rate used for a particular cash flow is the compounding together of these different rates from the current date to the date of the cash flow. These rates that apply over future periods of time are referred to as 'forward rates'.

To consider the relationship between these different interest rates let the (per period) yield to maturity on an n year bond be y_n (per dollar, and not per cent per annum) and the spot rate for a cash flow in t years' time be s_t (per dollar per period). The price of an n year maturity Treasury bond with semi-annual coupon of c p.a. and face value F can be written using the yield to maturity as:

■ *Equation 6.1*

$$\sum_{t=1}^{2n} \frac{\frac{1}{2}C}{(1+y_n)^t} + \frac{F}{(1+y_n)^{2n}}$$

where the v^t symbol used in chapter 3 has been written in full in this formula as $1/(1+y_n)^t$.

Using the spot rates the bond price becomes:

■ *Equation 6.2*

$$\sum_{t=1}^{2n} \frac{\frac{1}{2}C}{(1+s_t)^t} + \frac{F}{(1+s_{2n})^{2n}}$$

where the per period interest rate used to value each of the cash flows is now different.

Notice that the yield to maturity y_n does not vary with t—it is fixed and equal to y_n for all times. However i_t does vary across time t and the last value is s_{2n} which applies to the face value, F.

The yield to maturity and the spot rates used in equations 6.1 and 6.2 for Treasury bonds are per half year rates since coupons are paid semi-annually on these bonds. The per cent p.a. rates, which are more familiar, will be 200 times the y_n and s_t rates used in equations 6.1 and 6.2. The formulae are readily adapted to apply to any time interval and any frequency of compounding. In practice semi-annual compounding is common since Treasury bond yields are most often used to determine spot yield curves.

The yield curve of spot rates is referred to as the term structure of interest rates. In practice the yields to maturity are available from bonds trading in the market. A yield curve is fitted to these yields to maturity to produce a par yield curve that represents the yields to maturity that would apply to hypothetical bonds that have coupon rates equal to their yields to maturity. These par yields give bond prices equal to 100 (par or face value) for all maturity bonds. This par yield curve is then used to derive the spot yield curve for zero coupon bonds.

The procedure to do this works forward in time, solving for each spot yield one at a time. The value of the par yield bond (100) is equated to the value of the coupons and maturity value at the spot yields. By working forward in time, the only spot yield not known is the yield applying to the maturity amount including the final coupon. The first spot yield is equal to the first par yield, since the bond maturing at the first maturity has a price of 100 and pays 100 plus a coupon equal to the par yield to maturity. The spot yield must equal the par yield to maturity otherwise the price will not be par. The second spot yield is determined by equating the price of the par bond with maturity in 2 time periods to the value of the coupons, which are equal to the par yield for that maturity, and the maturity amount at the spot yields. Since the first spot yield has been determined previously, the second spot yield is the only unknown. In general the following equation holds for the n maturity spot yield:

$$100 = \frac{p_n}{(1 + s_1)} + \frac{p_n}{(1 + s_2)^2} + \ldots + \frac{100 + p_n}{(1 + s_n)^n}$$

where p_n is the par yield (per period, per $100 face value) for maturity n determined from the fitted par yield curve, s_1 to s_{n-1} are the (per period, per dollar) spot yields determined working forward in time and s_n is the spot yield to be determined. This can be rearranged to give:

$$(1 + s_n)^n = \frac{100 + p_n}{(100 - p_n a^*_{\overline{n-1}})}$$

where p_n is the per period par yield for the nth maturity and $a^*_{\overline{n-1}}$ is the value of $n - 1$ payments of 1 at the spot yields to maturity. This gives an expression for the spot yield for maturity n of:

■ *Equation 6.3*

$$s_n = \left[\frac{100 + p_n}{(100 - p_n a^*_{\overline{n-1}})} \right]^{\frac{1}{n}} - 1$$

Example 6.1

Calculate the spot yield curve corresponding to the par yield curve given in table 6.1.

Table 6.1

Time to maturity (yrs)	Par yield (% p.a. semi-annual)
0.5	8.00
1.0	8.25
1.5	8.50

Solution

The equation for the first period is:

$$100 = \frac{100 + 4}{(1 + s_1)}$$

since $p_1 = \dfrac{8}{200} \times 100 = 4$. Thus $s_1 = 4\%$ per half year or 8% p.a. semi-annual the same as the first par yield.

The equation for the second period is:

$$100 = \frac{4.125}{(1.04)} + \frac{100 + 4.125}{(1 + s_2)^2}$$

using s_1 from the previous period. Thus $a^*_{\overline{1}|} = 0.961538$. Solving for s_2 using equation 6.3 gives:

$$s_2 = \left[\frac{140.125}{(100 - 4.125 \times 0.961538)} \right]^{\frac{1}{2}} - 1$$

$$= 0.041276$$

or 8.255% p.a.

The equation for the third period is:

$$100 = \frac{4.25}{(1.04)} + \frac{4.25}{(1.041276)^2} + \frac{100 + 4.25}{(1 + s_3)^3}$$

and the value for s_3 is:

$$s_3 = \left[\frac{104.25}{(100 - 4.25 \times 1.883830)} \right]^{\frac{1}{3}} - 1$$

$$= 0.042572$$

or, after multiplying by 200, a spot yield of 8.514% p.a. (semi-annual compounding).

This procedure is most suited for calculation using a computer program or spreadsheet macro. The general principle should be readily understood from example 6.1.

Example 6.2

The yields, or 'spot rates', as given in table 6.2 are available on zero coupon government securities.

Table 6.2

Time to maturity (yrs)	Yield (% p.a. semi-annual)
0.5	7.25
1.0	7.50
1.5	7.75
2.0	7.80

Use these rates to calculate the price of a 12% 2 year Treasury bond per $100 face value.

Solution

Each coupon is for an amount of $6. The price is the present value of each coupon plus the maturity payment, each valued using the spot rate corresponding to the time to receipt. Thus:

$$\text{Price} = \frac{6}{\left(1 + \frac{7.25}{200}\right)} + \frac{6}{\left(1 + \frac{7.50}{200}\right)^2} + \frac{6}{\left(1 + \frac{7.75}{200}\right)^3} + \frac{106}{\left(1 + \frac{7.80}{200}\right)^4}$$

$$= 6 \times 0.9650181 + 6 \times 0.9290173 + 6 \times 0.8922096 + 106 \times 0.8580998$$

$$= 107.676 \ (107.676050)$$

Example 6.3

Calculate the yield to maturity for the bond in example 6.2 using the price given by the value of the bond at the spot rates ($107.676).

Solution

The yield to maturity y_2 is given by equating the price to the value of the cash flows at this yield. The yield to maturity is the solution to:

$$107.676 = \frac{6}{\left(1 + \frac{y_2}{200}\right)} + \frac{6}{\left(1 + \frac{y_2}{200}\right)^2} + \frac{6}{\left(1 + \frac{y_2}{200}\right)^3} + \frac{106}{\left(1 + \frac{y_2}{200}\right)^4}$$

$$= 6a_{\overline{4}|} + 100v^4 \text{ at } (y_2 + 2)\%$$

In order to determine the solution to this equation it is necessary to use an iterative trial and error method. Using the HP12C financial functions gives a yield to maturity of 7.782% per (semi-annual).

For any given set of spot rates, as represented in the form of a yield curve similar to that in example 6.2, it is possible to determine the yield to maturity which corresponds to these spot rates for any particular bond. This was illustrated in example 6.3.

The bond price can also be written in terms of the forward rates. If the forward rate which applies for time periods t to T is denoted by $f_{t,T}$ (per dollar per period) then the price of an n year Treasury bond can be written as:

■ *Equation 6.4*

$$\frac{\frac{1}{2}c}{(1 + f_{0,1})} + \frac{\frac{1}{2}c}{(1 + f_{0,1})(1 + f_{1,2})} + \ldots + \frac{F + \frac{1}{2}c}{(1 + f_{0,1})(1 + f_{1,2})\ldots(1 + f_{2n-1,2n})}$$

The price formula using the spot rates and the price formula using the forward rates will both give the same bond price for any particular bond.

The values of each of the coupons and of the face value will be equal using these 2 alternatives for valuing the bond. Equating the values of the first coupon gives:

$$\frac{1}{(1+s_1)} = \frac{1}{(1+f_{0,1})}$$

so that:

$$f_{0,1} = s_1$$

Similarly, equating the values of the second coupon gives:

$$\frac{1}{(1+s_2)^2} = \frac{1}{(1+f_{0,1})(1+f_{1,2})}$$

Substituting s_1 for $f_{0,1}$ in this expression and solving for $f_{1,2}$ gives:

$$f_{1,2} = \left[\frac{(1+s_2)^2}{(1+s_1)} - 1 \right]$$

This procedure is repeated for each coupon to determine each forward rate. In general the forward rate for time period $(t-1)$ to t, in terms of the spot rates, is given by:

■ *Equation 6.5*

$$f_{t-1,t} = \left[\frac{(1+s_t)^t}{(1+s_{t-1})^{t-1}} - 1 \right]$$

For a bond with semi-annual coupons the forward rates derived from equation 6.5 need to be multiplied by 200 to get per cent p.a. rates since in the bond case the rates derived from equation 6.5 will be half-yearly per dollar rates.

Example 6.4

Calculate the forward rates for each future half year corresponding to the spot rates given in example 6.2.

Solution

The forward rate for the first half year is the same as the spot rate. Hence $f_{0,1} = 7.25 \div 200 = 0.03625$ per half year. For the second half year:

$$f_{1,2} = 200 \times \left[\frac{(1+7.50/200)^2}{(1+7.25/200)} - 1 \right]$$

$$= 7.750\%$$

Similarly:

$$f_{2,3} = 200 \times \left[\frac{(1+7.75/200)^3}{(1+7.50/200)^2} - 1 \right]$$

$$= 8.251\%$$

and:

$$f_{3,4} = 200 \times \left[\frac{(1 + 7.80/200)^4}{(1 + 7.75/200)^3} - 1 \right]$$

$$= 7.950\%$$

The forward rates applying to future time periods corresponding to the spot rates in example 6.1 are therefore (see table 6.3):

Table 6.3

Forward time period (yrs)	Forward rate (% p.a. semi-annual)
0–0.5	7.250
0.5–1.0	7.750
1.0–1.5	8.251
1.5–2.0	7.950

Example 6.5

Calculate the price of the bond in example 6.2 using the forward rates derived in example 6.4.

Solution

Using equation 6.3 gives:

$$\text{Price} = \frac{6}{(1 + 7.250/200)} + \frac{6}{(1 + 7.250/200)\,(1 + 7.750/200)}$$
$$+ \frac{6}{(1 + 7.250/200)\,(1 + 7.750/200)\,(1 + 8.251/200)}$$
$$+ \frac{106}{(1 + 7.250/200)\,(1 + 7.750/200)\,(1 + 8.251/200)\,(1 + 7.950/200)}$$

$$= 6 \times 0.965018 + 6 \times 0.929019 + 6 \times 0.892210 + 106 \times 0.858101$$

$$= 107.676186 \ (107.676)$$

This answer differs in the fourth decimal place from the price calculated in example 6.2 because the forward interest rates were rounded to 3 decimal places in the calculations.

Spot and forward rates can be determined from any cash flows and can also be based on simple p.a. yields rather than on the semi-annual compounding rates considered so far. If the simple interest yields (spot rates) for a period of m days (s_m) and also for a period of n days (s_n) are available, then the forward rate for an investment commencing in n days for a period of $m - n$ days in simple interest yield terms is given by:

■ *Equation 6.6*

$$f_{n,m} = 100 \times \frac{365}{(m-n)} \times \left[\frac{\left(1 + \frac{m}{365} \times \frac{s_m}{100} \right)}{\left(1 + \frac{n}{365} \times \frac{s_n}{100} \right)} - 1 \right]$$

Example 6.6

A 90 day bank bill can be purchased at a yield of 7.75% p.a. and a 270 day bank bill at a yield of 7.50% p.a. Determine the forward rate applying to the 180 day period commencing in 90 days' time.

Solution

Since short-term securities such as bank bills only involve 1 cash flow, their yields to maturity and the spot rates are the same. Hence, using equation 6.6, s_{90} = 7.50% p.a., s_{270} = 7.75% p.a., and the forward rate applying in 90 days' time for a 180 day period is:

$$f_{90,270} = 100 \times \frac{365}{180} \times \left[\frac{\left(1 + \frac{270}{365} \times \frac{7.75}{100} \right)}{\left(1 + \frac{90}{365} \times \frac{7.50}{100} \right)} - 1 \right]$$

$$= 100 \times \frac{365}{180} \times \left[\frac{(1.057329)}{(1.018493)} - 1 \right]$$

$$= 7.732\% \text{ p.a.}$$

Spot and forward exchange rates

Exchange rates express the value of 1 currency in terms of another. They can be quoted in 'direct' terms, in which case the cost of 1 unit of a foreign currency is given in units of the domestic currency. They are also quoted in 'indirect' terms where the amount of foreign currency per unit of domestic currency is given. The UK pound is traditionally quoted in indirect terms where the units of foreign currency are given per pound sterling. The Commonwealth countries also tend to have followed the practice of quoting indirect rates.

Spot exchange rates are the rates that foreign currencies can be bought and sold at for settlement in 2 business days. The 2 business days allow the currencies being exchanged to be deposited into the relevant accounts at the international banks involved in the transactions. Rates can be obtained for settlement in 1 day rather than in 2 days. These rates are referred to as tomorrow rates (Tom.) or overnight points. If settlement falls on a weekend or public holiday then the settlement date will be the next business day.

Forward exchange rates are the rates at which foreign currencies can be bought and sold for delivery or settlement at future dates. Rates are quoted for even periods, typically at monthly intervals. If direct quotes are involved and the forward rate is higher than the spot rate, then the forward rate is at a premium over the spot and if it is lower it is at a discount on the spot rate. Forward rates are quoted in terms of premiums and discounts over the spot rate rather than in terms of the exchange rate. If indirect quotes are involved then the forward rate is at a premium when the forward rate is lower than the spot rate.

Exchange rates, like deposit and investment rates, are quoted with a spread between bid and offer rates. Bid rates are the rates at which the other party buys foreign currency, so it is the rate at which the holder of the currency will sell. Offer rates are the rates at which the currency is sold at or at which a purchaser of currency will buy from the party giving the quote. Exchange rates are quoted as:

Currency A/Currency B

or A/B which is the amount of currency B per unit of currency A and is not currency A divided by currency B. Thus a $/yen quote gives the amount of yen bought or sold for $1.

Forward exchange rates can be related to spot exchange rates by considering the relative levels of foreign and domestic interest rates. Consider a forward exchange rate for currency A in terms of currency B for delivery in M days. Let the spot rate be $S_{A/B}$ and the forward rate be $F_{A/B}$. Interest rates for an M day term are r_a in country A and r_b in country B. By buying currency A forward, a rate is fixed today at which settlement will occur in M days. Thus the effect of a forward purchase of currency A is that it will be purchased at a rate of $F_{A/B}$ per unit of currency A in M days' time.

Currency A can also be obtained in M days at a fixed rate using the following strategy. Borrow 1 unit of currency A and exchange this for currency B at the spot rate $S_{A/B}$. Invest this amount of currency B at rate r_b for M days. The loan in currency A has to be repaid out of these funds for an amount of 1 unit plus interest at rate r_a for M days. The forward rate will equal the ratio of the invested amount of currency B and the borrowed amount of currency A in M days, otherwise a profitable trading strategy (referred to as an arbitrage opportunity) will exist. This can best be seen with an example.

Example 6.7

The spot rate for the US$ in Australia is 0.75 A$/US$. This is an indirect quote since the US$ is priced in terms of foreign currency per domestic currency (or in indirect or foreign terms). The local A$ interest rate is 7.5% p.a. for a 90 day borrowing and the US$ investment rate for 90 days is 5.5% p.a. (a 360 day rate). Calculate the forward rate, based on this information, which will preclude any arbitrage opportunities.

Solution

Let the forward rate be f (A$/US$). If A$1 is borrowed at 7.5% for 90 days and this is exchanged for US$ at the spot rate, this will provide US$0.75. This can be invested at 5.5% p.a. for 90 days. At the same time take out a forward contract to convert the resulting US$ to A$ at the forward rate of f (A$/US$). The resulting A$ in 90 days can then be used to repay the original A$ borrowing with interest.

If the amount of A$ generated in 90 days through the forward market exceeds the original borrowing with interest, then an arbitrage opportunity exists since a profit can be made from this transaction without requiring any net investment (the funds required are borrowed at the start of the transaction). Similarly, if the A$ in 90 days are insufficient to repay the borrowing there is an arbitrage opportunity if the transaction is reversed. In this case the process would involve borrowing US$, spot exchanging the US$ for A$ and investing the proceeds in Australia while at the same time effecting a forward exchange for the A$s (with interest) at the forward rate.

This strategy can be used to calculate the forward rate as follows:

Borrow A$1.

Spot exchange to get US$0.75.

Invest US$ for 90 days to give:

$$0.75 \times \left(1 + \frac{90}{360} \times \frac{5.5}{100}\right) = 0.7603$$

Exchange the resulting US$ for A$ under the forward contract to get $0.7603/f$ A$.

This has to equal the repayment of the borrowing of:

$$\left(1 + \frac{90}{365} \times \frac{7.50}{100}\right) = 1.0185 \text{ A\$}$$

Hence the forward rate, to avoid arbitrage, will be:

$$f = 0.7603/1.0185 = 0.7465$$

In this example the quote is an indirect one which gives the exchange rate of A$ in terms of the US dollar. Because of this it is necessary to take the inverse of these exchange rates to obtain the exchange rate in A$ terms rather than in US$ terms as given. The forward rate in A$ terms is then seen to be higher than the spot rate in this example, which means that the US$ is at a forward premium, even though the forward rate (as an indirect quote) is lower than the spot rate. The difference between the spot rate and the forward rate is referred to as the 'forward points' or 'margin' and this is the way that forward rates are quoted. In this example the forward points are $0.75 - 0.7465 = 35$ points premium.

The result above generalises as follows. Let d indicate the domestic currency and f the foreign currency, t be the term (in years) for the forward rate, r_f and r_d, respectively, denote the foreign and domestic p.a. interest rates, S indicate the spot rate and F indicate the forward rate. The following results will apply, where rates and time periods are assumed to be on a 365 day convention so that if either or both of the rates r_f or r_d are on a 360 day convention then they will have to be multiplied by 365/360 before using these formulae.

Forward rate in indirect terms:

■ *Equation 6.7*

$$F_{d/f} = \frac{S_{d/f} \times (1 + t \times r_f)}{(1 + t \times r_d)}$$

Forward points, or margin, in indirect terms:

■ *Equation 6.8*

$$F_{d/f} - S_{d/f} = \frac{S_{d/f} \times t \times (r_f - r_d)}{(1 + t \times r_d)}$$

Forward rate in direct terms:

■ *Equation 6.9*

$$F_{f/d} = \frac{S_{f/d} \times (1 + t \times r_d)}{(1 + t \times r_f)}$$

Forward points, or margin, in direct terms:

■ *Equation 6.10*

$$F_{f/d} - S_{f/d} = \frac{S_{f/d} \times t \times (r_d - r_f)}{(1 + t \times r_f)}$$

These results are based on the assumption that the interest cost of borrowing in the domestic currency will be equated to the interest return on the foreign currency, expressed in domestic currency terms using the spot and forward foreign exchange rates. This is referred to as 'interest rate parity'. If these results do not hold then it is possible to use the transactions in example 6.7 to make profits. These transactions are referred to as 'covered interest arbitrage'.

Pricing forward contracts

Forward contracts are agreements to buy or sell an underlying asset such as a commodity or financial instrument on a prespecified future date for a fixed future price. Forward contracts can also be in the form of an agreement to make a net payment to the buyer or seller of the contract which represents the difference between the value of a financial instrument (or commodity) at a prespecified yield (or price) and the market yield (or price) at the future date. The market yield (or price) is determined under the rules set out in the forward contract. Contracts requiring the future purchase or sale of the underlying asset involve physical 'delivery', whereas contracts requiring a net payment on the settlement date involve 'cash settlement'.

If you are 'long' a forward contract then you have an obligation to buy a financial instrument or commodity on the maturity of the contract. Similarly, if you are 'short' a forward contract then you have an obligation to sell the underlying asset at the future date.

There are no payments between the parties to a forward contract until the future date when the forward purchase or sale takes place (or alternatively the net payment under the contract is made). Because there is no purchase price for a forward contract, the only variable that is 'priced' in a forward contract is the forward price at which sale or purchase takes place. Since no investment is made in the contract at inception this price must be determined so that the value of the forward contract is zero.

The difference between the forward price and the current price (spot price) of the financial instrument or commodity is called the basis. In the case of commodities this difference will be required to cover what are referred to as 'carrying' costs. Carrying costs are the costs of storage, insurance, inspection of the commodity plus the interest expense in financing the purchase of the commodity. Commodity forward contracts will not be considered in any detail. Instead attention will be given mainly to forward contracts on financial instruments. Similar principles apply to commodity forward contracts, except that many commodities do not have active markets, unlike financial instruments, and commodities are used in production. These factors influence commodity futures prices. For financial instruments the carrying costs are the financing costs on the spot purchase price. However, unlike commodities, financial instruments will usually pay a rate of return in the form of interest or dividends which will be available to offset the financing costs.

Consider a forward contract on a 90 day bank accepted bill (BAB) for delivery in 30 days' time. A relationship between spot prices and forward prices for bank bills can be determined as follows. Forward contracts on bank bills are quoted in terms of the purchase/sale yield which is used to determine the purchase/sale price on the delivery date. Let the 30 day forward rate on the 90 day bill be given by $f_{30,120}$. A 'long' position equivalent to that under the forward contract can be created by purchasing a 120 day bank bill today and holding this for 30 days. The result is a 90 day bank bill in 30 days' time which would be purchased under the forward contract at a yield of $f_{30,120}$. If the purchase yield for the 120 day bank bill is denoted by s_{120}, then the cost of purchasing a \$500 000 face value bank bill today (the spot price) is:

$$\text{Spot price} = \frac{500\,000}{\left(1 + \dfrac{120}{365} \times \dfrac{s_{120}}{100}\right)}$$

The effective cost of creating a 90 day bank bill in 30 days' time will equal the cost of the bill plus the 'carrying' or funding costs for 30 days at the 30 day rate, s_{30}, which will be:

$$\text{Spot price} \times \left(1 + \frac{30}{365} \times \frac{s_{30}}{100}\right)$$

The forward price will be equal to this if there is to be no difference between taking out a forward contract or creating an equivalent position by purchasing a 120 day bank bill and funding it for 30 days. The forward price under the forward contract is:

$$\text{Forward price} = \frac{500\,000}{\left(1 + \dfrac{90}{365} \times \dfrac{f_{30,120}}{100}\right)}$$

Equating the forward price to the effective cost in 30 days (determined today) gives:

$$\text{Forward price} = \text{Spot price} \times \left(1 + \frac{30}{365} \times \frac{s_{30}}{100}\right)$$

or:

$$\frac{500\,000}{\left(1 + \dfrac{90}{365} \times \dfrac{f_{30,120}}{100}\right)} = \frac{500\,000}{\left(1 + \dfrac{120}{365} \times \dfrac{s_{120}}{100}\right)} \times \left(1 + \frac{30}{365} \times \frac{s_{30}}{100}\right)$$

For these 2 expressions to be equal the forward interest rate must equal, after a little algebra:

$$f_{30,120} = 100 \times \frac{365}{90} \times \left[\frac{\left(1 + \dfrac{120}{365} \times \dfrac{s_{120}}{100}\right)}{\left(1 + \dfrac{30}{365} \times \dfrac{s_{30}}{100}\right)} - 1\right]$$

This is the identical relationship developed earlier between spot and forward interest rates. The techniques used to establish these relationships are referred to as 'arbitrage' arguments since, if they do not hold, then there is the opportunity to make arbitrage profits.

In the above case the 120 day bill was purchased in the spot market and sold in the forward market. The purchase was funded using borrowing. An equivalent result is obtained if the 120 day bill was borrowed for 30 days, for a fee, from an investor currently holding the security. The fee required would be equal to the funding cost of the physical security over the 30 days. Borrowing and lending securities are carried out under repurchase agreements which, in the US market, are referred to as 'repos'. The fee involved in borrowing the security is often called the 'repo' rate. These rates are typically overnight rates and can change from day to day so that, in practice, the 30 day rate would not be known at the time the transaction was carried out.

Example 6.8

The rates available in the bank bill market are given in table 6.4.

Table 6.4

Maturity (days)	Spot rates (% p.a.)	90 day forward rates (% p.a.)
30	7.5	7.3
90	7.4	7.0
120	7.4	
180	7.4	

Spot rates are assumed to apply for both purchasing and funding physical bills. Given these rates, identify any arbitrage opportunities in these market rates.

Solution

There are 2 basic strategies for making arbitrage profits.

Strategy 1 Buy 120 day bills at 7.4%, fund them for 30 days at 7.5% and sell them forward as 90 day bills in 30 days at 7.3%. Basing all calculations on a $500 000 face value gives:

$$\text{Purchase cost} = \frac{500\,000}{\left(1 + \frac{120}{365} \times \frac{7.4}{100}\right)}$$

$$= \$488\,124.53$$

$$\text{Plus funding cost} = 488\,124.53 \times \left(1 + \frac{30}{365} \times \frac{7.5}{100}\right)$$

$$= \$491\,133.52$$

$$\text{Sale price under forward contract} = \frac{500\,000}{\left(1 + \frac{90}{365} \times \frac{7.3}{100}\right)}$$

$$= \$491\,159.14$$

Hence there is a possible profit of $25.62 per $500 000 face value of bills which will hardly be sufficient to cover transaction costs and is not a very attractive arbitrage opportunity.

Strategy 2 Buy 180 day bills at 7.4%, fund them for 90 days at 7.4% and sell them forward as 90 day bills in 90 days' time at 7.0%.

$$\text{Purchase cost} = \frac{500\,000}{\left(1 + \frac{180}{365} \times \frac{7.4}{100}\right)}$$

$$= \$482\,395.86$$

$$\text{Plus funding cost} = 482\,395.86 \times \left(1 + \frac{90}{365} \times \frac{7.4}{100}\right)$$

$$= \$491\,197.93$$

$$\text{Sale price under forward contract} = \frac{500\,000}{\left(1 + \frac{90}{365} \times \frac{7}{100}\right)}$$

$$= \$491\,516.29$$

This strategy gives a profit of $318 per $500 000 face value. In order to make a profit it is necessary to buy 180 day bills at 7.4% and borrow the cost at 7.4% for 90 days, and then sell 90 day bills under the forward contract in 90 days' time at 7.0% p.a.

The above transactions could have been carried out by borrowing the security, selling it in the spot market, and, at the same time, purchasing the security at a fixed rate in the forward market. The cost of borrowing the security under a repurchase agreement would then be compared with the returns from the sale in the spot market and the purchase in the forward market. The reverse of this transaction would involve the purchase of the security in the spot market, the forward sale of the security and, at the same time, the lending of the security under a repurchase agreement.

Some financial instruments, such as bonds and shares, pay interest or dividends and a forward contract on such instruments will need to be priced to allow for these earnings. Consider a forward contract to buy 10% coupon 10 year Treasury bonds in 1 year's time (immediately after the coupon then due has been paid). These bonds are assumed to be currently available as 10% 11 year Treasury bonds at a yield of 8.5% p.a. (semi-annual). Funding costs for 1 year are 7.5% p.a. (monthly compounding). The forward rate in 1 year's time is determined as follows.

The cost of the bonds today (11 year maturity, 10% coupon at a market yield of 8.5%) is (per $100 face value):

$$\text{Price} = 5a_{\overline{22}|} + 100v^{22} \text{ at } 4.25\%$$
$$= 5 \times 14.111868 + 100 \times 0.400246$$
$$= 110.583901$$

If the funding cost for 1 year is added then the effective cost of the bonds, including the 'carrying' cost, in 1 year's time will be:

$$\text{Effective cost} = 110.583901 \times (1 + 7.5/1200)^{12}$$
$$= 110.583901 \times (1.0776326)$$
$$= 119.168816$$

Offsetting the funding cost will be the receipt of coupons on the bond in 1 half year and at the end of the year. These are accumulated to the end of the year at the funding cost on the assumption that they are most likely to be used to repay the purchase cost funding. The accumulated value of the coupons will be:

$$5 \times (1 + 7.50/1200)^6 + 5$$
$$= 5 \times (1.038091) + 5$$
$$= 10.190454$$

Note that we could also calculate the accumulated value of the coupons using the $s_{\overline{n}|}$ function covered in chapter 4. To do this, because the payments are half yearly and the funding rate is a monthly compounding rate, it is necessary to convert the funding rate to an equivalent semi-annual rate. This is given by:

$$\text{Semi-annual equivalent} = 200 \times \left[\left(1 + \frac{7.5}{1200} \right)^6 - 1 \right]$$
$$= 7.618\% \text{ p.a.}$$

The accumulated value of the coupons is then:

$$5s_{\overline{2}|} \text{ at } 7.618/2\% \text{ (3.809\% per half year)}$$
$$= 5 \times \left(\frac{(1.03809)^2 - 1}{0.03809} \right)$$
$$= 5 \times 2.038091$$
$$= 10.190454$$

The net effective forward price on the bonds will need to allow for both the funding cost and the reinvested value of the coupons and will equal:

$$119.168816 - 10.190454$$
$$= 108.978362$$

The theoretical yield to maturity on a forward contract for delivery in 1 year's time for the 10 year bonds will be for this price. The forward yield is determined from:

$$108.978362 = 5a_{\overline{20}|} + 100v^{20}$$

which, using the HP12C, gives 4.320% per half year or 8.641% p.a. (semi-annual).

In practice, forward prices are affected by a host of factors not discussed in the above analysis so that these theoretical relationships do not always hold. One important factor not covered is the effect of tax. In any analysis of arbitrage transactions it will be important to incorporate tax effects. Another factor not allowed for which can easily be incorporated is transaction costs. These can often wipe out any arbitrage profits except for the large market players whose transaction costs will be the lowest. In order to incorporate these factors the basic principles covered in this chapter still apply, especially when determining the profit possibilities from any arbitrage transactions.

Example 6.9

A forward contract is available on a share for delivery in 6 months. The current share price is $10.50 per share and the forward contract requires delivery of 10 000 shares. The share will pay a dividend in 3 months of $0.50 per share. Funding costs for 6 months are 8.5% p.a. with interest payable monthly. Transaction costs are 2% of the value of the shares purchased. Determine the forward price for sale of the shares in 6 months at which all net funding and other costs would be covered.

Solution

The purchase cost of the 10 000 shares will be, including the transaction costs:

$$1.02 \times (10\ 000 \times 10.50) = \$107\ 100$$

Funding costs for 6 months will be:

$$107\ 100 \times \left[\left(1 + \frac{8.5}{1200}\right)^{6} - 1\right] = \$4633.12$$

The funding costs will be offset by the dividends which are accumulated at 8.5% on the assumption that they are used to offset the financing of the purchase cost of the shares. The accumulated value of the dividends is:

$$0.50 \times 10\ 000 \times \left[\left(1 + \frac{8.5}{1200}\right)^{3}\right] = 5000 \times 1.021401$$
$$= \$5107.00$$

Hence the forward price in 6 months required to cover net funding costs is:

$$107\,100 + 4633.12 - 5107.00 = 106\,626.12$$

or $10.66 per share.

The valuation of outstanding forward contracts

Forward contracts issued in the past and currently outstanding have fixed and known forward prices. Such forward contracts will have a value, depending on movements in forward prices since the inception of the contract. The theoretical forward price at inception can be determined by allowing for net carrying costs to the delivery date of the contract as already covered. The value of a forward contract at any date during its life can also be determined in a similar way if the contract forward price and any future net carrying costs are known. To show this, consider a forward contract for settlement in T days' time with a forward price of F_T. For an investor who is long a forward contract the value of the contract on the settlement date is:

$$S_T - F_T$$

where S_T is the spot price on the settlement date. This will be so since the forward contract involves the purchase at a price of F_T of an asset worth S_T. The net value of the transaction is therefore the difference between S_T and F_T.

For an investor who is short a forward contract, the value of the contract on the settlement date will be:

$$F_T - S_T$$

since a commodity worth S_T is sold for a price of F_T for a net gain or loss (if negative) of $F_T - S_T$.

The value of the contract, given the forward price, is the present value of the amount the contract is worth on the delivery or settlement date. The present value for the long forward contract is the present value of:

$$S_T - F_T$$

which is equal to:

Present value of S_T − Present value of F_T

This present value is determined by creating a long forward contract by buying the underlying instrument (or commodity) for a current spot price of S_0 and borrowing this amount at rate r_T. The borrowing with interest will amount to:

$$S_0 \times \left(1 + \frac{T}{365} \times \frac{r_T}{100} \right)$$

on the delivery date and the underlying instrument can be sold for S_T to provide funds to repay the loan. The net proceeds of this transaction will be:

$$S_T - S_0 \times \left(1 + \frac{T}{365} \times \frac{r_T}{100}\right)$$

The difference between the settlement payment on the forward contract $(S_T - F_T)$ and this net proceeds is:

$$S_0 \times \left(1 + \frac{T}{365} \times \frac{r_T}{100}\right) - F_T$$

This amount has a present value of:

$$\frac{S_0 \times \left(1 + \frac{T}{365} \times \frac{r_T}{100}\right) - F_T}{\left(1 + \frac{T}{365} \times \frac{r_T}{100}\right)}$$

which is equal to:

■ *Equation 6.11*

$$S_0 - \frac{F_T}{\left(1 + \frac{T}{365} \times \frac{r_T}{100}\right)}$$

This is the value of a forward contract with a forward price of F_T for settlement in T days since it is the additional value of the contract over and above the equivalent of a forward contract taken out on the valuation date (which has zero current value). It is the difference between the current spot price and the present value, at the funding rate r_T, of the forward price. The current spot price is the present value of the spot price on the delivery date. Note that interest or dividends, as well as any carrying costs, have been ignored. These can easily be incorporated. Similar arguments can be used to value the short position in the futures contract. This can be determined more simply by noting that such a position is the reverse of the long position and has the equal but opposite value to that in equation 6.11.

Example 6.10

An investor holds a long position in a forward contract on gold for delivery in 90 days at $450 an ounce. The current spot price of gold is $420 an ounce and insurance and storage costs for gold are 2% p.a. Ninety day interest rates are 9.5% p.a. What is the value of this forward contract?

Solution

The long position in the forward contract will have a value on settlement of:

$$S_{90} - 450$$

per ounce in 90 days where S_{90} is the spot price of gold in 90 days' time.

Buy gold today at $420 an ounce and store and insure it for 90 days. Borrow the funds to purchase the gold for 90 days at 9.5%. In 90 days' time the ounce of gold will be worth S_{90} less the storage costs and a loan for $420 plus the funding costs will have to be repaid. The net value of this transaction will be:

$$S_{90} - \left(420 \times \frac{90}{365} \times \frac{2}{100}\right) - 420 \times \left(1 + \frac{90}{365} \times \frac{9.5}{100}\right)$$

$$= S_{90} - 431.91$$

The forward contract with a $450 forward price will have a payment in 90 days of $450 - 431.91 = 18.09$ less than the above transaction. The present value of this is:

$$\frac{-18.09}{\left(1 + \frac{90}{365} \times \frac{9.5}{100}\right)} = -17.68$$

This forward contract has a negative value of $17.68 per ounce.

Futures contracts—relationship with forwards

Futures contracts are similar to forward contracts in that they provide for the future sale or purchase of a commodity or financial instrument at a price specified at inception of the contract. Futures contracts differ from forward contracts in a number of respects. Firstly, a Clearing House is the counterparty with whom a futures contract is effectively written, so that the risk that the contract will not be fulfilled will be the risk that the Clearing House cannot meet its commitments. Forward contracts involve the risk that a specified counterparty to the contract will not perform and this will differ from counterparty to counterparty. All futures contracts have the same effective counterparty (the Clearing House) so that non-performance risk is the same for all these contracts.

The use of the Clearing House as counterparty also allows for the offsetting of bought and sold contracts or the 'closing out' of futures contracts. Since a bought and a sold contract both have the Clearing House as counterparty it is possible to settle any net payment due under the 2 contracts and to no longer have either of the contracts outstanding. The net payment required to do this is the difference between the futures price in the bought contract and the futures price in the sold contract.

The other significant difference between futures and forward contracts is the margin calls that arise from the mark-to-market practice used for futures contracts. This practice involves the daily revaluation of the futures contract by the daily change in the futures price. Margin calls are then made for this amount. In other words, the contract is revalued to the current futures market price or 'marked-to-market' on a daily basis.

Futures contracts require an initial deposit to be paid at inception. As the current futures price changes, margin calls are made to ensure that the protection provided by the initial deposit is not reduced by adverse changes in the value of the futures contract. The initial deposit is a security deposit required by the Clearing House to reduce the risk that a buyer or seller will be unable to perform under the contract in the event of adverse price movements.

Under the mark-to-market practice, margin calls are made for an amount equal to the daily change in the futures price. If futures prices move adversely, then payments are made by the contract holder to the Clearing House. Adverse price movements are increases in the futures price if the contract has been sold (short a contract) and decreases in the futures price if the contract has been bought (long a contract). Similarly, if price movements are favourable then potential profits can be realised through payments from the Clearing House. The practical effect of margin calls is that a futures contract is, in effect, settled up at the end of every day rather than wholly on the settlement date as in a forward contract. If margins calls are not met then the futures position is automatically closed out and the deposit used to cover any resulting losses.

Margin calls can be allowed for in futures pricing as follows. If the futures price on a particular contract on day t for settlement on day T (in $(T-t)$ days' time) is denoted as $f_{t,T}$, then at inception of the contract on day 0 the futures price will be $f_{0,T}$, assuming delivery under the contract is to be in T days' time.

The margin call at the end of the next day will be for an amount:

$$f_{1,T} - f_{0,T}$$

Similarly at the end of day m the margin call will be for an amount:

$$f_{m,T} - f_{m-1,T}$$

The futures price on the last day of trading of the contract will be equal to the spot price of the underlying instrument or commodity, otherwise there will be an arbitrage opportunity by way of buying the spot instrument or commodity and selling it immediately in the futures market for a profit. In practice the amount of this profit will depend upon the transaction costs involved, whether cash settlement or physical delivery is involved under the contract terms, and the timing of the actual settlement or delivery.

Margin calls will need to be funded if they are adverse and invested if they are favourable. If the interest rate at which funds can be borrowed or invested on each day from the current date to the delivery date is known in advance, then the following strategy can be used to handle margin calls.

For each margin call, borrow or invest the net amount involved from the day it occurs to the delivery date. Ignoring any initial deposit, on the first day a margin call occurs for an amount of:

$$f_{1,T} - f_{0,T}$$

The resulting cash flow effect on the delivery date from this margin call, including interest earnings/costs, will be:

$$\left[f_{1,T} - f_{0,T}\right] \times \left(1 + \frac{(T-1)}{365} \times \frac{r_{T-1}}{100}\right)$$

where r_{T-1} is the interest rate applying to the margin call borrowing or investing for $T-1$ days. If the above margin call is a negative amount then this indicates a payment by a short position, which must be funded, and a corresponding receipt by a long position which can be invested.

On the second day the variation margin will amount to:

$$f_{2,T} - f_{1,T}$$

which will have a cash flow effect on the delivery date of:

$$\left[f_{2,T} - f_{1,T}\right] \times \left(1 + \frac{(T-2)}{365} \times \frac{r_{T-2}}{100}\right)$$

This procedure is repeated for each variation margin. The total cash flow effects from all the margin calls on the delivery date will be:

$$\left[f_{1,T} - f_{0,T}\right] \times \left(1 + \frac{(T-1)}{365} \times \frac{r_{T-1}}{100}\right)$$
$$+ \left[f_{2,T} - f_{1,T}\right] \times \left(1 + \frac{(T-2)}{365} \times \frac{r_{T-2}}{100}\right)$$
$$+ \ldots$$
$$+ \left[f_{T,T} - f_{T-1,T}\right]$$

which can be simplified to:

$$\left[f_{T,T} - f_{0,T}\right]$$
$$+ \left[f_{1,T} - f_{0,T}\right] \times \left(\frac{(T-1)}{365} \times \frac{r_{T-1}}{100}\right)$$
$$+ \ldots$$
$$+ \left[f_{T-1,T} - f_{T-2,T}\right] \times \left(\frac{1}{365} \times \frac{r_1}{100}\right)$$
$$= \left[f_{T,T} - f_{0,T}\right] + \sum_{t=1}^{T-1}(mc_t) \times \left(\frac{T-t}{365} \times \frac{r_{T-t}}{100}\right)$$
$$= f_{T,T} - \{f - \text{net interest earnings on variation margins}\}$$

where mc_t is the margin call for day t.

Assuming that the futures price on the last day of the contract $(f_{T,T})$ is equal to the spot price on the settlement date (S_T), the cash flow effects of margin calls on the settlement date will equal:

$$S_T - \{f_{0,T} - \text{net interest earnings on variation margins}\}$$

Note that this is similar to the cash flow on the settlement date for a forward contract, except that in this case the effective forward price is the futures price minus the net interest earnings on the margin calls. In practice, because interest costs/earnings on margin calls will depend on interest rates at the time that the margin call occurs, the effective forward price on a futures contract will depend on unknown future interest rates and will not be totally fixed under a futures contract. This result holds, regardless of the type of the futures contract and arises from the daily mark-to-market feature of futures contracts. Thus the effect of margin calls is that a futures contract does not actually fix the purchase or sale price on the settlement date as in the case of a forward contract.

Example 6.11

A futures contract which requires the delivery of a $500 000 face value 90 day Bank Accepted Bill (BAB) is bought at a futures yield of 7.38% p.a. for delivery in 30 days' time. Table 6.5 gives the expected futures closing yields for the next 30 days and the assumed interest rates for funding/ investing variation margins.

Table 6.5

Days prior to delivery	Expected closing futures yield	Funding/investing interest rate
29–20	7.52	7.50
19–10	7.45	7.55
9–5	8.05	8.05
4–1	8.95	8.10
0	7.75 (spot)	–

Determine the variation margin calls based on the price value of the contract on days 1, 11, 21, 26 and 30. Also calculate the effective forward price allowing for the net interest earnings on the variation margins.

Solution

In practice 90 day BAB futures on the Sydney Futures Exchange are quoted in terms of an index equal to 100 minus the yield. Thus the above expected futures yields would be quoted as 100 minus the above yields. The price value of the BAB futures contract on the day it is bought is calculated using the futures yield of 7.38% p.a. to get:

$$\frac{500\,000}{\left(1+\dfrac{90}{365}\times\dfrac{7.38}{100}\right)}=\$491\,063.98$$

At the end of the first day the price value of the contract becomes:

$$\frac{500\,000}{\left(1+\dfrac{90}{365}\times\dfrac{7.52}{100}\right)}=\$490\,897.55$$

so that the margin call will be for 490 897.55 – 491 063.98 = –166.43. Note that the price value of the contract is always determined for the 90 day bill which underlies the contract at the then current futures yield. Similarly, at the end of day 11 the price value changes to:

$$\frac{500\,000}{\left(1+\dfrac{90}{365}\times\dfrac{7.45}{100}\right)}=\$490\,980.75$$

so that the variation margin is 490 980.75 – 490 897.55 = +83.20. This procedure is repeated for each expected change in futures yield to get table 6.6.

Table 6.6

Day	Price value of futures contract	Variation margin
1	490 897.55	–166.43
11	490 980.75	+83.20
21	490 268.51	–712.24
26	489 204.00	–1064.51
30	490 624.37	+1420.37

The total of the variation margin calls is –439.61 which is the difference between the value of the 90 day bank bill futures contract at the 'spot' or settlement yield of 7.75% on the closing date and the initial value of the futures contract at the fixed yield of 7.38% (490 624.37 – 491 063.98 = –439.61). This would be the settlement payment under a forward contract with a forward yield of 7.38%, but in the case of the forward contract, this would be paid on the settlement date. In the futures contract this amount is paid during the life of the contract.

Allowing for interest on the margin calls for the futures contract gives an effective forward price of:

$$491\,063.98-\{-166.43\times\frac{29}{365}\times\frac{7.5}{100}+83.20\times\frac{19}{365}\times\frac{7.55}{100}$$
$$+-712.24\times\frac{9}{365}\times\frac{8.05}{100}-1064.51\times\frac{4}{365}\times\frac{8.10}{100}\}$$

$$=491\,063.98-\{-0.99+0.33-1.41-0.94\}$$

$$=491\,063.98+3.01$$

$$=491\,066.99$$

The effective futures yield for this contract will be:

$$100 \times \frac{365}{90} \times \frac{(500\ 000 - 491\ 066.99)}{491\ 066.99} = 7.377\%\ \text{p.a.}$$

so that the effect of margin calls under the assumptions used in this example is not significant. The larger the movement in the futures price over the life of a futures contract, the larger will be the effect of interest on margin calls.

Example 6.12

A futures contract is sold on the Share Price Index for settlement in 15 months at an index value of 2510. Assuming that the futures price for the SPI contract moves to 2850 immediately and remains at this level to settlement and that the interest rates for margin calls are 8.5% (simple interest), calculate the effective forward index value for this contract.

Solution

The Sydney Futures Exchange SPI futures contract provides for a settlement payment in dollars equal to the difference between the spot value of the index and the futures value multiplied by 25. The dollar value of the contract is the index value times 25.

The dollar value of the futures contract at the index value of 2510 is $2510 \times 25 = \$62\ 750$. If the futures value of the index moves to 2850 then the dollar value of the contract becomes $2850 \times 25 = \$71\ 250$. If this move occurs a margin call of $71\ 250 - 62\ 750 = \$8500$ will be required by the sold futures position.

The interest cost of this variation margin will be:

$$8500 \times \frac{15}{12} \times \frac{8.5}{100} = \$903.13$$

The effective forward index value for the seller will be:

$$62\ 750 + (-903.13) = 61\ 846.87$$

or 2474 in index value terms. In this case the move in the index and the interest cost has a reasonably significant effect on the effective forward price in the futures contract, altering the contract value of 2510 to 2474.

The tail hedge

Futures contracts do not fix the forward price because of the unknown effect of interest earnings on margin calls. A technique that is used to handle the funding cost/interest earnings on margin calls is to use futures contracts to generate profits or losses that will offset these costs/earnings. These futures contracts are referred to as a 'tail hedge'. The aim of the tail hedge is to fix the futures price so that interest earnings/costs on margin calls are not a significant factor in determining the effective forward price on a futures contract. Using a tail hedge is also referred to as 'underhedging' since the tail hedge contracts are in opposite positions to the underlying futures position.

Consider an investor holding M futures contracts with d days to delivery/settlement. The previous day's closing value of the futures contract will be denoted by f_d. If the futures contract closes at the end of day d, with $(d-1)$ days to settlement, at f_{d-1} then the margin call on the contracts is:

$$M \times \left[f_{d-1} - f_d \right]$$

The interest at rate r_{d-1} on this margin call to the settlement date will be:

$$M \times \left[f_{d-1} - f_d \right] \times \frac{(d-1)}{365} \times \frac{r_{d-1}}{100}$$

In order to ensure that this interest does not affect the effective forward price, it is possible to take an offsetting position in the futures contract so that margin calls on the offsetting position are equal to this interest amount. Margin calls are received/paid at the current date whereas the interest benefit/cost of the margin call is received/paid on the settlement date. As a result it is necessary to generate the present value of the interest amount in profits or losses on the offsetting futures tail hedge.

If an offsetting position is taken in m futures contracts then the variation margin on these contracts (the required profit or loss) will be:

$$m \times \left[f_{d-1} - f_d \right]$$

and this has to be equal to the *present value* of the interest on the margin call on the underlying M contracts or:

$$\frac{M \times \left[f_{d-1} - f_d \right] \times \dfrac{(d-1)}{365} \times \dfrac{r_{d-1}}{100}}{\left(1 + \dfrac{d-1}{365} \times \dfrac{r_{d-1}}{100} \right)}$$

Equating these 2 gives an expression for the contracts required in the tail hedge of:

■ *Equation 6.12*

$$m = \frac{M \times \dfrac{d-1}{365} \times \dfrac{r_{d-1}}{100}}{\left(1 + \dfrac{d-1}{365} \times \dfrac{r_{d-1}}{100} \right)}$$

In practice the tail hedge contracts will be taken into account by reducing the underlying M futures contracts to give a net number of contracts of:

$$M - m = M - \dfrac{M \times \dfrac{d-1}{365} \times \dfrac{r_{d-1}}{100}}{\left(1 + \dfrac{d-1}{365} \times \dfrac{r_{d-1}}{100}\right)}$$

or, after simplifying:

■ *Equation 6.13*

$$M - m = \dfrac{M}{\left(1 + \dfrac{d-1}{365} \times \dfrac{r_{d-1}}{100}\right)}$$

Note that if M is a long position then M and m are positive, so that the net futures position will be less than M by the number of contracts in the tail hedge. Similarly, if M is a short position then M and m are negative. The net contracts $M - m$ will be a smaller negative than M by the number of contracts in the tail hedge (m).

Equation 6.13 shows that the adjusted number of net futures contracts required to fix a forward price is the present value of the number of forward contracts that would otherwise be required.

Note that one of the problems with using the tail hedge in practice is that the tail hedge is determined on the day that the futures price moves, but the margin call occurs on the following day and is funded/invested at interest rates on the day after the tail hedge is determined (r_{d-1}). This interest rate will not be known with certainty when setting the tail hedge and it is necessary to estimate it. Note also that the adjustment required is not related to the actual movement in the futures price in any way and the tail hedge applies to all futures contracts regardless of the underlying commodity/instrument.

Example 6.13

An investor who expects interest rates to rise has decided to sell $10 million face value of bank bills in 9 months' time at a fixed yield. The 90 day BAB futures contract on the Sydney Futures Exchange for delivery in 9 months is currently trading at 7.75% p.a. On the assumption that the futures yields and interest rates in table 6.7 apply during the period of the contract, determine the effective forward yield (with no tail hedge) and the number of contracts required in a tail hedge to fix the futures yield independent of the margin call requirements.

Table 6.7

Time from current date (months)	Assumed futures yield (% p.a.)	Variation margin interest rate
0	7.75	—
1	8.50	9.75
6	10.50	11.75
9	11.50 (spot)	—

Solution

To fix the yield on $10 million face value will require a short position in 90 day BAB futures contracts of:

$$\frac{10\,000\,000}{500\,000} = 20 \text{ contracts}$$

The initial price value of 1 futures contract will be:

$$\frac{500\,000}{\left(1 + \frac{90}{365} \times \frac{7.75}{100}\right)} = \$490\,624.37$$

Without a tail hedge the following margin calls and interest earnings/costs will occur.

After 1 month, the price value of 1 contract is:

$$\frac{500\,000}{\left(1 + \frac{90}{365} \times \frac{8.50}{100}\right)} = \$489\,735.68$$

The margin call on the short position is:

$$-(489\,735.68 - 490\,624.37) = +888.69$$

and interest on this margin call is:

$$+888.69 \times \frac{8}{12} \times \frac{9.75}{100} = +57.77$$

After 6 months, the price value of 1 contract becomes:

$$\frac{500\,000}{\left(1 + \frac{90}{365} \times \frac{10.50}{100}\right)} = \$487\,381.49$$

The margin call on the short position is:

$$-(487\,381.49 - 489\,735.68) = +2354.19$$

and interest on this variation margin is:

$$2354.19 \times \frac{3}{12} \times \frac{11.75}{100} = +69.15$$

On settlement after 9 months, the price value of 1 contract is:

$$\frac{500\ 000}{\left(1 + \dfrac{90}{365} \times \dfrac{11.50}{100}\right)} = \$486\ 212.87$$

The margin call on the short position is:

$$-(486\ 212.87 - 487\ 381.49) = +1168.62$$

The net value of 20 contracts incorporating the interest earnings on the margin calls is:

$$20 \times [490\ 624.37 - 486\ 212.87 + 57.77 + 69.15] = \$90\ 768.40$$

on the settlement date and the effective forward price per contract under these assumptions for the sold position will be:

$$490\ 624.37 + [57.77 + 69.15]$$

$$= 490\ 751.29$$

or an effective futures yield of:

$$100 \times \frac{365}{90} \times \frac{(500\ 000 - 490\ 751.29)}{490\ 751.29} = 7.643\% \text{ p.a.}$$

For the 20 contracts the effective sale proceeds will be $20 \times 490\ 751.29 = \$9\ 815\ 025.80$ (which is variable depending on margin calls) as against the proceeds based on the futures price $20 \times 490\ 624.37 = \$9\ 812\ 487.40$ ignoring margin calls.

In this example the movements in the futures yield have been beneficial. In practice they could just as easily be adverse. It is the adverse case that the tail hedge is usually designed to cover. However, the tail hedge eliminates profits *and* losses from the margin call interest effects. It aims to eliminate the risk that the effective forward price under a futures contract will be influenced by margin calls and attempts to fix the effective forward price.

The tail hedge in this example can be calculated by noting that prior to the delivery date of the futures contract, there is assumed to be a change in the futures price on only 2 days (at the end of the first month and at the end of the sixth month). Because there are no futures price changes on any other days, the tail hedge will have no financial effect but can still be determined using equation 6.12. On the days that margin calls are made—that is, when the futures price changes—the tail hedge will have a financial effect and must be correctly determined according to equation 6.12 on the day prior to any futures price change. Note also that the 20 contracts are sold contracts so that $M = -20$.

On the day prior to the end of the first month the tail hedge will be (from equation 6.12):

$$\frac{(20) \times \dfrac{d-1}{365} \times \dfrac{9.75}{100}}{1 + \dfrac{d-1}{365} \times \dfrac{9.75}{100}}$$

Because the exact number of days from the date these contracts are effected to the delivery date (d) is not given in this example, this time period will be calculated using months instead of days. In this case $(d-1)/365$ will be equal to 8/12 of a year since there will be 8 months from the date of the margin call to the delivery date. Hence the tail hedge at the end of the first month will be:

$$\frac{20 \times \frac{8}{12} \times \frac{9.75}{100}}{\left(1 + \frac{8}{12} \times \frac{9.75}{100}\right)} = 1.22 \text{ contracts}$$

Since the original M contracts were sold these offsetting contracts in the tail hedge are bought. Similarly, on the day prior to the end of the sixth month the tail hedge will be:

$$\frac{(20) \times \frac{3}{12} \times \frac{11.75}{100}}{\left(1 + \frac{3}{12} \times \frac{11.75}{100}\right)} = 0.57 \text{ contracts (bought)}$$

This equation uses the months to the delivery date $(9-6=3)$ to determine the time period in years for equation 6.12.

The tail hedge position calculated using equation 6.12 does not affect the calculations on any other days in this example and can be ignored for the other days.

The following margin calls occur on the net position (see table 6.8). The figures in brackets are based on a rounded number of futures contracts, whereas the non-bracketed figures are the theoretical figures assuming fractional contracts can be effected.

Table 6.8

Time (months)	Net contracts	Variation margin	Interest on variation margin
0–1	18.78 (19)	16 689.60 (16 885.11)	1084.92 (1097.63)
1–6	19.43 (19)	45 741.91 (44 729.61)	1343.59 (1313.85)
6–9	20.00 (20)	23 372.40 (23 372.40)	— —
Total		85 803.91 (84 987.12)	2428.51 (2411.48)

The effective sale proceeds on the settlement date allowing for the tail hedge will be:

$20 \times 486\ 212.87 + 85\ 803.91\ (84\ 987.12) + 2428.51\ (2411.48)$

$= 9\ 812\ 489.82\ (9\ 811\ 656.00)$

The figures in brackets allow for the fact that a whole number of contracts must be used. These figures differ from the expected sale proceeds using the futures yield of $20 \times 490\ 624.37 = 9\ 812\ 487.40$ by 2.42 (831.40). The effective forward sale yield using the tail hedge becomes:

$$100 \times \frac{365}{90} \times \frac{10\,000\,000 - 9\,812\,489.82\,(9\,811\,656.00)}{9\,812\,489.82\,(9\,811\,656.00)}$$

$$= 7.75\% \text{ p.a. } (7.785\% \text{ p.a.})$$

which demonstrates that the tail hedge has achieved the 7.75% p.a. yield of the futures contract.

The tail hedge is a risk reduction technique designed to cover variation margins on futures contracts. It in effect reduces a futures contract to an equivalent forward contract. As such it is a valuable technique. Not all risk is removed since the interest rates required to determine the tail hedge on any day must be estimated and the number of contracts will have to be rounded, resulting in a futures price which will differ slightly from that given in the futures contract.

Duration and convexity for futures contracts

The main Australian interest rate futures contracts are the $500 000 face value 90 day Bank Accepted Bill contract, the $100 000 face value 3 year 12% coupon Treasury bond contract and the $100 000 face value 10 year 12% coupon Treasury bond contract. All these contracts are quoted as an index equal to $(100 - \text{yield})$ where the yield is used to calculate the price of the security underlying the futures contract. Futures contracts have a significant effect on the interest rate sensitivity of interest-bearing security portfolios, even though they require no initial investment other than the initial deposit. Duration and convexity measures of interest rate risk for futures contracts are calculated in the same way as for physical securities as at the delivery date of the contract.

For the 90 day BAB contract the duration is simply the term to maturity or $90/365 = 0.2466$ years. Any zero coupon security, such as a 90 day BAB, has a duration equal to its term to maturity. The modified duration of the 90 day BAB contract is:

$$\frac{-P'(i)}{P} = \frac{\dfrac{90}{365}}{\left(1 + i \times \dfrac{90}{365}\right)}$$

where i is a per dollar yield, and the convexity of the BAB contract is:

$$\frac{P''(i)}{P} = \frac{2 \times \left(\dfrac{90}{365}\right)^2}{\left(1 + i \times \dfrac{90}{365}\right)^2}$$

and i is a per dollar yield so that convexity is per dollar.

Table 6.9   Duration and convexity (yrs) 90 day BAB contract

Price	Yield (%)	Duration	Modified duration	Convexity (%)	Convexity (per $)
92.50	7.50	0.2466	0.2421	0.00117	0.117
90.00	10.00	0.2466	0.2406	0.00116	0.116
87.50	12.50	0.2466	0.2392	0.00114	0.114
85.00	15.00	0.2466	0.2378	0.00113	0.113
82.50	17.50	0.2466	0.2364	0.00112	0.112
80.00	20.00	0.2466	0.2350	0.00110	0.110

Table 6.9 gives the duration, modified duration and convexity of the 90 day BAB contract for a range of futures yields.

The duration and convexity is calculated for the bond contracts in the same way as for physical bonds. Table 6.10 illustrates the calculations for the 3 year 12% coupon Treasury bond contract with a futures price of 90.00 (a yield of 10% p.a.). Note that all the figures in table 6.10 were calculated using a computer program which calculated all figures accurately with no rounding of intermediate calculations. For this reason products and totals derived using only the numbers shown in column (3) will differ slightly from those shown in the rest of the table owing to rounding.

Using the figures in table 6.10 gives:

$$\text{Duration} = \frac{274.995676}{105.075692} = 2.6171 \text{ years}$$

$$\text{Modified duration} = 0.952381 \times 2.6171 = 2.4925$$

$$\text{Convexity} = 0.907029 \times \frac{917.046973}{105.075692} = 7.916$$

These calculations have been performed for a range of yields for the 3 year bond contract to give table 6.11. Table 6.12 gives the duration, modified duration and convexity for the 10 year 12% coupon Treasury bond futures contract.

Table 6.10   Duration and convexity calculations—3 year Treasury bond contract

Time (yrs) (1)	Cash flow (2)	v^t (3)	(2) × (3) = (4)	(1) × (2) × (3) = (5)	(1) × [(1) + 0.5] × (2) × (3) = (6)
0.5	6	0.952381	5.714286	2.857143	2.857143
1.0	6	0.907029	5.442177	5.442177	8.163265
1.5	6	0.863838	5.183026	7.774538	15.549077
2.0	6	0.822702	4.936215	9.872430	24.681074
2.5	6	0.783526	4.701157	11.752892	35.258677
3.0	106	0.746215	79.098832	237.296496	830.537736
Total			105.075692	274.995676	917.046973

Table 6.11   Duration and convexity—3 year Treasury bond futures contract

Price	Yield (%)	Duration	Modified duration	Convexity (%)	Convexity (per $)
95.00	5.00	2.6437	2.5792	0.08418	8.418
92.50	7.50	2.6305	2.5355	0.08163	8.163
90.00	10.00	2.6171	2.4925	0.07916	7.916
87.50	12.50	2.6034	2.4503	0.07678	7.678
85.00	15.00	2.5894	2.4088	0.07448	7.448

Table 6.12   Duration and convexity—10 year Treasury bond futures contract

Price	Yield (%)	Duration	Modified duration	Convexity (%)	Convexity (per $)
95.00	5.00	6.8781	6.7103	0.5908	59.08
92.50	7.50	6.5976	6.3592	0.5446	54.46
90.00	10.00	6.1309	6.0104	0.4999	49.99
87.50	12.50	6.0209	5.6668	0.4572	45.72
85.00	15.00	5.7308	5.3310	0.4166	41.66

The duration of a portfolio of physical securities and futures contracts can be estimated using the formula:

■ *Equation 6.14*

$$D_p = D_s + D_f \times \frac{V_f}{V_s}$$

where:

- D_p is the portfolio duration,
- D_s is the duration of the physical securities at the current date,
- D_f is the duration of a futures contract on the delivery date,
- V_f is the value of the securities underlying the futures contracts, which is negative if the futures contracts are sold and positive if bought, and
- V_s is the current market value of the physical securities.

This formula is like a weighted average of the durations of the physical and futures contracts with an allowance for the fact that the net investment in a futures contract is zero if the initial margin is ignored. A similar formula can be used for convexity.

Example 6.14

An investor holds a portfolio of physical securities with a current market value of $5 179 000, a duration of 7.96 years and a convexity (%) of

0.5865. The investor has sold 10 three year Treasury bond futures contracts at a futures yield of 8.5%. Determine the duration and convexity of the portfolio including the futures contracts.

Solution

For this portfolio:

- $D_s = 7.96$,
- $V_s = 5\ 179\ 000$,
- $D_f = 2.6305$ (from table 6.11),
- $V_f = -10 \times 100\ 000 \times 109.0995/100 = -1\ 090\ 995.45$.

Note that the price of a 3 year 12% Treasury bond at 8.5% is:

$$6a\overline{_6|} + 100v^6 = 109.0995$$

Hence the duration of the portfolio, using equation 6.14, is:

$$7.96 + 2.63054 \times \frac{-1\ 090\ 995}{5\ 179\ 000} = 7.41 \text{ years}$$

Similarly, portfolio convexity is:

$$0.5865 + 0.08163 \times \frac{-1\ 090\ 995}{5\ 179\ 000} = 0.5693$$

Forward rate agreements

Forward rate agreements, or FRAs, are over-the-counter interest rate forward contracts where 2 counterparties agree to compensate each other for the difference between a specified interest rate and a market interest rate at a future date for a future period (commencing on the future date) on an agreed notional principal amount. FRAs are standardised contracts which are settled in cash. The market rate used for Australian dollar FRAs is the Bank Bill rate for the term of the agreement determined on the settlement date. The counterparty wishing to protect against rises in interest rates is referred to as the borrower and the counterparty wishing to protect against falls in interest rates is referred to as the lender. If the specified interest rate exceeds the market rate then the borrower pays the lender and vice versa.

Australian FRAs are based on the value of discount securities and are settled at the beginning of the forward period. FRAs can also be based on interest payments on a loan amount and be paid at the end of the forward period. Consider an FRA on a principal sum of F dollars for an m day period commencing in n days' time. For an Australian FRA the net settlement payment in n days' time will be the difference between the present value of the notional principal amount at the specified interest rate and the present value at the market rate. If the specified, or fixed, interest rate is denoted by $r_{f,m}$ and the market, or spot, rate is denoted by $r_{s,m}$ then the net settlement payment in n days' time, at the beginning of the forward period, will equal:

$$\frac{F}{\left(1+\dfrac{m}{365}\times\dfrac{r_{f,m}}{100}\right)}-\frac{F}{\left(1+\dfrac{m}{365}\times\dfrac{r_{s,m}}{100}\right)}$$

FRAs can be used to fix the interest payment on a variable rate loan in the Australian market. In this case an adjustment must be made to the notional principal and the fact that the settlement is at the beginning of the forward period must be taken into account. In some overseas markets FRAs are settled at the end of the period and the settlement amount is based on notional principal times the difference between the specified interest rate and the market interest rate.

Example 6.15

A borrower wishes to fix the interest cost on a $10 million variable rate borrowing for the 90 day period commencing in 25 days' time. Interest on the borrowing is paid in arrears. The borrower intends to use a standard FRA. The agreed rate for the FRA is 8.25% p.a. Calculate the notional principal sum for the FRA that will fix the interest cost at 8.25% p.a. on the $10 million borrowing.

Solution

If the 90 day variable rate in 25 days' time is r% p.a., then the borrower requires a net payment of:

$$10\ 000\ 000 \times \frac{90}{365} \times \left(\frac{8.25}{100}-\frac{r}{100}\right)$$

in 115 days' time to fix the borrowing cost at 8.25% p.a. If the FRA is for a notional principal of F then the net payment under the FRA in 25 days' time will be:

$$\frac{F}{\left(1+\dfrac{90}{365}\times\dfrac{r}{100}\right)}-\frac{F}{\left(1+\dfrac{90}{365}\times\dfrac{8.25}{100}\right)}$$

This amount must be accumulated at the market rate of r in 25 days' time for a period of 90 days to produce an in-arrears equivalent interest payment of:

$$\left[\frac{F}{\left(1+\dfrac{90}{365}\times\dfrac{r}{100}\right)}-\frac{F}{\left(1+\dfrac{90}{365}\times\dfrac{8.25}{100}\right)}\right]\times\left(1+\dfrac{90}{365}\times\dfrac{r}{100}\right)$$

This expression simplifies to:

$$\left[\frac{F}{\left(1+\dfrac{90}{365}\times\dfrac{8.25}{100}\right)}\right]\times\frac{90}{365}\times\left(\frac{8.25}{100}-\frac{r}{100}\right)$$

By comparing this with the amount required to fix the in-arrears interest on the borrowing, the notional principal in the FRA, F, can be determined:

$$\left[\frac{F}{\left(1 + \frac{90}{365} \times \frac{8.25}{100}\right)}\right] \times \frac{90}{365} \times \left(\frac{8.25}{100} - \frac{r}{100}\right)$$

$$= 10\,000\,000 \times \frac{90}{365} \times \left(\frac{8.25}{100} - \frac{r}{100}\right)$$

so that, solving for F:

$$F = 10\,000\,000 \times \left(1 + \frac{90}{365} \times \frac{8.25}{100}\right)$$

$$= \$10\,203\,424.66$$

This value of F is the future value of the borrowing at the agreed FRA interest rate.

7 Swaps

Swaps are used extensively in money and capital markets. These transactions have in common the exchange between 2 counterparties of cash flows of one sort or another. The main types of transactions are bill swaps, interest rate swaps, the foreign currency swap (or deposit swap) and foreign exchange or cross currency swaps. Bond switches are also referred to as bond swaps. Futures and forward contracts are similar to swaps in that they effectively involve an exchange of a variable amount for a fixed amount on a future date.

Bill swaps

The bank bill swap transaction is used to create a synthetic security which has a term to maturity not normally available in the physical short-term market. The synthetic security is created by the purchase of a physical security and the simultaneous purchase of a 'strip' of futures contracts. This synthetic security is then sold. The bill swap is the 'securitised' form of a 'reverse cash and carry' transaction in futures markets. It is called a swap because the transaction involves the swap of the synthetic security for a physical bank bill.

The rollover yield on a bank bill can be fixed using BAB interest rate futures contracts. The rollover yield is the purchase yield for a physical security on maturity of the security. A synthetic security with a longer maturity than is available in the physical bank bill market can be created by purchasing a strip of BAB futures contracts. A bill swap requires a number of bank bill transactions at future dates, since a physical bank bill is used to back the synthetic security.

In a bill swap a bank bill is sold at a price determined as the present value of the face value of the swap. For the purchaser of a bill swap the transaction is in effect the same as purchasing a long-term discount security. The proceeds of the bill swap are used by the seller of the swap to purchase a physical bank bill for the same face value as the swap. At each rollover of the physical bank bill a new bill is 'swapped' for the maturing bill. No payment is made between the buyer and seller of the bill swap on these rollover dates. On maturity of the bill swap the face value is paid to the buyer of the swap. This maturity payment will equal the face value on maturity of the final physical bank bill. The rollover dates for the physical bank bills coincide with the BAB futures contract settlement dates.

The seller of the swap locks-in interest rates on the rollover of the physical bank bills by purchasing BAB futures contracts. The seller also has to finance part of the purchase cost of the physical bank bill on settlement of the bill swap and will receive cash flows at each rollover date, representing the difference between the maturity value of the bank bill and the purchase cost of the replacement bank bill. The purchase cost on rollover is fixed using the BAB futures contracts.

Pricing a bill swap involves determining the yield to use to calculate the present value of the face amount of the swap. This is determined by compounding together the strip of BAB futures yields to the maturity date of the swap.

Example 7.1

A merchant bank can purchase a 70 day bank bill at 8.00% p.a. and can purchase 90 day BAB futures for delivery in 70 days at 8.50%, for delivery in 160 days at 8.75%, for delivery in 250 days at 8.75% and for delivery in 340 days at 9.00%. Calculate the simple p.a. yield that can be obtained over a 430 day period using the physical bank bill and a strip of futures contracts. Convert this yield to a semi-annual compound yield equivalent.

Solution

The accumulated value of $1 over the 430 days will be:

$$\left(1 + 0.08 \times \frac{70}{365}\right) \times \left(1 + 0.085 \times \frac{90}{365}\right) \times \left(1 + 0.0875 \times \frac{90}{365}\right)$$

$$\times \left(1 + 0.0875 \times \frac{90}{365}\right) \times \left(1 + 0.09 \times \frac{90}{365}\right)$$

$$= (1.0153425)\,(1.0209589)\,(1.0215753)\,(1.0215753)\,(1.0221918)$$

$$= 1.1058443$$

Thus the simple p.a. yield is given by:

$$100 \times \frac{365}{430} \times \frac{0.1058443}{1.0000000} = 8.985\%\,\text{p.a.}$$

This can be converted to a semi-annual compound equivalent. Let the per half year yield per dollar be i so that the annualised per cent yield is $200i\%$. Then:

$$(1 + i)^2 = (1.1058443)^{365/430}$$

$$(1 + i)^2 = 1.0891535$$

or:

$$i = 0.043625$$

Now multiply i by 200 to get the semi-annual compound equivalent of 8.725% p.a.

The bill swap is sold at a price to reflect this yield over the term of the swap. In practice, adjustments will need to be made to this yield to allow for costs and a profit margin on the deal.

Example 7.2

The merchant bank in example 7.1 agrees with a customer to undertake a bill swap with a face value of $500 000 and a maturity of 430 days at a semi-annual compound yield of 8.725% p.a. Calculate the settlement proceeds for the swap.

Solution

The settlement proceeds will be the present value of the $500 000 at a discount rate of 8.725% p.a. semi-annual over 430 days. This is:

$$500\,000 \times v^{(430/365 \times 2)} \text{ at } 8.725/2\%$$

$$= 500\,000 \times v^{2.35616}$$

$$= 500\,000 \times 0.904287$$

$$= \$452\,143.38$$

The settlement proceeds could also have been determined using the simple interest yield in example 7.1 since this is equivalent to the semi-annual compound yield used above. However, a difference in answers will arise from the rounding of the semi-annual equivalent yield. The settlement proceeds would be:

$$\frac{500\,000}{1.1058443} = 452\,143.22$$

The bill swap generates cash flows on the maturity date of the physical bank bills, since replacement bills are purchased at the futures yields and the full face value of the maturing bank bill is available to meet this cost. There is also an initial cash flow when the first physical bank bill is purchased, since the sale proceeds for the swap will be the present value for the maturity term of the swap which is longer than the term of the physical bank bill. This will be insufficient to meet the full cost of the first physical bank bill. Thus the seller of bill swaps will invest funds in

the transaction on the sale of the swap and will receive funds on the
rollover dates of the bank bills.

Example 7.3

A merchant bank can purchase 120 day physical bills at 8.9% p.a. and
can purchase 90 day BAB futures contracts for delivery at the following
dates and yields:

- in 120 days at 9.1% p.a.,
- in 210 days at 9.4% p.a., and
- in 300 days at 10.2% p.a.

(a) Calculate a simple p.a. yield that can be fixed over the 390 day
period using a strip of futures contracts. Convert this simple yield
rate to a p.a. equivalent semi-annual compounding yield.

(b) The merchant bank agrees to pay $500 000 to a client in 390 days'
time in return for a payment today and uses a physical bank bill
plus a strip of futures transactions to fix a yield for the period.
Calculate the payment the merchant bank would require at settlement from the client.

(c) The transaction in (b) is carried out by the merchant bank purchasing physical bank bills initially for 120 days and fixing
subsequent 90 day rollover yields using a strip of BAB futures
contracts, each with face values of $500 000. Calculate the net
cash flow that the bank experiences at settlement and at each
rollover of the bank bills.

(d) Determine the yield that the merchant bank earns on the net cash flows.

Solution

(a) The simple p.a. yield over the 390 day period is given by firstly
compounding the futures yields to get:

$$\left(1 + 0.089 \times \frac{120}{365}\right) \times \left(1 + 0.091 \times \frac{90}{365}\right)$$

$$\times \left(1 + 0.094 \times \frac{90}{365}\right) \times \left(1 + 0.102 \times \frac{90}{365}\right)$$

$$= (1.0292603)\,(1.0224384)\,(1.0231781)\,(1.0251507)$$

$$= 1.1038277 \text{ (accumulated over 390 days)}$$

The simple p.a. yield is:

$$100 \times 365/390 \times 0.1038277 = 9.7172\% \text{ p.a.}$$

The equivalent semi-annual compounding yield, $200i\%$, is given
by:

$$(1 + i)^2 = (1.1038277)^{(365/390)}$$

$$i = (1.096860)^{\frac{1}{2}} - 1$$

$$= 0.04731$$

so that it equals 9.4622% p.a.

(b) The settlement payment is the present value of $500 000 over the 390 day period. Using the simple yield and simple interest formula gives:

$$\frac{500\ 000}{\left[1 + 0.097172 \times \dfrac{390}{365}\right]} = \$452\ 969.28$$

Using the semi-annual compounding yield and a compound interest formula gives:

$$\frac{500\ 000}{(1.04731)^{(390/365 \times 2)}} = \$452\ 970.03$$

Note that the answers differ due to the rounding of the semi-annual yield.

(c) The cash flows on the bill swap for the seller will be as given in table 7.1.

Table 7.1

Time	Maturity value	Purchase cost	Bill swap cash flow	Net cash flow
Settlement	—	−485 785.78	+452 969.28	−32 816.50
120 days	+500 000	−489 027.04	—	10 972.96
210 days	+500 000	−488 673.49	—	11 326.51
300 days	+500 000	−487 733.18	—	12 266.82
390 days	+500 000	—	−500 000.00	—

Note that the purchase cost figures for the physical bank bills are:

$$\frac{500\ 000}{(1 + 0.089 \times 120/365)} = 485\ 785.78$$

$$\frac{500\ 000}{(1 + 0.091 \times 90/365)} = 489\ 027.04$$

$$\frac{500\ 000}{(1 + 0.094 \times 90/365)} = 488\ 673.49$$

$$\frac{500\ 000}{(1 + 0.102 \times 90/365)} = 487\ 733.18$$

(d) To determine the yield on the net cash flows the internal rate of return (*IRR*) is calculated for the net cash flows using the equation:

$$32\ 816.50 = 10\ 972.96v^{(2 \times 120/365)} + 11\ 326.51v^{(2 \times 210/365)}$$
$$+ 12\ 266.82v^{(2 \times 300/365)}$$

where the yield *i* is on a semi-annual basis. Trial and error has to be used to determine *i* since financial calculators do not calculate the internal rate of return for cash flows at uneven intervals. Spreadsheets include goalseek and solver functions that can determine the yield on these cash flows. This was determined to be 9.116% p.a. (semi-annual) using a spreadsheet.

This can be checked by calculating the value of the net cash flows at 9.116/2% = 4.558% to get:

$$10\ 972.96 \times 0.971118 + 11\ 326.51 \times 0.950005$$
$$+\ 12\ 266.82 \times 0.929351 = 32\ 816.46$$

which agrees with the initial cash flow.

The cash flows can be discounted at the simple interest rates that apply in each period as follows:

$$10\ 972.96 \times \left(1 + \frac{8.9}{100} \times \frac{120}{365}\right)^{-1} +$$

$$11\ 326.51 \times \left(1 + \frac{8.9}{100} \times \frac{120}{365}\right)^{-1} \times \left(1 + \frac{9.1}{100} \times \frac{90}{365}\right)^{-1} +$$

$$12\ 266.82 \times \left(1 + \frac{8.9}{100} \times \frac{120}{365}\right)^{-1} \times \left(1 + \frac{9.1}{100} \times \frac{90}{365}\right)^{-1} \times$$

$$\left(1 + \frac{9.4}{100} \times \frac{90}{365}\right)^{-1}$$

$$= 32\ 816.51$$

From this it can be seen that the yield on the cash flows is actually fixed by the BAB futures yields for each rollover date. The semi-annual compounding yield is equivalent to a weighted average of these yields.

Foreign exchange swaps

Foreign currency swaps are an often used over-the-counter contract. In the foreign exchange market a swap involves the simultaneous purchase and sale of a foreign currency with delivery under the purchase and sale on 2 different dates. If 1 of the transactions is a spot purchase or sale and the transaction will be reversed at a future date, then the swap is referred to as a spot against forward swap. Where both purchase and sale occur at future dates the swap is referred to as a forward/forward swap. Foreign exchange swaps are sometimes referred to as deposit swaps to avoid confusion with cross currency foreign exchange swaps (which will be covered shortly).

Swap rates are quoted in terms of the forward margin or forward points. The difference between the purchase and sale exchange rates, and not the actual exchange rates, determines the cost/benefit of a deposit swap. A deposit swap, in effect, is identical to borrowing 1 currency, exchanging it for another currency at an agreed exchange rate, investing this currency to the date the transaction will be reversed and then exchanging the invested amount of currency into the original currency at a fixed forward rate to repay the original borrowing. Swaps are the foreign exchange market equivalent of the repurchase agreements in the bond market, where a bond is sold and an agreement for its repurchase at a fixed price at a future date undertaken at the time of sale.

Example 7.4

Table 7.2 lists the rates that are available in the money and foreign exchange markets.

Table 7.2   Market rates for example 7.4

Maturity (months)	US$ interest rates (% p.a.)	A$ interest rates (% p.a.)	Spot rate A$/US$ (0.75)
3 (90 days)	6.50	8.50	
6 (180 days)	7.00	9.00	

Use this information to determine the theoretical swap rate if a company wishes to:

(a) enter a spot against forward swap in which the A$ would be bought against the US$ today and sold against the US$ in 90 days, and

(b) enter a forward/forward swap in which the US$ would be bought against the A$ in 90 days' time and sold against the A$ in 180 days.

Solution

(a) In this case the company would buy 1/0.75 = 1.33333 A$ per US$ spot. In 90 days' time the US$ will accumulate to:

$$\left(1 + \frac{6.50}{100} \times \frac{90}{360}\right) = 1.016250$$

and the 1.33333 A$ will accumulate to:

$$1.33333 \times \left(1 + \frac{8.50}{100} \times \frac{90}{365}\right) = 1.361279$$

The theoretical exchange rate for the sale of the A$ in 90 days will be 1.016250/1.361279A$/US$ or 0.7465. The spot against 3 month swap rate should therefore be 0.7465 − 0.75 = −0.0035 or 35 points premium.

(b) Assume that the 90 day forward exchange rate for A$/US$ is 0.7465. Under this swap the company buys 0.7465 US$ per A$ in 90 days' time. In order to fix the forward/forward swap rate now it is necessary to invest/borrow funds at fixed forward interest rates. The theoretical 90 day forward interest rates for a 90 day term can be derived for US$ and A$ as follows:

US$:

$$100 \times \frac{360}{90} \times \left[\frac{\left(1 + \frac{7.00}{100} \times \frac{180}{360} \right)}{\left(1 + \frac{6.50}{100} \times \frac{90}{360} \right)} - 1 \right] = 7.3801\%$$

A$:

$$100 \times \frac{365}{90} \times \left[\frac{\left(1 + \frac{9.00}{100} \times \frac{180}{365} \right)}{\left(1 + \frac{8.50}{100} \times \frac{90}{365} \right)} - 1 \right] = 9.3050\%$$

In 180 days' time the 0.7465 US$ received in 90 days will accumulate to:

$$0.7465 \times \left(1 + \frac{7.3801}{100} \times \frac{90}{360} \right) = 0.7603$$

and the A$ will accumulate to:

$$1 \times \left(1 + \frac{9.3050}{100} \times \frac{90}{365} \right) = 1.0229$$

The theoretical exchange rate for the sale of the US$ in 90 days will be 0.7603/1.0229A$/US$ or 0.7432. The 3 month against 6 month swap rate should therefore be 0.7432 – 0.7465 = 33 points premium.

Note that the spot against 6 month swap rate can be determined by adding the 2 swap rates in (a) and (b) to get 66 points premium. This can be checked as follows. The company would buy 1/0.75 = 1.3333A$ per US$ spot. In 180 days' time the US$ will accumulate to:

$$\left(1 + \frac{7.00}{100} \times \frac{180}{360} \right) = 1.035$$

and the 1.3333 A$ will accumulate to:

$$1.3333 \times \left(1 + \frac{9.00}{100} \times \frac{180}{365} \right) = 1.3925$$

The theoretical exchange rate for the sale of the A$ in 180 days will be 1.035/1.3925A$/US$ or 0.7433. The spot against 6 month swap rate should therefore be 0.7433 – 0.75 = –0.072 or 67 points premium, which allowing for rounding is the same as the sum of the 2 premiums.

In practice the calculation of swap rates has to allow for the bid/offer spread. To do this any purchase of a currency should use the offer rate and any sale should use the bid rate. Bid/offer rates should similarly be used for any borrowing or investment transactions.

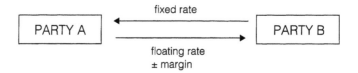

Figure 7.1   Interest rate swap

Interest rate swaps

An interest rate swap involves 2 counterparties who exchange interest payments based on a notional principal amount. Because all payments are in the same currency the principal amount does not change hands. Interest rate swaps can either be from fixed rate to floating rate, referred to as a coupon swap, or from 1 floating rate to another floating rate, referred to as a basis swap.

In the fixed to floating swap 1 of the counterparties pays a fixed rate to the other and is referred to as the fixed rate payer. This fixed rate is specified in the swap agreement. The other party, in return for receiving the fixed rate payment, pays a floating rate to the fixed rate payer. This floating rate will be based on a market rate such as LIBOR or Bank Bill rate plus or minus a margin. Interest payments for the fixed rate will generally be annual or semi-annual. The frequency of floating rate payments will be determined by the floating rate used so that if a 180 day Bank Bill rate was used it would be every 180 days. The days in the year convention used to determine the payment amounts will also be determined by the index. Swaps based on 6 month LIBOR will determine a floating rate payment based on actual days over 360. Figure 7.1 sets out a simple interest rate swap structure. In this swap Party A is the floating rate payer and Party B is the fixed rate payer.

Swaps will involve fees and expenses related to the arrangement of the swap and often an intermediary to assume the credit risk in the transaction. Often a bank will act as intermediary between the counterparties to the swap. The effect of these fees depends on which party pays them. They are usually incurred up-front.

Valuation or pricing of swaps will be needed for a number of purposes, including assessing the relative cost of funds under a swap at commencement of the contract, which may include an allowance for fees and expenses, and for use in calculating termination values if the swap has to be terminated prior to the maturity date. The convention for assessing swaps is to determine the fixed rate applying under the swap if the floating rate payer were to pay only the floating rate flat (with no plus or minus adjustment). This fixed rate is determined as the internal rate of return of the net cash flows in the swap adjusted for the floating rate margin. This fixed rate is often expressed as a margin over a Treasury bond yield of the same maturity as the swap.

Swaps will have a range of different features that make it difficult to generalise any particular formula. These features include different day in the year conventions, different frequencies of interest payment for fixed and floating rates, a first interest payment based on a fractional period and not equal to subsequent payments, and a net payment at settlement because of fees and charges. These add to the complexity of the analysis. The basic techniques for analysing these transactions are the same no matter how complex the swap. These techniques use the internal rate of return and the net present value of the underlying cash flows.

Example 7.5

An interest rate swap is settled on 15 May XX based on the following rates:

- Fixed payment: 12.5% p.a. semi-annually on 15 May and 15 November of each year
- Floating payment: 6 month LIBOR less 25 points, payable 15 May and 15 November. Interest payments are calculated using number of days in period over 360.

The swap is for a notional principal amount of $10 million, with a maturity date of 15 May XX + 3. The year XX + 1 is assumed to be a leap year.

Ignoring fees and other charges, calculate the effective fixed rate of the swap against 6 month LIBOR.

Solution

The interest payments under the swap are given in table 7.3.

Table 7.3 Swap payments for example 7.5

	Fixed payment	Days	Floating rate per payment (%)
15 November XX	625 000	184	(LIBOR − 0.25) × (184/360)
15 May XX + 1	625 000	182	(LIBOR − 0.25) × (182/360)
15 November XX + 1	625 000	184	(LIBOR − 0.25) × (184/360)
15 May XX + 2	625 000	181	(LIBOR − 0.25) × (181/360)
15 November XX + 2	625 000	184	(LIBOR − 0.25) × (184/360)
15 May XX + 3	625 000	181	(LIBOR − 0.25) × (181/360)

LIBOR is a variable interest rate which is not known for all future periods—only the current rate is known.

The floating payment here is:

$$[\text{LIBOR (6 month rate)} - 0.25]\% \text{ p.a.}$$

hence each (unknown) payment is:

$$\$10\ 000\ 000 \times \frac{(\text{LIBOR} - 0.25)}{100} \times \frac{\text{days}}{360}$$

LIBOR flat is LIBOR with no minus (or plus) adjustment. Hence the fixed rate payments against LIBOR flat are those obtained by adjusting the floating rate payments to be:

$$10\ 000\ 000 \times \frac{\text{LIBOR}}{100} \times \frac{\text{days}}{360}$$

that is, we *add*:

$$10\ 000\ 000 \times \frac{0.25}{100} \times \frac{\text{days}}{360}$$

to each fixed (and floating) payment to give adjusted cash flows against LIBOR flat of:

- 15 November XX:
  $625\ 000 + 10\ 000\ 000 \times (0.0025) \times (184/360) = 637\ 777.78$
- 15 May XX + 1:
  $625\ 000 + 10\ 000\ 000 \times (0.0025) \times (182/360) = 637\ 638.89$
- 15 November XX + 1:
  $625\ 000 + 10\ 000\ 000 \times (0.0025) \times (184/360) = 637\ 777.78$
- 15 May XX + 2:
  $625\ 000 + 10\ 000\ 000 \times (0.0025) \times (181/360) = 637\ 569.44$
- 15 November XX + 2:
  $625\ 000 + 10\ 000\ 000 \times (0.0025) \times (184/360) = 637\ 777.78$
- 15 May XX + 3:
  $625\ 000 + 10\ 000\ 000 \times (0.0025) \times (181/360) = 637\ 569.44$

To calculate the fixed rate against the LIBOR flat, the notional principal amount is used as the settlement price and is added to the 15 May XX + 3 payment as a maturity payment. The *IRR* on these adjusted payments is then determined. This requires a trial and error procedure, which with 6 cash flows is time consuming to do manually and is readily calculated using a financial calculator such as the HP12C or using a spreadsheet. The fixed rate against LIBOR flat is 6.3769% per half year or 12.7538% p.a. semi-annual.

Fees and other swap arrangement costs can readily be incorporated into the calculations.

Example 7.6

For the swap in example 7.5 the fixed rate payer agrees to meet arrangement costs of 0.5% of the notional principal amount. Calculate the effective fixed rate against LIBOR flat, allowing for these costs.

Solution

To do this calculation it is necessary to adjust the initial 10 million for the up-front costs of 50 000. This gives a net settlement figure of 9 950 000. This is then used along with the same adjusted fixed rate cash flows against LIBOR flat from example 7.5 to determine an *IRR*

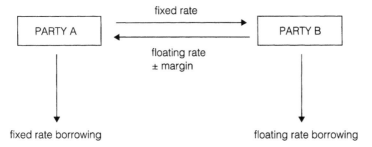

Figure 7.2   Interest rate swap with underlying borrowings

which will be the effective fixed rate allowing for costs, measured against LIBOR flat.

The cash flows are: 9 950 000, 637 777 78, 637 638.89, 637 777.78, 637 569.44, 637 777.78, 10 637 569.44. The *IRR* is determined (using the HP12C) as 6.4801% per half year or 12.9602% p.a. Thus the up-front 0.5% costs add approximately 0.2% p.a. to the fixed rate.

The analysis of swaps covered above considers the swap in isolation. Often there will be an underlying borrowing on each side of the swap and each party will be interested in their effective borrowing cost allowing for the swap. This arrangement is illustrated in figure 7.2. The fixed rate payer will usually have a floating rate borrowing and the floating rate payer will have a fixed rate borrowing. The fixed rate payer receives floating rate payments which will offset the floating rate borrowing costs and the result of the swap is a net borrowing cash flow which is at a fixed rate. The floating rate payer is in a similar position, receiving a fixed rate and using this to meet the fixed rate borrowing costs. The analysis in these cases involves determining the effective borrowing interest payments allowing for the original borrowing plus the net swap cash flows and any fees and other costs. These effective interest payments are then used to determine an effective borrowing interest rate by calculating an *IRR* on the adjusted borrowing cash flows.

Example 7.7

A borrower raises $10 million of Eurobonds with semi-annual coupons of 12% maturing in 10 years. Costs amount to 2.5% of the principal and are netted from the total borrowing. The borrower enters an interest rate swap agreement with a notional principal of $10 million under which it will receive fixed payments of 12.5% p.a. semi-annually and pay semi-annual floating payments of LIBOR plus 0.25% (25 points). The floating rate payments are based on actual days divided by 360. Calculate the effective fixed rate applying under the swap against LIBOR flat, ignoring costs. At what effective floating rate does the borrower raise funds allowing for the Eurobond costs?

Solution

In order to allow accurately for the number of days in the floating rate payment, assume a settlement date of 1 July XX. The fixed rate payments are $10\,000\,000 \times (0.125/2) = 625\,000$. These fixed rate payments are adjusted for the margin on the floating rate payments in table 7.4.

Table 7.4   Adjusted fixed swap cash flows

Period	Days	$0.25\% \times \dfrac{days}{360}$	Adjusted fixed cash flows
1/7/XX–1/1/XX + 1	184	12 777.78	612 222.22
a1/1/XX + 1–1/7/XX + 1	182	12 638.89	612 361.11
1/7/XX + 1–1/1/XX + 2	184	12 777.78	612 222.22
1/1/XX + 2–1/7/XX + 2	181	12 569.44	612 430.56
1/7/XX + 2–1/1/XX + 3	184	12 777.78	612 222.22
1/1/XX + 3–1/7/XX + 3	181	12 569.44	612 430.56
1/7/XX + 3–1/1/XX + 4	184	12 777.78	612 222.22
1/1/XX + 4–1/7/XX + 4	181	12 569.44	612 430.56
1/7/XX + 4–1/1/XX + 5	184	12 777.78	612 222.22
a1/1/XX + 5–1/7/XX + 5	182	12 638.89	612 361.11
1/7/XX + 5–1/1/XX + 6	184	12 777.78	612 222.22
1/1/XX + 6–1/7/XX + 6	181	12 569.44	612 430.56
1/7/XX + 6–1/1/XX + 7	184	12 777.78	612 222.22
1/1/XX + 7–1/7/XX + 7	181	12 569.44	612 430.56
1/7/XX + 7–1/1/XX + 8	184	12 777.78	612 222.22
1/1/XX + 8–1/7/XX + 8	181	12 569.44	612 430.56
1/7/XX + 8–1/1/XX + 9	184	12 777.78	612 222.22
a1/1/XX + 9–1/7/XX + 9	182	12 638.89	612 361.11
1/7/XX + 9–1/1/XX + 10	184	12 777.78	612 222.22
1/1/XX + 10–1/7/XX + 10	181	12 569.44	612 430.56

a Assumed to be a leap year.

The days in the period 1 July to 1 January are always 184 days and the period 1 January to 1 July always has 181 days except for the leap years XX + 1, and XX + 5 and XX + 9 which have 182 days.

The *IRR* on the last column in table 7.4 using the cash flows −10 000 000, plus the last column with +10 000 000 added to the last cash flow (+10 612 430.56), is 6.1231% or 12.2462% p.a. semi-annual. This is the fixed rate against LIBOR flat in the swap. The adjusted fixed payment is 12.5% p.a. (semi-annual) minus 0.25% on a days/360 basis, so that the margin has changed from −0.25% on a days/360 basis to −0.2538% on a semi-annual basis (12.5 − 0.2538 = 12.2462).

The effective floating rate allowing for costs can be determined by using the floating rate note formula developed in chapter 4. The settlement proceeds net of costs is 10 000 000 − 250 000 = 9 750 000. This can be used as the equivalent of the purchase price of an FRN. The effective margin over LIBOR, ignoring costs, will be:

12% p.a. (semi-annual) − 12.2462% p.a. (semi-annual) + LIBOR

= LIBOR − 0.2462% p.a.

where the margin is now expressed as a semi-annual rate.

If an average LIBOR of 10% is assumed, an effective margin using the FRN formula is calculated as follows:

$$\text{Spread or margin} = -0.2462$$

Respread the costs which are equivalent to the discount in the FRN formula using:

$$s_{\overline{20}} = \frac{(1.05)^{20} - 1}{0.05} = 33.06595$$

to get:

$$\frac{(100 - 97.5)}{33.06595} \times 2 = 0.1512$$

Interest on the costs will be:

$$(100 - 97.5) \times 0.1 = 0.25$$

so that the effective margin, combining all the above components, is:

$$\frac{(-0.2462 + 0.1512 + 0.25)}{97.5} \times 100 = 0.159\% \text{ p.a.}$$

Since LIBOR is on a 360 days basis, the above margin must be converted to the same basis. This can be done using the ratio of the swap margin on a 360 day basis to the margin on a semi-annual basis previously calculated. Hence the effective margin, allowing for costs, is $0.159 \times (0.25/0.2538) = 0.157\%$ p.a. on a days/360 basis.

An alternative approach is to assume 10% for LIBOR and to set out the actual cash flows to the borrower which will be +12% (semi-annual) –12.5% (semi-annual) + 10.25% (days/360). These cash flows are: –9 750 000, 498 888.89, 493 194.44, 498 888.89, 490 347.22, 498 888.89, 490 347.22, 498 888.89, 490 347.22, 498 888.89, 493 194.44, 498 888.89, 490 347.22, 498 888.89, 490 347.22, 498 888.89, 490 347.22, 498 888.89, 493 194.44, 498 889.89, 10 490, 347.22, which gives an *IRR* of 5.1549% or 10.3099% p.a. (semi-annual).

This value is then converted to a days/360 basis to get:

$$10.3099 \times \frac{0.25}{0.2538} = 10.156\% \text{ p.a.}$$

Hence the margin is 0.156% p.a. on a days/360 basis, allowing for costs, which is almost exactly equal to that already derived using the FRN formula.

Example 7.8

The counterparty to the swap in example 7.7 has raised floating rate funds at LIBOR plus 0.125%. What is the fixed rate cost at which this borrower raises funds, allowing for the swap?

Solution

The counterparty payments are (where a negative sign indicates a payment of interest):

Borrowing	Swap
–(LIBOR + 0.125)	–12.5% + (LIBOR+ 0.25)

which gives a net payment, combining the underlying borrowing and the swap, of –12.5% (semi-annual) +0.125% (days/360). The swap margin is not on a semi-annual basis. On a semi-annual basis the margin of 0.125 is:

$$0.125 \times \frac{0.2538}{0.25} = 0.1269$$

The fixed rate cost will therefore be –12.5% + 0.1269% = 12.3731% (semi-annual) allowing for the swap.

The alternative method is to determine the combined net cash flows of the borrowing and swap and to then calculate the *IRR* on these cash flows. The cash flows are: +10 000 000, –618 611.11, –618 680.55, –618 611.11, –618 715.28, –618 611.11, –618 715.28, –618 611.11, –618 715.28, –618 611.11, –618 680.55, –618 611.11, –618 715.28, –618 611.11, –618 715.28, –618 611.11, –618 715.28, –618 611.11, –618 680.55, –618 611.11, –10 618 715.28. The *IRR* is 6.1866% or 12.3731% p.a. (semi-annual) which confirms the previous answer.

Interest rate swaps can also be evaluated using net present values rather than *IRR*s. The difficulty in using this methodology is that the cash flows are for variable amounts and so it is necessary to assume some average floating rate over the life of the swap to determine the cash flows to use in the present value calculations. It is also necessary to determine the appropriate interest rate to use to present value the derived cash flows.

Interest rate swaps are a useful instrument for the purpose of valuing floating rate securities. A combination of a floating rate security along with an interest rate swap, in which the floating rate is paid away and the fixed rate is received, provides the same cash flows as a fixed rate security. Fixed rate securities are readily valued in financial markets using the conventions covered in chapter 3. This allows floating rate securities to be valued by equating them to a fixed rate security plus an interest rate swap.

Example 7.9

Ten year 10.0% Treasury bonds can be purchased at a market yield of 9.0% p.a. yield to maturity (semi-annual). An interest rate swap with semi-annual payments pays floating payments of the 6 month Bank Accepted Bill rate plus 0.75% in return for fixed payments of 9.0% p.a. semi-annual with interest payments on the coupon dates of the 10.0% Treasury bond. A $500 000 10 year floating rate security pays 6 month

BAB rate plus 1.2% p.a. (semi-annual). Use this information to determine the price of the floating rate security, ignoring credit risk factors.

Solution

If $500 000 face value of the 10.0% 10 year Treasury bonds are purchased, the cost will be:

$$25\,000a_{\overline{20}|} + 500\,000v^{20} \text{ at } 4.5\%$$

$$= 25\,000 \times 13.007936 + 500\,000 \times 0.414643$$

$$= \$532\,519.84$$

The fixed rate receipts on the bond can be swapped into floating rate payments by doing a swap with a $500 000 face value. Under the swap the semi-annual cash flows will be:

- Fixed rate payment:

$$\frac{9}{200} \times 500\,000 = 22\,500$$

- Floating rate receipt:

$$\frac{(6\,\text{month BAB} + 0.75)}{200} \times 500\,000$$

$$= \frac{(6\,\text{month BAB})}{200} \times 500\,000 + 1875$$

If $2500 (fixed rate payment of $22 500 minus coupon cash flow on the bond of $25 000) is added to both fixed and floating rate payments, then the resulting swap cash flows will be:

- Fixed rate payment:

$$25\,000 \text{ or } 10\% \text{ semi–annual}$$

- Floating rate receipt:

$$\frac{(6\,\text{month BAB})}{200} \times 500\,000 + 4375$$

$$= \frac{(6\,\text{month BAB} + 1.75)}{200} \times 500\,000$$

Hence the 10.0% coupons on the bond can be swapped into floating payments of 6 month BAB plus 1.75%. The floating rate security pays 6 month BAB plus 1.2% on $500 000 so that it has to be worth (1.75 – 1.2)% on $500 000 (semi-annual) less than the bond plus the swap.

The value of the floating rate security must be the value of the bond less the value of the additional margin, or:

$$532\,519.84 - \frac{(1.75 - 1.2)}{200} \times 500\,000a_{\overline{20}|} \text{ at } 4.5\%$$

$$= 532\,519.84 - 1375 \times 13.007936$$

$$= \$514\,633.93$$

Another way of pricing the floating rate security is to note that, under the swap, a floating payment of 6 month BAB flat is effectively equivalent to a fixed rate of 9% − 0.75% = 8.25%, so that the floating rate security in effect pays 8.25 + 1.2 = 9.45% as a fixed coupon. Its price is therefore:

$$\left(\frac{9.45}{200} \times 500\ 000\right) a_{\overline{20}|} + 500\ 000 v^{20} \text{ at } 4.5\%$$

$$= 2325 \times 13.007936 + 500\ 000 \times 0.414643$$

$$= \$514\ 633.93$$

which is identical to the value derived above.

This example shows how the fixed rate security market and the floating rate security market are linked through the interest rate swap market.

On settlement

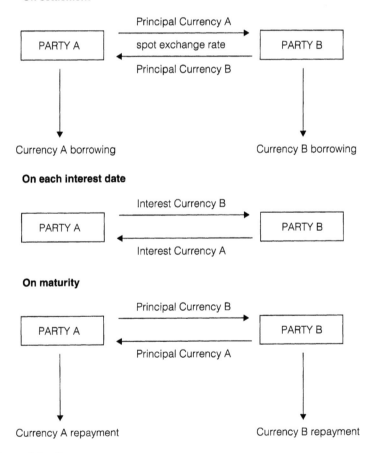

On each interest date

On maturity

Figure 7.3   Cross currency swap

Cross currency swaps

Cross currency swaps are similar in concept to interest rate swaps, except that the principal sum is actually swapped at the spot exchange rate from 1 currency to another on settlement of the swap. Interest payments in the 2 different currencies involved in the transaction are then swapped on interest payment dates. On maturity of the swap the principal amount is re-exchanged, usually at the spot rate used on settlement of the transaction. Figure 7.3 sets out a typical cross currency swap. Cross currency swaps can involve the exchange of fixed interest payments in both currencies or the exchange of a floating rate in 1 currency and a fixed rate in the other. In the case where the cross currency swap involves fixed to floating interest payments, the swap is usually referred to as a CIRCUS swap or cross interest rate and currency swap.

Foreign currency swaps usually arise when a party has a borrowing in 1 currency and prefers to have a borrowing in another currency. The counterparty will have a borrowing in the other currency and will prefer to have a borrowing in the currency that the first party has. Under a foreign currency swap these parties swap the interest payments on their debt as well as the initial borrowed amount and the principal repayment.

In effect a foreign currency swap is a portfolio of forward exchange agreements to exchange the interest payments and principal payments on loans in different currencies at rates fixed today. These rates are fixed by the cash flows of the swap agreement. To analyse a cross currency swap, the net payments under the underlying borrowing and the swap in each currency are determined and the *IRR* or net present value of the net payments for each currency can be separately determined.

Example 7.10

A company borrows 1400 million Japanese yen for 10 years at an interest rate of 4% p.a. with annual interest payments. A cross currency swap is entered into in which the Japanese yen are exchanged for A$10 million. In the swap the company will pay away Australian dollar interest of 12% p.a. annually and receive Japanese yen of 4% p.a. On maturity of the swap a payment of A$10.1 million will be made in exchange for 1400 million Japanese yen. The company will pay fees of 3% of the principal amount of the swap in fees in Australian dollars on settlement of the swap. Calculate the effective Australian dollar borrowing rate that the company achieves, allowing for the fees.

Solution

The Australian dollar cash flows achieved by combining the swap and the yen borrowing will be:

- On settlement: 10 million – fees of 300 000 or A$9 700 000
- Annual interest payments: A$1 200 000

- On maturity: A$10 100 000

The Japanese yen cash flows under the swap exactly match the Japanese yen borrowing cash flows and cancel out.

The effective Australian dollar borrowing rate is given by the yield on these cash flows determined from the equation:

$$9\ 700\ 000 = 1\ 200\ 000 a_{\overline{10}|} + 10\ 100\ 000 v^{10}$$

which is 12.5994%p.a. This rate allows for the fees and the premium paid on the maturity date under the swap.

8 Options

Introduction to options

An option contract is one which gives the holder the right to either buy or to sell an underlying commodity or financial instrument (usually referred to as the underlying asset) on or before a future date (referred to as the expiration date) for a price (referred to as the exercise or strike price) which is fixed on the inception date of the contract. Call options give the holder the right to buy the asset, and put options give the holder the right to sell the asset.

An option does not involve an obligation to buy or sell the commodity or financial instrument as does a futures/forward contract, so that the holder has the flexibility to only exercise the option if it is worthwhile doing so. If the option can be exercised on any day prior to the expiration date then it is an American option, and if it can only be exercised on the expiration date it is a European option. Whether an option is American or European has nothing to do with the geographical location of the market in which it is traded. Most exchange-traded options are American options. Most over-the-counter options—that is, options which are custom designed and issued primarily by banks and institutions—are European options—for example, interbank traded foreign currency options are European options.

Options have been in existence at least since the seventeenth century when tulip bulb put options were sold in Holland. Standardised option contracts are traded in most major financial centres including Sydney, London, Montreal, Geneva, Amsterdam, New York, Chicago and Phila-delphia. The first significant regulated options market was the Chicago Board of Options Exchange (CBOE), which began trading options on stocks in April 1973. In the US, the American Stock Exchange, Philadel-phia Stock Exchange, Pacific Stock Exchange and New York Stock Exchange all have options contracts on stocks (referred to as shares in Australia). In Australia option contracts on ordinary shares are traded on the Australian Options Market, and options on futures contracts are traded on the Sydney Futures Exchange. Over-the-counter markets in interest rate options, including bond options, swaptions, caps and floors, are also significant.

Buying a call or put option is referred to as 'opening' a long position in the put or call option, and selling a call or put option is referred to as 'opening' a short position. The seller of an option, who receives the option price or premium from the buyer, is called the writer of the option.

Option features also exist in a wide range of financial instruments such as convertible bonds, mortgage-backed securities, warrants and callable bonds with optional redemption dates. Chapter 9 introduces the valuation models used for interest rate derivatives, including interest rate options.

Option payoffs

The payoffs to the holder of a European option on the expiration date can easily be determined. There are no payoffs prior to the exercise date.

American options have added flexibility in that they can be exercised prior to the date that a European option would be exercised, so that they will be worth at least as much as a European option. An American option is a European option with something extra—the right to exercise prior to maturity. If the holder is rational the American option will usually only be exercised prior to maturity if it is worth exercising early. Thus the American option must be worth at least as much as the European option.

A European call option with an exercise price of E will have payoffs (on the expiration date) of:

■ *Equation 8.1*

$$\boxed{\begin{array}{l} S - E \text{ if } S > E \\ \text{and } 0 \text{ if } S \leq E \end{array}}$$

where S is the underlying asset price on the expiration date.

This result will be so since, if the underlying asset price is greater than the exercise price, then the option will be exercised and the underlying asset purchased for a price of E, for which an asset with value S is obtained (or equivalently the underlying asset could be immediately sold for a price of S). Hence the value of the option is the difference in the asset price and the exercise price on the expiration date if $S > E$.

If the underlying asset price is less than the exercise price then the option is not worth exercising and so it has a value of zero. It is cheaper to buy the underlying asset at a price of S than to exercise the option.

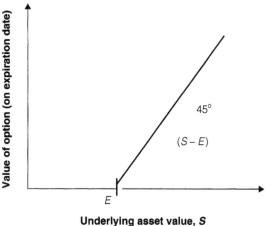

Figure 8.1   Call option payoff

Call option payoffs can be written as the maximum of $(S - E, 0)$ which is often written as:

$$\max (S - E, 0) \text{ or } (S - E)^+$$

or shown graphically in a 'hockey stick' diagram, as given in figure 8.1.

A put option is only worth exercising if the underlying asset value is less than the exercise price, since it will pay to sell an asset worth S at the higher exercise price E for a net gain of $E - S$. The put option payoffs are:

■ *Equation 8.2*

$$E - S \text{ if } S < E$$
$$\text{and } 0 \text{ if } S \geq E$$

Put option payoffs can also be written as:

$$\max (E - S, 0) \text{ or } (E - S)^+$$

or in a payoff diagram as given in figure 8.2.

Options that have a positive value if they were exercised at the current time are said to be 'in the money options'. These are call options where the underlying asset price is above the exercise price or put options where the exercise price is above the underlying asset price. 'At the money' options are those where the exercise price is equal to the underlying asset price. Other options are said to be 'out of the money'.

The payoffs on the expiration date for call and put options, based on the current price of the underlying asset, are referred to as the 'intrinsic

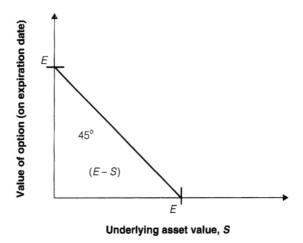

Figure 8.2   Put option payoff

value' of the option. Any difference between the intrinsic value and the option price is referred to as the 'time value', since it reflects the difference between the value of the option on the exercise date (based on the current asset price) and the option value at the current date which is a time difference. If the intrinsic value is positive then the option is 'in the money'. 'Out of the money' options have only time value.

Example 8.1

Put and call options expiring in September are available on BHP stock for exercise prices of $18.20, $19.10 and $20.00. The current share price for BHP is $19.20. Determine the intrinsic value of these put and call options.

Solution

The intrinsic values in table 8.1 are determined using equations 8.1 and 8.2, noting that max (negative value, 0) is 0.

Table 8.1   Intrinsic value of BHP options

Exercise price	Intrinsic value
Call options	
$18.20	max (19.20 – 18.20) = 1.00
$19.10	max (19.20 – 19.10) = 0.10
$20.00	max (19.20 – 20.00) = 0.00
Put options	
$18.20	max (18.20 – 19.20) = 0.00
$19.10	max (19.10 – 19.20) = 0.00
$20.00	max (20.00 – 19.60) = 0.40

Asset price distributions

The value of an option is determined by the payoffs that the option provides to the holder. These payoffs depend on the underlying asset value on future dates. In order to value the option it is necessary to make assumptions about the probability that the underlying asset will have particular values on future dates. Although the behaviour of the underlying asset values for stock prices and other assets can never be known for certain, there are statistical models of this behaviour that work reasonably well for practical purposes. It should always be remembered that when valuing or pricing options there will be a statistical assumption about the price of the underlying asset which will be an approximation of the actual behaviour of this price.

Two statistical models of asset prices have found wide acceptance as practical option valuation models. These are the binomial distribution model, a discrete model of asset prices, and the lognormal distribution model, a continuous model of asset prices. Other statistical models are acceptable and the true test of these models is how closely the resulting option prices reflect actual market prices.

The binomial model

If the current asset price is S_0 and the price in each subsequent time period is assumed to either go up by a multiplicative factor u to uS_0 or down by a multiplicative factor d to dS_0, then the asset price follows a multiplicative binomial model.

The probability that the asset price goes up is assumed to be p and the probability that the asset price goes down is $q = 1 - p$. Asset values take on discrete values at discrete points of time under this model. The possible asset prices over 2 time periods can be set out using a binomial tree or lattice diagram as in figure 8.3. The points in the lattice where the share

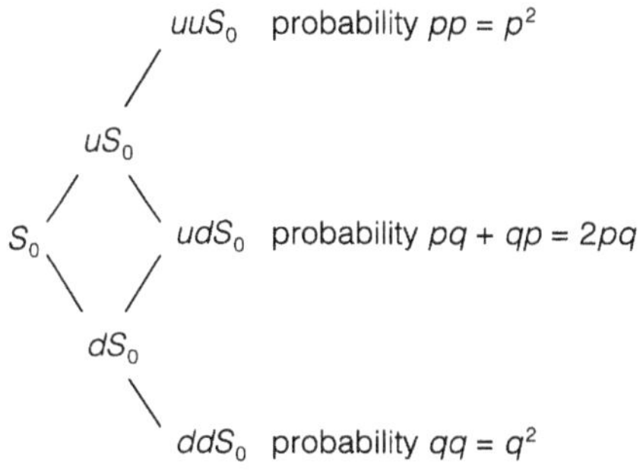

Figure 8.3 Asset price binomial tree or lattice

Table 8.2   Two period binomial distribution

Period 1	Period 2	Asset price	Probability
Up	Up	$u \times u \times S_0$	$p \times p$
Up	Down	$u \times d \times S_0$	$p \times q$
Down	Up	$d \times u \times S_0$	$q \times p$
Down	Down	$d \times d \times S_0$	$q \times q$

prices occur are referred to as 'nodes' of the lattice. This binomial tree is easily extended to n time periods.

The asset prices at the nodes of the lattice at the end of 2 periods are given by the alternative combinations of up and down movements in each period. The alternatives are given in table 8.2.

This means that there are 3 different possible asset prices: uuS_0, udS_0 and ddS_0. In this lattice the size of the up and down movements are such that $udS_0 = duS_0$ and the lattice is said to recombine. Because of this the middle 2 possibilities are combined in figure 8.3 and the probabilities are added.

For n time periods the probability that the asset price will include j up movements and $(n - j)$ down movements, resulting in an asset price of $u^j d^{(n-j)} S_0$, is given by the binomial probability function:

■ *Equation 8.3*

$$^n C_j p^j q^{(n-j)}$$

where:

■ *Equation 8.4*

$$^n C_j = \frac{n!}{j!(n-j)!}$$

where:

$$n! = n(n - 1)(n - 2) \dots (2)(1)$$

The notation $n!$ is referred to as 'n factorial' and is the product of the integers from 1 to n. It should also be noted that u is equal to $(1 + r_u)$ where r_u is the rate of return on the asset if the price goes up and d is equal to $(1 + r_d)$ where r_d is the rate of return on the asset if the price goes down.

Example 8.2

A share is currently priced at $110. Possible price movements over each period are an increase by 20% with probability 0.6 and a decrease by

15% with probability 0.4. What is the probability that the share price will exceed $120 in 4 periods' time?

Solution

In this case we have:

$$u = \frac{uS_0}{S_0} = \frac{110 + (20\% \times 110)}{110}$$

$$= \frac{132}{110}$$

$$u = 1.2$$

$$p = 0.6$$

$$d = \frac{dS_0}{S_0} = \frac{110 - (15\% \times 110)}{110}$$

$$= \frac{93.5}{110}$$

$$d = 0.85$$

$$q = 0.4$$

Figure 8.4 sets out the share price movements and figure 8.5 gives the respective probabilities over the 4 periods. The probability of each share price is obtained by following the paths through time that give each possible price and then summing the probabilities of each of these paths. For example, the price of $161.568 resulting from 3 up movements and 1 down movement can be reached by 4 different paths each with probability $(0.4)(0.6)^3$ so that its probability is 4 times this or 0.3456.

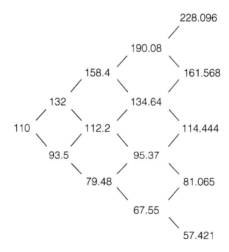

Figure 8.4　Share price movements for example 8.2

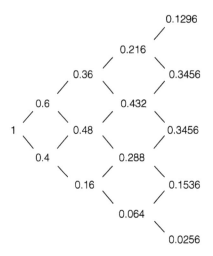

Figure 8.5   Share price probabilities for example 8.2

Doing this for a large number of periods can be rather awkward and prone to error. In this example it is not too difficult.

The required probability is the probability that the share price will be greater than $120, which occurs for the case of 4 up movements and also 4 up movements and 1 down movement, giving prices of $228.096 and $161.568, respectively. Hence the required probability is $0.1296 + 0.3456 = 0.4752$

The solution can also be obtained using the binomial probability distribution directly. To use this we need to know the minimum number of up movements such that the share price will exceed the specified price of $120. This is given by m in equation 8.5.

■ *Equation 8.5*

$$S_0 (u)^m (d)^{(n-m)} > K$$

where S_0 is the current share price, n is the number of periods and K is the specified price.

To solve for m using equation 8.5, take logarithms of both sides to get:

$$\log(S_0) + m\log(u) + (n-m)\log(d) > \log(K)$$

or:

$$m[\log(u) - \log(d)] > \log(K) - \log(S_0) - n\log(d)$$

$$m\log(u/d) > \log(K) - \log(S_0) - \log(d^n)$$

$$m\log(u/d) > \log\left(\frac{K}{S_0 d^n}\right)$$

which gives:

■ *Equation 8.6*

$$m > \frac{\log (K/S_0 d^n)}{\log (u/d)}$$

Remember in taking logarithms that:

$$\log(a^x) = x\log(a)$$

$$\log(a/b) = \log(a) - \log(b)$$

$$\log(a \times b) = \log(a) + \log(b)$$

In equation 8.6 m is the first integer number of increases that satisfies the inequality.

In example 8.2 we have:

$$n = 4, \ u = 1.2, \ d = 0.85, \ K = 120, \text{ and } S_0 = 110$$

so that:

$$m > \frac{\log[120/(110 \times 0.85^4)]}{\log(1.2/0.85)} = \frac{\log(2.08984)}{\log(1.411765)} = 2.137$$

or $m = 3$. The required probability is then the probability that the share price has 3 or more up movements which, using equation 8.3, is:

$$^4C_4(0.6)^4 + {}^4C_3(0.6)^3(0.4)$$

$$= \frac{4!}{4!0!}(0.6)^4 + \frac{4!}{3!1!}(0.6)^3(0.4)$$

$$= \frac{4 \times 3 \times 2 \times 1}{4 \times 3 \times 2 \times 1 \times 1}(0.6)^4 + \frac{4 \times 3 \times 2 \times 1}{3 \times 2 \times 1 \times 1}(0.6)^3(0.4)$$

(since $0! = 1$)

$$= (0.6)^4 + 4(0.6)^3(0.4)$$

$$= 0.4752$$

as before.

Example 8.3

On any trading day a share price is assumed to either increase by 0.05% with probability 0.7 or decrease by 0.05% with probability 0.3. The current share price is $10.50. Calculate the probability that the price will be less than $10.59 after 20 trading days.

Solution

Because there are 20 possible increases or decreases in the share price, it is not practical to set out a diagram as in the previous example and determine the probability by totalling the number of possible ways of getting a price less than $10.59. It is easier to use the binomial probability function. To do this determine the minimum number of up price movements that will give a price more than $10.59. This is the first integer larger than:

$$\frac{\log\{10.59/(10.5 \times 0.9995^{20})\}}{\log(1.0005/0.9995)} = \frac{\log(1.018713)}{\log(1.001005)} = 18.53$$

which is 19. Hence the share price will be less than $10.59 if there are 18 or fewer up movements in the 20 trading days. We could work out the probability of 1, 2, 3, all the way to 18 up movements and then add all these together to get the required probability, but it is not necessary to do this since the calculations can be reduced by noting that the required probability is:

1 – Probability (share price after 20 days is > $10.59)

$= 1 - [\text{Prob}(19 \text{ up movements}) + \text{Prob}(20 \text{ up movements})]$

$= 1 - [^{20}C_{19}(0.7)^{19}(0.3) + {}^{20}C_{20}(0.7)^{20}]$

$= 1 - [20 \times (0.7)^{19}(0.3) + (0.7)^{20}]$

$= 1 - [0.006839 + 0.000798]$

$= 0.9924$

which is a 99.24% chance that the price will be less than $10.59.

As the size of the period used in the binomial model becomes shorter and shorter, the distribution of prices becomes closer to a continuous distribution since the number of possible share prices at the end of any fixed period increases. The most common assumed price distribution model for continuous price distributions is the lognormal distribution. As the binomial model time interval is made smaller and smaller the binomial share price behaviour, provided the up and down movements and the associated probabilities are chosen suitably, becomes closer and closer to the lognormal distribution.

Distributions of share prices can be summarised using their mean and variance. The mean is the average or expected value and the variance is a measure of the dispersion or spread of the actual values around the mean. In option pricing the mean and variance used are those of the continuously compounding rate of return on the underlying asset. This rate of return is given by the natural logarithm (base e = 2.718282) of the price relatives, the ratio of 2 successive prices. Hence if δ is the continuously compounding rate of return over any single time interval in the binomial model then:

■ *Equation 8.7*

$$\delta = \log\left[\frac{S_{k+1}}{S_k}\right]$$

so that:

$$\delta = \begin{cases} \log(u) = \text{with probability } p, \text{ and} \\ \log(d) = \text{with probability } q = 1 - p \end{cases}$$

The expected value of δ is:

$$[p \times \log(u) + q \times \log(d)]$$

and its variance is:

$$[\log(u) - \log(d)]^2 \times p \times q$$

The square root of the variance is the standard deviation which is usually referred to as the option 'volatility'.

The mean and variance for the price after n time intervals can be determined by noting that:

$$\log(S_n/S_0) = \sum_n \delta$$

so that the continuously compounded return over n time intervals in the binomial model is the sum of the single time interval continuously compounding returns which are assumed to be statistically independent. This means that the expected value of the continuously compounding rate of return over n time periods is the sum of the n single time interval means or:

■ *Equation 8.8*

$$\boxed{n \times [p \times \log(u) + q \times \log(d)]}$$

and its variance is the sum of the n single time interval variances:

■ *Equation 8.9*

$$\boxed{n \times [\{\log(u) - \log(d)\}^2 \times p \times q]}$$

If n is chosen as the number of periods per year then these values are the p.a. mean and variance of the rate of return on the underlying asset.

Example 8.4

For the share in example 8.3 determine the expected p.a. continuously compounding rate of return and the p.a. variance. Also determine the volatility. Assume that there are 250 trading days in a year.

Solution

For the share in example 8.3, for a single day:

$$u = 1.0005 \text{ and } d = 0.9995$$

and:

$$\log(1.0005) = 0.000499 \text{ and } \log(0.9995) = -0.000500$$

Hence the expected p.a. return is:

$$250 \times [0.7 \times 0.000499 + 0.3 \times -0.000500] = 0.049969 \text{ or } 4.997\% \text{ p.a.}$$

and the p.a. variance is:

$$250 \times [\{0.000499 - (-0.000500)\}^2 \times 0.7 \times 0.3]$$
$$= 0.0000525 \text{ or } 0.00525\% \text{ p.a.}$$

The volatility is the square root of the variance or 0.007246 or 0.725% p.a.

The lognormal model

Instead of modelling the return on an asset with discrete values at discrete points of time as in the binomial model, the lognormal model generates the asset price for a continuous range of values at any point of time by modelling the continuous rate of return earned on the asset. Consider an asset with current price S_0 that increases in value at a known continuous rate of δ_i p.a for time interval i. The price in t interval's time will be given by:

$$S_t = S_0 e^{\delta_1} e^{\delta_2} \ldots e^{\delta_t} = S_0 \, e^{\sum_{i=1}^{t} \delta_i}$$

where e denotes the exponential function which is sometimes written as exp(.). In this expression δ_i is referred to as the 'force of interest' or the continuous rate of return for time interval i. The asset price experiences exponential growth and is said to be continuously compounding. Option pricing is based on very small time intervals for δ_i. As the time interval becomes small the multiplicative binomial model converges to a lognormal distribution.

The characteristics of a continuous lognormal probability distribution which are important in determining prices are the mean μ and the variance σ^2 of the continuous compounding rate of return. If the continuous rate of return over a particular time period is assumed to be generated statistically by a normal distribution, then the ratio of the price at the end of the time interval to that at the beginning of the time interval, called the price relative, is generated by a lognormal distribution.

The normal distribution is used to give the probability that the continuous rate of return will be less than or equal to a particular value over a particular time interval. It is a very commonly used probability distribution in statistics. A normal distribution results from the sum of a large number of additive random shocks. The continuous rate of return can be considered as the additive result of a large number of random economic influences.

If the continuous rate of return δ over a single time interval has a normal distribution with mean μ and variance σ^2, then e^δ will have a lognormal distribution with mean $\exp\{\mu + \frac{1}{2}\sigma^2\}$ and variance $\exp(2\mu + \sigma^2)$ $\{\exp(\sigma^2) - 1\}$. If δ has a normal distribution with constant mean μ and variance σ^2 then $\Sigma\delta$, the sum of the returns from t independent intervals, will have a normal distribution with mean μt and variance $\sigma^2 t$ (and standard deviation, or volatility, of $\sigma\sqrt{t}$). Hence price relatives given by:

$$\frac{S_t}{S_0} = e^{\Sigma\delta}$$

will have a lognormal distribution.

The probability that an asset price will be less than any given value can be determined using the lognormal distribution. Taking logarithms of the price relative produces a random variable with a normal probability distribution. The probability that a normal random variable exceeds any given value can be readily determined. These probabilities are tabulated in statistical tables which give the probability that a normally distributed random variable with a mean of zero and a variance of 1, referred to as a standard normal random variable, is less than or equal to specified values. To transform a normally distributed random variable to 1 with a mean of zero and a variance of 1 it is necessary to subtract the mean and divide by the square root of the variance. The square root of the variance is the standard deviation. The standard deviation of the rate of return is referred to as the volatility in option pricing. The standard normal probabilities can also be calculated using an approximate formula and most spreadsheets have an in-built function that calculates such probabilities. One approximation for the normal probability is:

$$N(x) = \frac{1}{2} + \frac{1}{2}(1 - e^{\frac{-2x^2}{\pi}})^{\frac{1}{2}} \quad \text{for } x > 0$$

where $\pi = 3.1415926536$. For $x < 0$ the value for $N(x)$ is equal to $1 - N(-x)$. There are other polynomial approximations that can be used.

Example 8.5

The continuous p.a. rate of return on a share is constant and normally distributed with mean 0.16 (16%) and variance 0.03 (3%). The current price is $25. Calculate the probability that the price in 5 years' time will be greater than $50. What will the expected share price be in 5 years' time?

Solution

In this case the probability required is the probability that $S_5 > 50 or that:

$$\frac{S_5}{S_0} > \frac{50}{25} = 2$$

Now the probability that this price relative is greater than 2 is:

$$\text{Probability } [e^{\Sigma\delta} > 2]$$

which, after taking logarithms inside the probability, is:

$$\text{Probability } [\Sigma\delta > \log(2)]$$

Since $\Sigma\delta$ is normally distributed with mean $0.16 \times 5 = 0.8$ and variance $0.03 \times 5 = 0.15$, this probability can be determined using the normal distribution probabilities. This gives the required probability as:

$$Pr\left\{\frac{(\Sigma\delta - 0.8)}{\sqrt{0.15}} > \frac{[\log(2) - 0.8]}{\sqrt{0.15}}\right\} = Pr\{Z > -0.2759\} = N(0.2759)$$

where Z has a normal distribution with mean 0 and variance 1 (the standard normal distribution). This can be determined using standard normal tables to get 0.6087 or 61%. The approximate formula gives:

$$N(0.2759) = 0.5 + 0.5[1 - e^{(-0.0484575)}]^{0.5} = 0.6087 = 0.61$$
$$\text{to 2 decimal places}$$

The expected value of the price relative S_t/S_0 is $\exp\{\mu t + \frac{1}{2}\sigma^2 t\}$ so that the expected share price in 5 years will be:

$$S_5 = S_0 \times \exp\{\mu t + \frac{1}{2}\sigma^2 t\}$$
$$= 25 \times \exp\{0.16 \times 5 + \frac{1}{2}(0.03 \times 5)\}$$
$$= 25 \times \exp\{0.875\}$$
$$= 25 \times 2.398875$$
$$= \$59.97$$

Option valuation

These models for asset prices can be used to value the payoffs of an option. The technique used to value an option is to assume it is possible to replicate the payoffs of an option, using a portfolio of the underlying asset along with borrowing and or lending. This portfolio is constructed to have the same value as the option by 'rebalancing' it over time. Rebalancing involves adjustments to the proportion of the portfolio made up of the underlying asset. To avoid any arbitrage or profitable trading opportunities between the option and this replicating portfolio, the price of the option and the value of the replicating portfolio must be the same. Hence the value of the option is determined by the value of the replicating portfolio which is made up of assets that have market prices. The replicating portfolio must be 'self-financing' which means that once the initial funds, which are equal to the option price, are used to construct the portfolio no net additional investment is required over the life of the option. Any additional borrowing (or lending) which occurs through rebalancing has to be offset (along with interest) by future cash flows from future rebalancing of the portfolio.

Binomial option pricing formula

The simplest model for illustrating the valuation of options is the binomial model. This is used extensively in practice for option valuation. The binomial model is used to value an option by working backwards in time from the expiration date. Over the last period before expiration the share price movements are assumed to be:

$$
S \quad
\begin{array}{l}
\text{Expiration date} \\
uS \text{ with probability } p \\
\\
dS \text{ with probability } q = 1 - p
\end{array}
$$

and the corresponding call option value (C) with exercise price (K) 1 period prior to expiration is given by:

$$
C \quad
\begin{array}{l}
\text{Expiration date} \\
C_u = \max(uS - K, 0) \\
\\
C_d = \max(dS - K, 0)
\end{array}
$$

Denote the interest rate over the last period for borrowing by i and let $r = (1 + i)$. Note that it is always assumed that any borrowing will be fully repaid so that there is no default risk. This borrowing is called risk free for this reason and the interest rate is referred to as the risk-free rate. Consider the following portfolio 1 period prior to expiration:

- Buy h shares at price S
- Borrow B dollars (guaranteed to be repaid)
- (h and B to be determined)

The payoff on this portfolio on the option expiration date will be:

$$
hS - B \quad
\begin{array}{l}
\text{Expiration date} \\
h(uS) - Br \\
\\
h(dS) - Br
\end{array}
$$

Now choose h and B so that these payoffs are the same as those for the call option. This gives:

$$h(uS) - Br = C_u[= \max (uS - K, 0)]$$
$$h(dS) - Br = C_d[= \max (dS - K, 0)]$$

These equations can be solved for h and B by first subtracting the second equation from the first equation to give:

$$h(uS) - Br - \{h(dS) - Br\} = C_u - C_d$$

or:

$$h = \frac{C_u - C_d}{S(u - d)}$$

This value for h is then substituted into the first equation to solve for B, giving:

■ *Equation 8.10*

$$h = \frac{C_u - C_d}{S(u - d)}$$

$$B = \frac{dC_u - uC_d}{(u - d)r}$$

Because this portfolio gives the same payoffs as the option at the end of the period, the value of the option 1 period prior to the expiration date has to be the same as the value of this portfolio if the option and asset markets are to be arbitrage free. This means that the option price will be:

$$C = hS - B$$

$$= \frac{(C_u - C_d)S}{S(u - d)} - \frac{dC_u - uC_d}{(u - d)r}$$

$$= \left[\frac{(r - d)}{(u - d)} C_u + \frac{(u - r)}{(u - d)} C_d \right] \frac{1}{r}$$

$$= [p'C_u + (1 - p') C_d] \div r$$

with p' equal to $(r - d)/(u - d)$.

Note that this expression for the call option price is in the form of a discounted expected value. The expected value of the call option at the end of the period is calculated with the probability p' and then it is discounted to the start of the time interval at the interest rate $r = (1 + i)$.

This process can be repeated recursively over each time interval from the expiration date back to the current date. Over each time interval a replicating portfolio is constructed and the value of the option is equal to the value of the replicating portfolio at the start of the time interval in order for the option and underlying asset market to be arbitrage free. To illustrate this recursive process, consider asset prices over the final 3 periods prior to expiration as set out in figure 8.6. The corresponding call option values are given in figure 8.7.

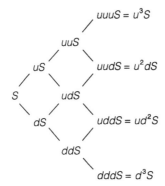

Figure 8.6   Asset prices

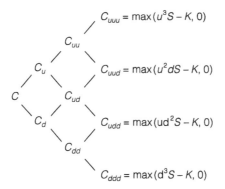

Figure 8.7   Call option values

The option prices 1 period before the expiration date can be written down in terms of the expiration option values as:

$$C_{uu} = [p'C_{uuu} + (1 - p')C_{uud}] \div r$$
$$C_{ud} = [p'C_{uud} + (1 - p')C_{udd}] \div r$$
$$C_{dd} = [p'C_{udd} + (1 - p')C_{ddd}] \div r$$

Repeating this for the next period gives:

$$C_u = [p'C_{uu} + (1 - p')C_{ud}] \div r$$

and since expressions for C_{uu} and C_{ud} have been derived these can be substituted into the expression for C_u to get:

$$C_u = [p'\{p'C_{uuu} + (1 - p')C_{uud}\} \div r + (1 - p')\{p'C_{uud} + (1 - p')C_{udd}\} \div r] \div r$$
$$= [(p')^2 C_{uuu} + 2p'(1 - p')C_{uud} + (1 - p')^2 C_{udd}] \div r^2$$

and similarly:

$$C_d = [(p')^2 C_{uud} + 2p'(1 - p')C_{udd} + (1 - p')^2 C_{ddd}] \div r^2$$

The option value C can be derived by repeating this recursive procedure to get:

$$C = [p'C_u + (1 - p')C_d] \div r$$

which, when the expressions for C_u and C_d derived above are substituted into this formula and simplified, gives:

$$C = [(p')^3 C_{uuu} + 3(p')^2(1 - p')C_{uud} + 3p'(1 - p')^2 C_{udd} + (1 - p')^3 C_{ddd}] \div r^3$$

This can be rewritten using the binomial notation and the summation sign as:

■ **Equation 8.11**

$$C = \left[\sum_{j=0}^{3} \left\{ {}^3C_j \, (p')^j \, (1 - p')^{3-j} \, C(j, 3 - j) \right\} \right] \div r^3$$

where $C(j, n - j)$ is the option value on the expiration date if the asset price has j up movements and $n - j$ down movements and n is the number of periods to the expiration date which is 3 in this case.

In words, the option price is the expected option value on the expiration date where the option values are weighted by binomial probabilities using p' as the probability of an up movement, present valued to the current date at the rate i using discount factor $r = 1 + i$.

The p' probabilities can be interpreted as special probabilities of an up (or $(1 - p')$ for a down) movement in the price. Over any period 1 plus the expected return on the asset will be:

$$\frac{puS + (1 - p)dS}{S}$$

In general 1 plus the asset return will be greater than r, since investors will usually require a higher return for the asset because its return is not guaranteed. If, instead of using the actual probabilities to determine the expected value, these probabilities are replaced with p' and $(1 - p')$ so that 1 plus the expected return on the asset is the same as the risk-free rate r, then:

$$\frac{p'uS + (1 - p')dS}{S} = r$$

or, after simplifying this expression:

$$p'(u - d) = (r - d)$$

so that:

$$p' = \frac{(r-d)}{(u-d)}$$

and:

$$1 - p' = 1 - \frac{(r-d)}{(u-d)}$$

$$= \frac{(u-d)-(r-d)}{(u-d)}$$

$$= \frac{(u-r)}{(u-d)}$$

The probabilities in the call option value derived earlier can be seen to be those that give an expected return on the asset equal to the risk-free interest rate. The expected call option payoff is present valued at the risk-free interest rate because the probabilities used to derive the expected payoff are consistent with this interest rate.

The option value for n time intervals prior to the expiration date follows from the 3 period example and is given in equation 8.12.

■ *Equation 8.12*

$$C = \left[\sum_{j=0}^{n} \left\{ {}^{n}C_{j} \, (p')^{j} \, (1-p')^{n-j} \, C(j, n-j) \right\} \right] \div r^{n}$$

where $C(j, n-j) = \max(u^{j}d^{n-j} S - K, 0)$ is the option value for j up movements and $n-j$ down movements.

Let m be the first integer value for j which makes $u^{j}d^{n-j}S$ greater than K for the first time. The payoff on the call option, $C(j, n-j)$, will be 0 for values of j less than this.

To determine m use the inequality that gives the number of up jumps for which the asset price will exceed the exercise price:

$$u^{m}d^{n-m} S > K$$

Taking logarithms and rearranging gives m as the first integer such that:

■ *Equation 8.13*

$$m > \frac{\log(K/d^{n}S)}{\log(u/d)}$$

The call option value in equation 8.12 becomes:

$$\left[\sum_{j=m}^{n} \left\{ {}^nC_j\,(p')^j\,(1-p')^{n-j}\,(u^j d^{n-j} S - K) \right\} \right] \div r^n$$

which simplifies further by expanding the expression in the summation sign into 2 separate components, 1 containing the asset price S and 1 containing the exercise price K. The result is equation 8.14:

■ *Equation 8.14*

$$C = S \left[\sum_{j=m}^{n} \left\{ {}^nC_j\,(up')^j\,(d(1-p'))^{n-j} \right\} \right] \div r^n$$

$$- (K \div r^n) \left[\sum_{j=m}^{n} \left\{ {}^nC_j\,(p')^j\,(1-p')^{n-j} \right\} \right]$$

In words, equation 8.14 says that the call option value is the expected value of the asset price given that the option will be worth exercising on the expiration date (it will be 'in the money') *minus* the present value of the exercise price *times* the probability the option will be in the money on the expiration date, where the probabilities are the special probabilities that make the expected return on the asset equal to the risk-free interest rate.

Example 8.6

Assume that a share with current price $110 can increase by 20% with probability 0.6 or decrease by 15% with probability 0.4 over any time interval. Calculate the value of a European call option with exercise price $120 and expiration date in 4 time intervals if the risk-free rate for borrowing over any time interval is 10%.

Solution

Using equation 8.14 the option value is:

$$110 \left[\sum_{j=m}^{4} \left\{ {}^4C_j\,(up')^j\,(d(1-p'))^{4-j} \right\} \right] \div (1.1)^4$$

$$- (120 \div (1.1)^4) \left[\sum_{j=m}^{4} \left\{ {}^4C_j\,(p')^j\,(1-p')^{4-j} \right\} \right]$$

where:

$$u = 1.2$$

$$d = 0.85$$

$$p' = \frac{(1.1 - 0.85)}{(1.2 - 0.85)} = \frac{0.25}{0.35} = 0.714286$$

and m is the first integer greater than $\dfrac{\log(120 + \{(0.85)^4 110\})}{\log(1.2/0.85)}$

$= 2.137473$ which is 3.

Substituting these values into the expression for the option value gives:

$110 \times \{4 \times (0.85714^3) (0.24286^1) + 0.85714^4\} + (1.1)^4$

$\quad - 81.9616 \times \{4 \times (0.71429^3) (0.28571^1) + 0.71429^4\}$

$\quad = 110 \times [0.41783 + 0.36867] - 81.9616 [0.41649 + 0.260308]$

$\quad = 110 \times 0.7865 - 81.9616 \times 0.6768$

$\quad = \$31.04$

Example 8.7

Determine the portfolio that will replicate the call option payoffs for the option in example 8.6 after 2 periods if the share price is then 158.4 and after 3 periods if the share price is then 134.64.

Solution

From example 8.6:

$$p' = \frac{(1.1 - 0.85)}{(1.2 - 0.85)} = \frac{0.25}{0.35}$$

$$q' = 1 - \frac{0.25}{0.35}$$

The share prices come from figure 8.8. After 2 periods figure 8.8 is:

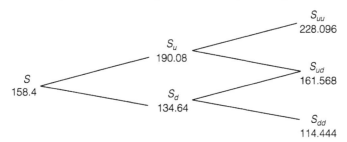

Figure 8.8

The formula for the call option value is:

$[p'(S_{uu} - K) + q'(S_{ud} - K)] \div r$

$= \{[0.25/0.35 \times (228.096 - 120)] + [(1 - 0.25/0.35) \times (161.658 - 120)]\} \div 1.1$

$= 80.9891$ if the share price goes up (to 190.08)

and:

$\{[0.25/0.35 \times (161.568 - 120)] + [(1 - 0.25/0.35) \times 0]\} \div 1.1$

$= 29.6914$ if the share price goes down (to 134.64)

After 2 periods with the share price at 158.4 buy h shares and borrow B to replicate the option value at the end of the third period. The value of this portfolio at the end of the third period will be:

$$h \times 190.08 - B(1.1) \text{ if the stock price goes up}$$

and:

$$h \times 134.64 - B(1.1) \text{ if the stock price goes down}$$

To determine h and B equate these payoffs to the option payoffs so that:

$$h \times 190.08 - B(1.1) = 80.9891 \text{ (if price goes up)}$$

$$h \times 134.64 - B(1.1) = 29.6914 \text{ (if price goes down)}$$

which gives, using equation 8.10:

$$h = \frac{C_u - C_d}{S(u - d)}$$

with:

$$C_u = 80.9891 \text{ (up)}$$

$$C_d = 29.6914 \text{ (down)}$$

$$uS = 158.4u = 190.08$$

$$dS = 158.4d = 134.64$$

$$r = 1.1$$

$$\therefore h = \frac{80.9891 - 29.6914}{190.08 - 134.64}$$

$$= 0.9253$$

and:

$$B = \frac{dC_u - uC_d}{(u - d)r}$$

$$= \frac{dSC_u - uSC_d}{(uS - dS)r} \left(\text{multiplying by } \frac{S}{S} \right)$$

$$= \frac{(134.64 \times 80.9891) - (190.08 \times 29.6914)}{(190.088 - 134.64)(1.1)}$$

$$= 86.26248$$

Hence the replicating portfolio requires 0.9253 shares for each option and borrowing of $86.26 per option if the share price is 158.4 after 2 periods.

After 3 periods with the share price at 134.64 the option value at expiration will be either $161.568 - 120 = 41.568$ if the stock price goes up, or 0 if the stock price goes down, so that the replicating portfolio will be such that:

$$h \times 161.568 - B(1.1) = 41.568$$

$$h \times 114.444 - B(1.1) = 0$$

which gives:

$$h = \frac{41.568 - 0}{161.568 - 114.444} = 0.8821$$

and:

$$B = \frac{114.444 \times 41.568 - 0}{(161.568 - 114.444)(1.1)} = 91.7735$$

So if the share price goes up in the third period to 134.64, the theoretical replicating portfolio needs to be revised to include 0.8821 shares and borrowing of 91.7735 per option.

The ratio of the number of shares per option denoted by h above is referred to as the hedge ratio. The hedge ratio is the option 'delta', which is the ratio of the dollar change in the option price to the dollar change in the share price. This can be seen by examining equation 8.10 for h which is the ratio of the difference in the up and the down option values to the difference i in the up and down asset prices.

The binomial model is a very flexible method for valuing options since it is easily adapted to handle dividend payments and also the early exercise possibility for American options, particularly American put options. To allow for early exercise, the value of the option at the end of each time interval is determined for each possible asset price working backward from expiration. If the early exercise value exceeds the value of the option at any time, then this early exercise value is used instead of the option value. A formula equivalent to equation 8.14 for early exercise options cannot be written down if the option is worth exercising early and it is necessary to compute option values numerically using the recursive procedure of calculating expected values and discounting over each time interval.

Binomial model parameters

In order to use the binomial model in practice it is necessary to choose the number of time intervals for the time to expiration and the values for u and d over any single time interval. If there are n time intervals and the time to expiration of the option is T years, then the length of each time interval is $t = T/n$. In practice n is usually chosen to be at least 50 to ensure accurate answers. The values of u and d are often chosen so that $\log(u) = \sigma\sqrt{t}$ and $d = 1/u$ where σ is the p.a. volatility of the option and $p' = \frac{(r-d)}{(u-d)}$. If R is the p.a. risk-free interest rate then the per single interval interest factor is chosen so that $r = (1 + i) = (1 + R)^t$. This choice of parameters ensures that the binomial tree or lattice recombines and will usually be adequate for small time intervals. However, for larger time intervals and larger volatility, the probability p' can be negative or greater than 1 and the binomial method will not produce reliable answers whenever the probability p' is less than 0 or greater than 1. There are a number of alternative methods of selecting the binomial parameters. Parameters should be selected to equate the expected value and variance of the price change to the lognormal distribution parameters as follows:

■ *Equation 8.15*

$$p'u + (1 - p')d = (1 + i)$$

■ *Equation 8.16*

$$p'u^2 + (1 - p')d^2 = e^{\sigma^2 t}(1 + i)^2$$

It is important to check that the probabilities are between 0 and 1 and that u and d are positive for any selection of parameters in order to ensure that the binomial model will produce meaningful results. An often used set of parameters determined using equations 8.15 and 8.16 that ensures the probabilities are between 0 and 1 is:

$$p' = \frac{1}{2}, \ u = (1 + i)(1 + \sqrt{e^{\sigma^2 t} - 1}), \text{ and } d = (1 + i)(1 - \sqrt{e^{\sigma^2 t} - 1}).$$

Example 8.8

Determine the per period parameters for the binomial model if the risk-free rate is 10% p.a., the volatility of the rate of return on the underlying stock is 20% p.a., the term to expiration is 3 months (0.25 of a year) and the number of time intervals is 20. Comment on the suitability of these parameters.

Solution

The per subperiod present value factor is:

$$r = (1 + i) = 1.1^{0.25/20} = 1.001192$$

The value of u is $e^{0.2 \times \sqrt{(0.25/20)}} = 1.022613$, the value of d is $1/1.022613 = 0.977887$ and the value of p' is –0.4736. Because the probability is negative this selection of parameters is unlikely to produce sensible or accurate answers. The alternative set of parameters gives $p' = 0.5$, $u = 1.0236$ and $d = 0.9788$ which would be more suitable.

Black–Scholes option pricing formula

One of the most used formulae in financial markets is the Black–Scholes option pricing formula. If the asset price is modelled using the lognormal probability distribution, then the resulting option pricing formula is the Black–Scholes formula which was derived by Fischer Black and Myron Scholes and has become the standard option pricing formula. The mathematics involved in doing this are more technical than for the binomial model, since they require stochastic calculus and the solution of partial differential equations. However, the replicating portfolio concepts are the same as those used for the binomial model.

The Black–Scholes formula for a call option is:

$$C = SN(d_1) - Kr^{-T}N(d_2)$$

where:

- $d_1 = \dfrac{\log(S/Kr^{-T}) + \dfrac{1}{2}\sigma^2 T}{\sigma\sqrt{T}}$,
- $d_2 = d_1 - \sigma\sqrt{T}$,
- $N(.)$ is the cumulative standard normal probability distribution function, determined from standard normal statistical tables or an approximate formula,
- $r = (1 + i) = e^\delta$ is 1 plus the per period interest rate i or the exponential of the continuously compounding interest rate δ,
- K is the exercise price,
- S is the current stock price,
- T is the time to maturity, and
- σ is the instantaneous standard deviation of the continuously compounded rate of return of the asset, usually referred to as the volatility of the option. The standard deviation is the square root of the variance σ^2.

Although commonly used, this formula lacks the flexibility of the binomial model, especially when allowing for early exercise of American options and for dividends. An approximate allowance for dividends is made by subtracting the present value of any dividends expected between the current date and the expiration date from the current asset price and using this adjusted price in the formula.

Example 8.9

The following information relates to options on BHP shares on the Australian Options Market. Each option is for delivery of 1000 shares at the exercise price.

- Last sale price for BHP shares: $19.34
- Volatility for 5 month call option: 20.5%

- Simple interest rate for 4 and 5 month borrowing: 7.5% p.a.
- Expected dividend in 4 months: 26 cents per share

Use the Black-Scholes formula to estimate the option price for a BHP 5 month 19.55 strike call option, using the above information and making approximate allowance for the dividend.

Solution

The value of the call, ignoring early exercise, is given by the Black-Scholes formula where the current share price is modified to allow for the dividend. The modification required is to deduct the present value of the dividend from the current share price. A commonly used alternative way of writing the Black-Scholes formula is with a continuously compounding interest rate as follows:

$$c = S^*N(d_1) - Xe^{-\delta T}N(d_2)$$

where:

$$d_1 = \left[\ln\left(\frac{S^*}{X}\right) + (\delta + \frac{1}{2}\sigma^2)T\right]/\sigma\sqrt{T}$$

and:

$$d_2 = d_1 - \sigma\sqrt{T}$$

The modified share price after deducting the present value of the dividend is:

$$S^* = 19.34 - 0.26\left(1 + 0.075 \times \frac{4}{12}\right)^{-1} = 19.0863$$

the exercise price is:

$$X = 19.55$$

the continuous compounding interest rate is:

$$\delta = \frac{12}{5}\ln\left[1 + 0.075 \times \frac{5}{12}\right] = 0.073852$$

and:

$$Xe^{-\delta\frac{5}{12}} = 18.9576$$

$$d_1 = \left[\ln\left(\frac{19.0863}{18.9576}\right) + \frac{1}{2}0.205^2\frac{5}{12}\right]/0.205\sqrt{\frac{5}{12}} = 0.117303$$

$$d_2 = 0.117303 - 0.205\sqrt{\frac{5}{12}} = -0.015024$$

$$N(d_1) \approx 0.5467 \qquad , \quad N(d_2) \approx 0.4940$$

so that the call option value is:

$$c = 19.0863 \times 0.5467 - 18.9576 \times 0.494 = 1.07$$

The Black-Scholes formula does not allow for early exercise. Options on dividend-paying shares are often worth exercising early. The dividend and early exercise are readily allowed for using the binomial model.

Put option pricing

Values for put options can be determined using portfolio replication arguments similar to those used to determine call option values. A useful result that allows the derivation of put option values from call option values for European options is called put–call parity. To illustrate this consider the following 2 portfolios:

- Portfolio A: A call option with exercise price K and a zero coupon bond with face value K maturing on the expiration date.
- Portfolio B: The underlying asset (with price S) and a put option on the share with exercise price K.

At the expiration date the payoffs on these 2 portfolios are as follows:

	$S \geq K$	$S < K$
Portfolio A		
Call option	$S - K$	0
Bond	K	K
Total payoff	S	K
Portfolio B		
Share	S	S
Put option	0	$K - S$
Total payoff	S	K

Because the portfolios provide the same payoffs, regardless of the asset price on the expiration date, they should have equal current values. Thus:

Current value portfolio A = Current value of portfolio B

Call option value + Value of bond = Share value + Put option value

or expressed in symbols as:

■ *Equation 8.17*

$$C + Kr^{-T} = S + P$$

where P = Put option value.

This result is called put–call parity. The put option value can be determined from equation 8.17 as:

$$P = C + Kr^{-T} - S$$

This relationship can be used with the Black–Scholes call option formula to derive the value of a European put option on a non-dividend paying asset as:

$$P = SN(d_1) - Kr^{-T}N(d_2) + Kr^{-T} - S$$
$$= Kr^{-T}[1 - N(d_2)] - S[1 - N(d_1)]$$
$$= Kr^{-T}[N(-d_2)] - SN(-d_1)$$

This is the Black–Scholes put option pricing formula.

Example 8.10

A European call option on BHP with an exercise price of $18.60 and time to maturity of 3 months can be purchased for a premium of $1.25. BHP shares have a market price of $19.20 and the interest rate for 3 month funds is 8% p.a effective. A European put option on BHP with exercise price $18.60 is trading at a market price of $0.40. If put–call parity holds, determine the value of the put option. What factors may explain any difference between this value and the actual market price of the put?

Solution

Put–call parity gives:

$$P = C + Kr^{-T} - S$$
$$= 1.25 + 18.60 \times (1.08)^{-3/12} - 19.20$$
$$= \$0.30$$

This value is below the $0.40 market price so it appears that put options are overvalued. One could take advantage of this by selling the put option at $0.40 and then buying the call option, investing the present value of the exercise price and short selling a share for a total net cost of $0.30 and hence generating a sure profit of $0.10. This latter strategy will have the same payoffs as the put option under put–call parity.

One of the factors that would explain the difference in the prices is dividend payments. The put–call parity relationship above ignores the value of dividend payments which will make the put option more valuable. An adjustment can be made for dividends in the put–call parity formula, provided the amount of dividend is known or can be approximated.

Other factors to be allowed for in option valuation

The development of option valuation set out above is very basic and only introduces this important and mathematical/statistical area. Other factors that need to be considered in practice are:

Dividend or interest payments on the underlying asset An approximate allowance for dividends between the current date and the expiration date can be made using the Black–Scholes formula, by deducting the present value of dividends from the current share price and using the non-dividend formulae. This is so since the value of the share that is bought/sold under the option will be less by the amount of any dividends paid on the share. In practice dividends will need to be allowed for using the binomial lattice or some other numerical valuation technique.

American options and early exercise American options can be more valuable than European options because it can pay to exercise the option prior to the expiration date. This is particularly so for underlying assets paying dividends or interest between the current date and the expiration date. In general the optimum time to exercise a call option will be immediately prior to a dividend payment. If the dividend will exceed the interest on the exercise price to the expiration date then it will pay to exercise the option to buy the share rather than wait until the expiration date. Since most traded options are American options this is a very important practical consideration.

Unknown future interest rates Most option valuation formulae assume that future interest rates are fixed and known. In practice this is not the case and this factor will be very important for options on interest-bearing securities where varying future interest rates are 1 of the reasons for the option. Allowance for varying interest rates is often made approximately by an adjustment to the volatility or variance parameter. The valuation of interest rate derivatives with varying interest rates is introduced in chapter 9.

Transaction costs and discrete rebalancing In practice the replicating portfolio will not produce exactly the same payoffs as the option, since the portfolio will not be continuously rebalanced (as required in the continuous returns model) and every rebalancing will involve transaction costs. The option value will reflect this in practice. Approximate allowance for transaction costs can be made by a suitable adjustment to the volatility (standard deviation) parameter in the Black–Scholes formula.

Forward contracts and options

There is a relationship between the payoffs on forward contracts and the payoffs on options. To see this consider a portfolio of a long put and a short call option, both with exercise price K and maturity T months. The payoffs on the maturity date are:

	$S \geq K$	$S < K$
Short call option:	$-(S - K)$	0
Long put option:	0	$K - S$
	$-(S - K)$	$K - S$

Hence, regardless of the asset value on the expiration date, this portfolio pays $K - S$ (since $-(S - K) = K - S$). This is the identical payoff to a short forward contract with forward price K. The value of this portfolio and the short forward contract must be the same, so:

$$P - C = -F$$

For non-dividend-paying European options put–call parity gives:

$$P - C = Kr^{-T} - S$$

which gives the value of the forward contract as:

$$F = S - Kr^{-T}$$

At inception of a forward contract its value is zero so that:

$$0 = S - Kr^{-T}$$

or:

$$K = Sr^{T}$$

Thus the forward price at inception of the forward contract is the spot price of the asset accumulated with interest to the delivery date. This result was also derived in chapter 6 using arbitrage arguments.

Example 8.11

A call option on gold with exercise price $420 expiring in 4 months can be bought for $5.20 and a put option on gold with the same exercise price and expiration date can be sold for a premium of $12.07. The spot price of gold is $400 and interest rate is 10% p.a. A forward contract on gold for delivery in 4 months with a forward price of $420 is held by an investor. Based on the option values, what is the value of the forward contract?

Solution

A long forward contract with forward price $420 can be created by buying the call option and selling the put option. Hence the value of the forward contract is:

$$5.20 - 12.07 = -6.87$$

If the current spot price of gold is $400 then the forward price of gold will be (ignoring storage and insurance costs):

$$400(1.1)^{4/12} = 412.91$$

The actual forward price for the contract is $420 so that there is an effective future loss on the forward contract of:

$$420 - 412.91 = 7.09$$

which has a present value of:

$$-7.09(1.1)^{-4/12} = -6.87$$

This is the value of the forward contract.

Convertible bonds and warrants

Convertible bonds are bonds which are issued as debt instruments, with the option to convert these securities to shares at fixed prices on or before specified future dates (e.g. the maturity date). Some require an initial waiting period before conversion (for tax reasons in Australia). Sometimes bonds are issued with 'warrants' attached which give the holder the option to purchase a specified number of shares on or before future dates at specified prices. Convertible securities are the same as conventional debt instruments (which can be valued using the techniques in chapters 1 to 4) combined with some option features.

The option valuation techniques can be used to value the option features on convertible bonds and also to value warrants. One major difference between these convertible bond option features and the options discussed in this chapter is that these options (or warrants) bring into being new shares and there is a dilution effect on the share price which does not occur with traded options on existing shares. Warrants and convertibles are issued by companies, and traded options are issued by individuals.

Example 8.12

A company whose shares are worth $8 has 1 million shares outstanding and 100 000 warrants worth $1 with exercise price $6. Determine the share price, assuming all warrants are exercised immediately. At what current share price will it not pay to exercise the warrants?

Solution

The current value of the equity in the company is the value of the shares plus the value of the warrants:

$$8 \times 1\,000\,000 + 1 \times 100\,000 = 8\,100\,000$$

If all warrants are exercised immediately, the total value of the equity in the company is the old value plus the exercise money paid by the warrant holders or:

$$8\,100\,000 + 6 \times 100\,000 = 8\,700\,000$$

The number of shares will be the old number plus the new shares issued through the exercise of the warrants or:

$$1\,000\,000 + 100\,000 = 1\,100\,000$$

The new share price will be:

$$\frac{8\,700\,000}{1\,100\,000} = \$7.91$$

This reduction in the share price is referred to as 'dilution'. It occurs because the warrant holders receive their shares for less than $8.

It will not pay to exercise the warrants if the value of the share *after* exercising is less than or equal to the warrant exercise price.

The actual payoff to a warrant is somewhat different to that of a call option because of the dilution effect. If the share price on the expiration date is S, the number of shares on issue is n_s, the warrant exercise price is X, the current warrant value is W and the number of warrants is n_w, then the warrant payoff will be the maximum of 0 and the difference between the diluted share price and the warrant exercise price. This maximum is:

$$\max\left[0, \frac{n_s S + n_w W + n_w X}{n_s + n_w} - X\right]$$

$$= \max\left[0, \frac{n_s(V-X)}{n_s + n_w}\right]$$

$$= \frac{n_s}{n_s + n_w} \times \max(0, V - X)$$

$$= \frac{n_s}{n_s + n_w} \times [\text{Payoff on a call option on the equity value of the company}]$$

where $V = \dfrac{n_s S + n_w W}{n_s}$.

Hence the value of the warrant W equals the dilution factor times the value of an equivalent call option on the total equity of the company. Notice that the value V depends on W, the value of the warrants, so that an iterative procedure will be required to determine the value of the warrants.

Example 8.13

A company issues 100 000 2 year convertible bonds paying 12% annual coupon interest payments with face value $100. If it had issued conventional debt it would have paid a yield to maturity of 13% p.a. The bonds are convertible into shares at a conversion price of $10 a share, so that each bond can be converted into 10 shares (a conversion ratio of 10). The current share price is $8, there are 10 million shares outstanding and a theoretical call option on the total value of the equity of the company with an exercise price of $10 is assumed to be valued at $1.50. Calculate the value of the convertible bonds.

Solution

The value of the convertible bonds will be the value of the conventional debt plus the value of the conversion 'warrant'.
Value of bonds as debt:

$$12a_{\overline{2}|} + 100v^2 \text{ at } 13\%$$

$$= 20.01723 + 100 \times 0.78315$$

$$= 98.3319$$

Value of conversion feature is:

$$10 \times \left[\frac{10}{10 + 1} \times 1.50 \right] = 13.6364$$

where $n_w = 100\ 000 \times 10 = 1\ 000\ 000$

$n_s = 10\ 000\ 000$

So that:

$$\text{Total value} = 98.3319 + 13.6364 = 111.9683$$

If this price was obtained for conventional debt, the effective yield would be given by the rate which solved:

$$111.9683 = 12a_{\overline{2}|} + 100v^2$$

or a rate of 5.52% p.a. Thus the value of the conversion feature is added to the convertible bond price, resulting in a lower effective yield.

Guaranteed indexed notes

Securities are issued which are indexed in value to a specific index such as the gold price or a Share Price Index, with a guarantee that a minimum repayment will be made if the index does not increase by at least a specified percentage. These securities have built-in option features and can be valued as the security without a guarantee, plus the value of the guarantee which is equal to the value of a put option. An example of this type of security issued in the Australian market is the ASPRIN (All Ordinaries Share Price Riskless Indexed Note) issued by the NSW Treasury Corporation and underwritten by Bankers Trust Australia. This security is a 4 year zero coupon bond indexed to the All Ordinaries Share Price Index with a minimum repayment of the amount subscribed.

Example 8.14

A security is issued for a cost of $100 000. The issuer guarantees to pay the larger of the cost of the security or the cost increased by the rate of increase of the All Ordinaries Share Price Index in 4 years' time. Show that the security is effectively a zero coupon bond plus an option on the Share Price Index.

Solution

The payment on maturity in 4 years' time is:

$$\max [100\ 000, 100\ 000 \times (1 + R_{SPI})]$$

where R_{SPI} is the rate of increase in the Share Price Index (*SPI*) over the 4 years:

$$\max [100\ 000, 100\ 000\ (SPI_4/SPI_0)]$$

where SPI_4 is the level of the index in 4 years' time, and SPI_0 is the current level of the index:

$$= 100\,000 + \max [0, 100\,000 \times (SPI_4/SPI_0) - 100\,000]$$

$$= 100\,000 + \frac{1000}{SPI_0} \times \max [0, 100 \times SPI_4 - 100 \times SPI_0]$$

$$= \text{Payoff on a zero coupon bond} + \frac{1000}{SPI_0} \times \text{Payoff on an}$$

'at-the-money' call option on the Share Price Index

Exotic options

There are many over-the-counter options on assets, interest rates and foreign currency that are non-standard in their payoffs. These options include Asian options, which are options that have either a strike price equal to the average asset price, interest rate or exchange rate or have a fixed strike price and have a payoff based on the average asset price, interest rate or exchange rate during the life of the option. There are chooser options that allow the holder to decide if the option is to be a put or a call option. There are barrier options that either 'knock-in' or 'knock-out' if the asset price reaches a specific barrier. All these options are designed to meet the needs of investors and companies. The valuation and analysis techniques required for these options is beyond the level of this book, but the technology exists to value the most complex of options.

9 Interest rate derivatives

Many securities have cash flows whose timing or amount is dependent on the future level of interest rates. Some examples are swaps, bond options and futures, interest rate caps, housing loans with capped interest rates, insurance bonds with guaranteed minimum rates of return, bonds with optional redemption dates because they can be called by the lender (callable bonds or bonds with call features), bonds with optional redemption dates because they can be put by the borrower (puttable bonds), and many more.

In order to value these securities it is necessary to model future interest rates as random variables. It is also necessary to ensure that the model of interest rates values fixed interest securities consistently and does not allow profitable trading opportunities between different interest rate derivatives. An interest rate model with these properties is arbitrage free.

A flexible method of valuing interest rate derivatives is to use a discrete interest rate model which allows future interest rates to take discrete values at discrete points of time. The most common model is the binomial model of interest rates where interest rates form a binomial tree or lattice. This model also allows the consistent and efficient computation of values of many different interest rate derivatives using a computer. The Black-Scholes option pricing formula can be adapted to value some interest rate derivatives and this formula is often used in practice for bond options, swaptions and caps and floors.

This chapter outlines how to construct simple discrete time binomial models of interest rates and shows how these can be used to value cash flows whose values are functions of interest rates. It shows how the parameters of these models can be fitted to the zero coupon yield curve so that the model is arbitrage free.

The concepts used in constructing discrete time interest rate models and fitting these to yield curves are similar to those used for pricing options

185

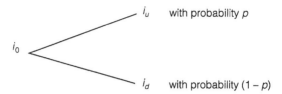

Figure 9.1   One period binomial model of the one period interest rate

on shares and other types of options. These were covered in chapter 8. For some interest rate derivatives, binomial models become cumbersome even on the most powerful computer and it is necessary to approximate the required answers using simulation.

The binomial lattice

Binomial lattices are most often constructed for one period spot interest rates. All other interest rates are related to the one period spot interest rate in these models. Models of forward interest rates and zero coupon bond prices can also be used. The basis for an interest rate binomial lattice is the assumption that over each time period the one period interest rate can move to 2 possible values as in figure 9.1.

In this case the 2 possible interest rates correspond to an up move in the interest rate from i_0 to i_u and a down move from i_0 to i_d. The interest rate for investing for the first time period will be i_0 which is fixed and known today and is referred to as the one period spot interest rate. The one period interest rate for investing in the second time period is a random variable taking the values of i_u or i_d. The mean and variance of the one period interest rate for the second period, taking the first period interest rate value as given, are:

■ *Equation 9.1*

$$E(i) = pi_u + (1 - p)i_d$$

and:

■ *Equation 9.2*

$$\mathrm{Var}(i) = pi_u^2 + (1 - p)i_d^2 - [E(i)]^2 = p(1 - p)(i_u - i_d)^2$$

In this model the distribution of an amount invested today will be related to future one period interest rates. An amount of \$1 invested today will have value \$$(1 + i_0)$ with certainty at the end of one period and will take the values $\$(1 + i_0)(1 + i_u)$ with probability p and $\$(1 + i_0)(1 + i_d)$ with probability $(1 - p)$ at the end of 2 time periods.

Example 9.1

Assume that, over any time period, the one period interest rates can either increase by a multiplicative factor of 1.15 or decrease by a factor of 0.95 with equal probability. The current interest rate is 6% per period. Determine the distribution of the accumulated value of $1000 in 3 years' time.

Solution

The distribution of one period interest rates is given in table 9.1.

Table 9.1   One period interest rate distribution

Time period 1		Time period 2		Time period 3	
Rate	Prob.	Rate	Prob.	Rate	Prob.
				0.07935 = 0.069(1.15)	0.25
		0.069 = 0.06(1.15)	0.5		
0.06	1.0			0.06555 = 0.069(0.95) = 0.057(1.15)	0.5
		0.057 = 0.06(0.95)	0.5		
				0.05415 = 0.057(0.95)	0.25

The distribution of 1000 accumulated over 3 periods will be as given in table 9.2.

Table 9.2   Distribution of accumulated values

End time period 1		End time period 2		End time period 3	
Amount	Prob.	Amount	Prob.	Amount	Prob.
				1000(1.06)(1.069)(1.07935)	0.25
		1000(1.06)(1.069)	0.5	1000(1.06)(1.069)(1.06555)	0.25
1000(1.06) = 1060	1.0				
		1000(1.06)(1.057)	0.5	1000(1.06)(1.057)(1.06555)	0.25
				1000(1.06)(1.057)(1.05415)	0.25

In this case the one period interest rate lattice recombines in time period 3, since the up move followed by the down move in the interest rate produces the same change in the interest rate as the down move followed by the up move. A binomial lattice with this property is said to be path independent. In the case of the accumulated value, the end of period 3 values depend on the order of the up and down movements in interest rates. Where values in a binomial lattice depend on the actual path taken through the lattice they are said to be path dependent. Thus the accumulated values are path dependent.

The accumulation of \$1 at the one period interest rates is equivalent to the return earned from investing in a deposit or money market account. The value of such an investment is usually referred to in journal articles on interest rate derivatives as the value of a money market account.

There are 2 common methods of relating next time period interest rates to the prior period interest rates in a binomial lattice. One is an additive model in which $i_u = i_0 + k_u$ and $i_d = i_0 - k_d$ where k_u and k_d are constants, that could vary from one time period to another, and the other is a multiplicative model in which $i_u = i_0 k_u$ and $i_d = i_0 k_d$. In practice the multiplicative model is often used since it gives a lognormal continuous equivalent distribution for interest rates.

In the multiplicative case, if $0 < k_d < 1$ then the lowest interest rate possible in the model will be $i_0 (k_d)^n$ and as $n \rightarrow \infty$, the lowest one period interest rate will be 0%. If the lowest one period interest rate was negative then it would be possible to borrow at a negative interest rate and hold the cash earning no interest for 1 time period. At the end of the time period the amount to be repaid would be less than the amount borrowed and a profit could be made. Hence negative one period interest rates allow arbitrage profits to be made and are not a sensible feature in these models. In practice the probability of a negative one period rate can be low enough in an additive model for it not to matter.

In practice interest rate models use monthly time intervals for a time period of up to 30 years, depending on the longest maturity of the security to be valued with the model. Thus the simple one period model in figure 9.1 must be extended to multiple time periods. This is done for 2 time periods in figure 9.2 for the multiplicative model. In this diagram the up and down movements in interest rates are different for each period. The points at the end of the branches of the lattice are referred to as nodes.

In this 2 period model the number of nodes in the lattice doubles over each time period so that the number of possible interest rates for the nth time period will be 2^n. In practice, even for a reasonable number of time periods, the number of nodes in this case will be too large. For example, for a monthly time interval and a time period of 15 years, the number of nodes will be $2^{(12 \times 15)} = 1.5 \times 10^{54}$! Such a binomial lattice is path dependent, with the interest rate at any time period depending on the number of

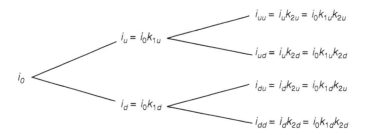

Figure 9.2 **Two period binomial model of the one period interest rate**

up moves from the start of the lattice and the order in which the up moves occur.

In order to make this problem manageable it is common to assume in the binomial lattice that an up followed by a down movement in interest rates results in the same value for future interest rates as a down followed by an up movement. A lattice that has this feature recombines and, because the values of future interest rates depend on only the number of up movements in interest rates, the lattice is path independent. The requirement for the lattice to recombine in a 2 period model is that $i_{ud} = i_{du}$ or that $k_{1u}k_{2d} = k_{1d}k_{2u}$. Under this assumption the number of nodes in the lattice will increase by only 1 over each time period so that after n time intervals the number of nodes will be $(n + 1)$. One method of ensuring that the nodes recombine is to set $\dfrac{k_{iu}}{k_{id}} = c$, a constant for all time periods i.

This binomial model is used to value interest rate derivatives by applying an arbitrage free requirement. Assume that the investments currently available in the market are a one period investment yielding a return of i_0 and 2 bonds with different maturities whose returns over the next time period depend on the one period interest rate in period 2. These bonds can have any maturities, with the key assumption that both bonds have values at the end of the period that are functions only of the one period interest. Assume that the current price of 1 of the bonds is known and the other is to be determined. Figure 9.3 illustrates the information that is assumed to be known.

Consider the following strategy. Borrow an amount of L dollars for one period at the one period interest rate and use this to purchase Δ units of bond 2 each for a price of B_2. The amount of the borrowing and the number of units of bond 2 will be determined so that the net amount of this strategy at the end of the first period will equal the value of bond 1 regardless of whether interest rates rise or fall. The portfolio of borrowing

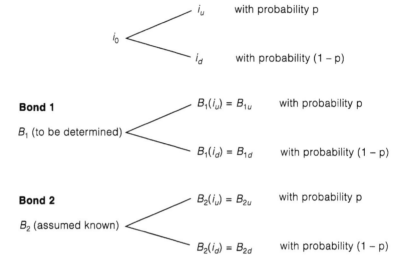

Figure 9.3   One period interest rates

and investing in bond 2 is the 'hedge portfolio', since this portfolio will be designed to hedge against movements in the value of bond 1.

This gives 2 equations to solve with 2 unknowns (L and Δ) as follows:

$$\Delta B_{2u} - L(1 + i_0) = B_{1u}$$

and:

$$\Delta B_{2d} - L(1 + i_0) = B_{1d}$$

for which the solutions are:

$$\Delta = \frac{B_{1u} - B_{1d}}{B_{2u} - B_{2d}}$$

and:

$$L = \frac{1}{1 + i_0} \left[\frac{B_{2d}B_{1u} - B_{1d}B_{2u}}{B_{2u} - B_{2d}} \right]$$

The strategy of borrowing and investing in bond 2 (the hedge portfolio) has been designed to produce the same value in 1 period as for bond 1. If the values of bond 1 and bond 2 are to be arbitrage free then the current value of this strategy must equal the current value of bond 1. In other words:

$$B_1 = \Delta B_2 - L$$

and substituting the expressions for L and Δ will give the value of bond 1 in terms of known values as follows:

$$B_1 = \left[\frac{B_{1u} - B_{1d}}{B_{2u} - B_{2d}} \right] B_2 - \frac{1}{1 + i_0} \left[\frac{B_{2d}B_{1u} - B_{1d}B_{2u}}{B_{2u} - B_{2d}} \right]$$

Rearranging gives:

$$B_1 = \frac{1}{1 + i_0} \left[\left\{ \frac{(1 + i_0) B_2 - B_{2d}}{B_{2u} - B_{2d}} \right\} B_{1u} + \left\{ \frac{B_{2u} - (1 + i_0) B_2}{B_{2u} - B_{2d}} \right\} B_{1d} \right]$$

$$= \frac{1}{1 + i_0} \left[pB_{1u} + qB_{1d} \right]$$

where:

$$p = \left\{ \frac{(1 + i_0) B_2 - B_{2d}}{B_{2u} - B_{2d}} \right\}$$

and:

$$q = \left\{ \frac{B_{2u} - (1 + i_0) B_2}{B_{2u} - B_{2d}} \right\}$$

with:

$$p + q = 1$$

This shows that the value of a bond can be written as an expected value of the bond values at the end of the next time period, present valued by the one period spot interest rate for the next time period. The expected value is calculated using special probabilities based on the price and price movements of another bond.

The important point is that the binomial model will value bonds consistently, so that no arbitrage profits can be made, if the value of bonds is determined by taking the expected bond value at the end of each node, using appropriately determined probabilities, and present valuing at the one period spot interest rate for that node.

In general this procedure applies at all nodes in the lattice and, provided the future cash flows on the bond are known at each node, they can be present valued in this manner by working back down the lattice. Such a procedure, that starts at the maturity date of the bond and works backward down the lattice, is referred to as 'backward recursion'.

Provided the probabilities on the binomial model are determined correctly, the backward recursion procedure can be used to value any set of cash flows whose values depend on the interest rates in the lattice. This includes bonds, swaptions, caps, floors and interest rate swaps. These models are therefore quite general in their application.

Example 9.2

Assume that interest rate derivatives can be valued with the binomial model of one period interest rates in example 9.1 so that over any time period the one period interest rates can either increase by a factor of 1.15 or decrease by a factor of 0.95 with equal probability. The current interest rate is 6% per period.

(a) Calculate, using backward recursion, the value of a bond paying a coupon of $6 per period, at the end of each period, and $100 on maturity at the end of 3 periods.
(b) Calculate the value of a security that pays the greater of the bond value determined in (a) minus $100 and zero at the end of each period for 3 periods—that is, the security pays max $(A - B, 0)$ at the end of each period where A = the bond price immediately after the coupon has been paid and $B = 100$.

Solution

(a) The cash flows on the bond at each node, where node (A) is the current date, nodes (B) and (C) are at the end of the first year and nodes (D), (E) and (F) are at the end of the second year, are as follows:

		Node (D) 6 _____ 100 + 6
	Node (B) 6	
Node (A)		Node (E) 6 _____ 100 + 6
	Node (C) 6	
		Node (F) 6 _____ 100 + 6

The value of the bond at the end of the third year is 106 immediately prior to maturity, and immediately prior to payment of the last coupon, regardless of the level of interest rates over the third year. Backward recursion is used to derive the values at each of the nodes using the discounted expected value formula. The procedure starts at the maturity date and works sequentially back through the lattice to the current date. The values are:

Node (D):

$$Value = \frac{1}{1.07935}\left[\frac{1}{2}\{106 + 106\}\right]$$

$$= 98.20725$$

Node (E):

$$Value = \frac{1}{1.06555}\left[\frac{1}{2}\{106 + 106\}\right]$$

$$= 99.47914$$

Node (F):

$$Value = \frac{1}{1.05415}\left[\frac{1}{2}\{106 + 106\}\right]$$

$$= 100.55495$$

Node (B):

$$\text{Value} = \frac{1}{1.069}\left[\frac{1}{2}\{(98.20725 + 6) + (99.47914 + 6)\}\right]$$

$$= 98.07595$$

Node (C):

$$\text{Value} = \frac{1}{1.057}\left[\frac{1}{2}\{(99.47914 + 6) + (100.55495 + 6)\}\right]$$

$$= 100.29995$$

and finally node (A) gives the value of the bond:

$$\text{Value} = \frac{1}{1.06}\left[\frac{1}{2}\{(98.07595 + 6) + (100.29995 + 6)\}\right]$$

$$= 99.23392$$

(b) The cash flows to be valued on this security are as follows:

Node (D)　　max. $(100 - 100,0) = 0$
max. $(98.20725 - 100,0) = 0$

Node (B)
max. $(98.07595 - 100,0) = 0$

Node (A)　　　　　　Node (E)　　max. $(100 - 100,0) = 0$
max. $(99.47914 - 100,0) = 0$

Node (C)
max. $(100.29995 - 100,0) = 0.2995$

Node (F)　　max. $(100 - 100,0) = 0$
max. $(100.55495 - 100,0) = 0.55495$

Then the value is determined using backward recursion as in (a). The values at nodes (D), (E) and (F) are clearly zero as is the value at node (B), since the cash flows being valued are zero regardless of movements in interest rates.
For node (C) the value is:

$$\text{Value} = \frac{1}{1.057}\left[\frac{1}{2}\{(0) + (0.55495)\}\right]$$

$$= 0.26251$$

and the value at node (A), adding in the payment at that node, is then:

$$\text{Value} = \frac{1}{1.06}\left[\frac{1}{2}\{(0) + (0.26251 + 0.2995)\}\right]$$

$$= 0.2651$$

Any interest rate derivative or interest rate dependent security can be valued using this procedure provided the payoff at each node can be determined from the contractual provisions of the security.

Parameters of the binomial interest rate model

The parameters for the binomial model are the probabilities of up movements in one period interest rates and the size of the up and down movements in one period interest rates. In practice the parameters are usually chosen so that the model will value zero coupon bonds for maturities at the end of each time period consistently with market values. The spot interest rates on bonds for each maturity are used as input. These spot interest rates are derived from the yields of traded coupon or par bonds using the techniques covered in chapter 6.

For interest rate derivatives it is important to ensure that the variances of interest rates and bond prices in the model are consistent with the variability of interest rates and bond prices actually observed. For this purpose historical estimates of the variance could be used to fit the parameters or the variance parameter could be estimated from traded interest rate derivative prices. For example, the assumption could be made that the logarithm of the one period interest rate is normally distributed with a constant variance equal to σ^2, and this could be estimated from historical data. In practice the data available for estimating volatility are historical bond prices and forward interest rates, as well as option prices for bond options and forward interest rate contracts. It is necessary to construct the interest rate lattice so that the volatility of the one period interest rates is consistent with the observed volatility of bond prices and forward interest rates. This can be done directly by constructing a lattice for forward interest rates or bond prices. The procedure used here is based on a one period spot interest rate lattice. In practice more advanced models are often used, based on forward rates. Also the interest rate model illustrated here assumes interest rates are subject to a single random 'shock' over any time period. In practice a model with at least 2 or 3 random 'shocks' is required for a realistic model. The underlying ideas are similar to those developed here but also more complex.

The procedure used to fit the probabilities is referred to as forward recursion. In this procedure the parameters for each time period are fitted by working forward from the current time period to the ultimate time period in the lattice.

Consider the following binomial lattice of one period interest rates, where all rates are per period per dollar rates:

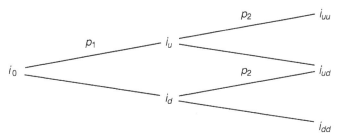

The probability of an up move in interest rates is p_1 in period 1 and p_2 in period 2 and these are to be determined. The sizes of the up and down jumps in each period are also to be determined and the lattice is required to recombine for ease of computation. There are many different ways of selecting these parameters. In practice the following selection for a multiplicative interest rate model is often used:

$$p_1 = p_2 = \frac{1}{2}$$
$$i_u = i_d \, e^{\sigma_2}$$
$$i_{ud} = i_{dd} \, e^{\sigma_3}$$
$$i_{uu} = i_{ud} \, e^{\sigma_3}$$

where σ_t is the per period (proportionate) volatility of the one period spot rate for time period t which is determined from historical data or from interest rate option volatilities. This selection of parameters ensures that the lattice recombines and has the property that the values of interest rate derivatives will approach the theoretical value as the size of the time interval in the binomial lattice gets smaller. The binomial model with these parameters is an approximation of a lognormal distribution of the one period interest rate.

The yields to maturity on 1, 2 and 3 period zero coupon bonds will be denoted by y_1, y_2 and y_3. The corresponding values of the zero coupon bonds maturing in 1, 2 and 3 periods will be denoted by B_1, B_2 and B_3, respectively.

The value of a 1 period zero coupon bond, paying \$1 in 1 time period, using the lattice will be:

$$\frac{1}{1 + i_0} \{p_1 1 + (1 - p_1)1\} = \frac{1}{2} \frac{1}{(1 + i_0)} + \frac{1}{2} \frac{1}{(1 + i_0)} = \frac{1}{1 + i_0}$$

The 1 period zero coupon bond can be considered as consisting of 2 basic interest rate derivative securities or 'primitive' securities. These 2 primitive securities are a derivative that pays \$1 if interest rates rise and zero otherwise, plus a derivative that pays \$1 if interest rates fall and zero otherwise. Denote the value of these derivatives by G_u and G_d, respectively, so that:

$$G_u = p_1 \frac{1}{1+i_0} = \frac{1}{2} \frac{1}{(1+i_0)}$$

$$G_d = (1-p_1) \frac{1}{1+i_0} = \frac{1}{2} \frac{1}{(1+i_0)}$$

The value of the 1 period zero coupon bond determined from the model is required to be equal to the market price so that i_0 is determined and so that:

$$B_1 = G_u + G_d$$

The market value of this bond, using the yield to maturity is:

$$B_1 = \frac{1}{1+y_1}$$

Equating these indicates the value of i_0 in the lattice must be the 1 period zero coupon bond yield to maturity y_1.

The value of a 2 period zero coupon bond, paying \$1 in 2 periods, derived from the lattice by taking expected values and discounting, will be:

$$\frac{1}{1+i_0} \left[p_1 \left\{ \frac{1}{1+i_u} (p_2 1 + (1-p_2)1) \right\} + (1-p_1) \left\{ \frac{1}{1+i_d} (p_2 + (1-p_2)1) \right\} \right]$$

This can be rewritten term by term by expanding this expression to get:

$$p_1 p_2 \frac{1}{1+i_0} \frac{1}{1+i_u} + p_1(1-p_2) \frac{1}{1+i_0} \frac{1}{1+i_u}$$

$$+ (1-p_1) p_2 \frac{1}{1+i_0} \frac{1}{1+i_d} + (1-p_1)(1-p_2) \frac{1}{1+i_0} \frac{1}{1+i_d}$$

This can be seen to be the value of a portfolio of basic interest rate derivative contracts. These are: a derivative that pays \$1 if interest rates rise in both the first and second period and zero otherwise; plus a derivative that pays \$1 if interest rates rise in the first period and fall in the second period and zero otherwise; plus a derivative that pays \$1 if interest rates fall in the first period and rise in the second period and zero otherwise; plus a derivative that pays \$1 if interest rates fall in both the first and second periods. Denote the value of these derivatives as G_{uu}, G_{ud}, G_{du} and G_{dd} so that:

$$G_{uu} = p_1 p_2 \frac{1}{1+i_0} \frac{1}{1+i_u}$$

$$G_{ud} = p_1(1-p_2) \frac{1}{1+i_0} \frac{1}{1+i_u}$$

$$G_{du} = (1-p_1)(p_2) \frac{1}{(1+i_0)} \frac{1}{(1+i_d)}$$

$$G_{dd} = (1-p_1)(1-p_2) \frac{1}{(1+i_0)} \frac{1}{(1+i_d)}$$

These values are equal to the present value of $1 payable at the end of each path of interest rates in the lattice, multiplied by the probability of the path. These values can be written in terms of values determined for the first period and the parameters for the probabilities and up and down jumps as follows:

$$G_{uu} = G_u p_2 \frac{1}{1+i_u} = G_u \frac{1}{2} \frac{1}{(1+i_d e^{\sigma_2})}$$

$$G_{ud} = G_u(1-p_2) \frac{1}{1+i_u} = G_u \frac{1}{2} \frac{1}{(1+i_d e^{\sigma_2})}$$

$$G_{du} = G_d p_2 \frac{1}{1+i_d} = G_d \frac{1}{2} \frac{1}{(1+i_d)}$$

$$G_{dd} = G_d (1-p_2) \frac{1}{1+i_d} = G_d \frac{1}{2} \frac{1}{(1+i_d)}$$

The value of the 2 period zero coupon bond from the lattice will be:

$$B_2 = G_{uu} + G_{ud} + G_{du} + G_{dd}$$

where the only parameter that is not known in this value is that for i_d, since all parameters have been specified (p_1, p_2 and σ_2) or solved for in the first period (G_u and G_d).

The value of this bond using the zero coupon yield curve is:

$$B_2 = \frac{1}{(1+y_2)^2}$$

Equating these 2 gives the equation for solving for i_d that fits the zero coupon yield curve. In this case the equation is non-linear in i_d and this must be solved using an iterative method such as the Newton-Raphson or secant method. Note that additive binomial models do not require a numerical solution method.

The procedure is the same for the next period. A 3 period zero coupon bond paying $1 on maturity will have a value derived from the lattice given by:

$$\frac{1}{1+i_0} \left\{ p_1 \left[\frac{1}{1+i_u} \left(p_2 \left\{ \frac{1}{1+i_{uu}} [p_3 1 + (1-p_3)1] \right\} + \right. \right. \right.$$

$$\left. (1-p_2) \left\{ \frac{1}{1+i_{ud}} [p_3 1 + (1-p_3)1] \right\} \right) \right] +$$

$$(1-p_1) \left[\frac{1}{1+i_d} \left(p_2 \left\{ \frac{1}{1+i_{ud}} [p_3 1 + (1-p_3)1] \right\} + \right. \right.$$

$$\left. \left. (1-p_2) \left\{ \frac{1}{1+i_{dd}} [p_3 1 + (1-p_3)1] \right\} \right) \right\}$$

which can be written in terms of the basic interest rate derivative contracts as previously. These values are determined from the previous periods' values and the parameters of the lattice. The only parameter to be solved for is i_{dd}, which is determined by equating the model value for the 3 period zero coupon bond and the value from the zero coupon yield curve given by:

$$B_3 = \frac{1}{(1+y_3)^3}$$

This procedure is repeated recursively to the longest maturity required. In practice it is readily programmed using a computer. The benefit of deriving the values for the basic interest rate derivative contracts, denoted by G, is that these can then be used to value other derivative securities since any interest rate derivative will be a portfolio of these basic contracts. The only contracts that will require special treatment are American early exercise options and other exotic interest rate options.

Example 9.3

The zero coupon bond yields given in table 9.3 are available in the market.

Table 9.3   Market yields

Term (months)	Yield to maturity y (% p.a. semi-annual)
1	6.0
2	6.1
3	6.2

The annualised (proportionate) volatility for monthly spot interest rates for future monthly periods given in table 9.4 are assumed to have been determined from interest rate option volatility data.

Table 9.4   One period interest rate volatility

Period (months)	Volatility (% p.a.)
1	n.a.
2	20
3	15

Note: To convert annualised volatility to monthly volatility, multiply by the square root of the time interval so that for a 1 month volatility the annualised volatility is multiplied by $\sqrt{\frac{1}{12}}$.

Use these data and a multiplicative binomial model, with probability of a half, to fit the parameters for a recombining interest rate lattice for the 1 month spot interest rate in order to derive the prices of the basic interest rate derivative contracts (primitive securities). Express the interest rates in the lattice as p.a. semi-annual compounding yields.

Solution

The initial value of the 1 month interest rate in the lattice will be the first period zero coupon yield. Hence $i_0 = 6.0\%$ p.a. The basic interest rate securities have values:

$$G_u = \frac{1}{2}\left(1 + \frac{6}{200}\right)^{-2 \times \frac{1}{12}} = 0.497543$$

$$G_d = \frac{1}{2}\left(1 + \frac{6}{200}\right)^{-2 \times \frac{1}{12}} = 0.497543$$

For the second period $\sigma_2 = 20\sqrt{\frac{1}{12}} = 5.7735\%$ or 0.057735 so that:

$$G_{uu} = G_u \frac{1}{2}\frac{1}{1 + i_d e^{\sigma_2}} = 0.248771 \frac{1}{1 + i_d e^{0.057735}}$$

$$G_{ud} = G_u \frac{1}{2}\frac{1}{1 + i_d e^{\sigma_2}} = 0.248771 \frac{1}{1 + i_d e^{0.057735}}$$

$$G_{du} = G_d \frac{1}{2}\frac{1}{1 + i_d} = 0.248771 \frac{1}{1 + i_d}$$

$$G_{dd} = G_d \frac{1}{2}\frac{1}{1 + i_d} = 0.248771 \frac{1}{1 + i_d}$$

so that from the lattice:

$$B_2 = G_{uu} + G_{ud} + G_{du} + G_{dd} = 0.497543 \left\{ \frac{1}{1 + i_d e^{0.057735}} + \frac{1}{1 + i_d} \right\}$$

Note that since the lattice recombines, the primitive securities that pay $1 if one period interest rates rise and fall or fall and rise have the same payoff so that they can be combined for valuation purposes.

The value of the 2 period zero coupon bond from the yield curve is:

$$B_2 = \frac{1}{\left(1 + \frac{6.1}{200}\right)^{2 \times \frac{2}{12}}} = 0.990035$$

These 2 are equated and solved numerically, using a spreadsheet, to get $i_d = 0.004954$ which is a per month per dollar rate so that, on a % p.a. semi-annual compounding basis, it is equal to:

$$200 \times \{(1 + 0.004954)^6 - 1\} = 6.0190\% \text{ p.a.}$$

This gives $i_u = i_d e^{0.057735} = 0.005248$ and a % p.a. semi-annual compounding equivalent of 6.3814% p.a.

This procedure is repeated for the next period. The following figures are taken from a spreadsheet used to calculate the model values:

Zero coupon bond prices	0.9950856	0.9900353	0.9848513

Primitive security values

			$G_{uuu} = 0.1230602$
		$G_{uu} = 0.2474726$	
	$G_u = 0.4975428$		$0.3692736 = G_{uud} + G_{udu}$
1		$0.4950176 = G_{ud} + G_{du}$	
	$G_d = 0.4975428$		$0.3693655 = G_{dud} + G_{ddu}$
		$G_{dd} = 0.2475451$	
			$G_{ddd} = 0.1231521$

One period spot interest rate lattice
(per month, per dollar)

		$i_{uu} = 0.0054941$
	$i_u = 0.0052485$	
$i_0 = 0.0049386$		$i_{ud} = 0.0052613$
	$i_d = 0.004954$	
		$i_{dd} = 0.0050383$

One period spot interest rate lattice
(% p.a. semi-annual compounding)

		6.6841
	6.3814	
6.0000		6.3972
	6.0190	
		6.1226

Example 9.4

Use the interest rate model in example 9.3 to value a derivative that guarantees that the minimum interest rate earned by an investor on a 1 month discount security in 2 months' time with face value $500 000 will be the monthly equivalent of 6.5% p.a. (semi-annual). Note that this derivative is referred to as an interest rate floor agreement.

Solution

The model interest rates in 2 months for a 1 month investment will be 6.6841%, 6.3972% or 6.1226%. The value of the $500 000 face value 1 month discount security at 6.6841% will be:

$$500\ 000 \left(1 + \frac{6.6841}{200}\right)^{-2 \times \frac{1}{12}} = 497\ 205.09$$

and in this case the derivative pays zero. The values at each of the other rates will be 497 383.11 and 497 493.49. The value of the discount security at 6.5% is 497 341.84. In order to guarantee a rate of 6.5% a payment of $497\ 383.11 - 497\ 341.84 = 41.27$ will be made to the investor if the interest rate is 6.3972% and a payment of $497\ 493.49 - 497\ 341.84 = 151.65$ will be made if the interest rate is 6.1226%. The value of these payments can be determined in a number of ways. The simplest method is to recognise it as a portfolio of the basic interest rate derivatives and to multiply the payoffs by the values of the basic interest rate derivatives and then sum to get:

$$0 \times 0.2474726 + 41.27 \times 0.4950176 + 151.65 \times 0.2475451 = 57.97$$

The value can be determined by calculating expected values and discounting using backward recursion down the lattice. In this case the value will be:

$$\frac{1}{1.0049386}\left[\frac{1}{2}\frac{1}{1.0052485}\left\{\frac{1}{2}\times 0 + \frac{1}{2}\times 41.27\right\}\right.$$

$$\left. +\frac{1}{2}\frac{1}{1.004954}\left\{\frac{1}{2}\times 41.27 + \frac{1}{2}\times 151.65\right\}\right] = 57.97$$

which agrees with the first method.

Simulation

For some valuation problems a path dependent lattice of interest rates is required. In these situations the binomial model involves too many nodes, since they grow exponentially in this case, and cannot be computed efficiently, if at all. One approach to avoiding this problem is to use simulation. Simulation is usually used to value interest-sensitive cash flows using path-wise valuation. In this approach the interest rates are generated randomly for each path and the cash flows of the derivative as a function of the generated interest rates are determined. These cash flows are then present valued back to the current time along this same path. This procedure is repeated many times, 1000 or 10 000 times being common, and the resulting value averaged since each path is generated to be equally likely.

The parameters used to simulate the interest rates are determined by using the procedure to value zero coupon bonds for different maturities and selecting parameters that produce values that are consistent with market values. This approach is similar to the valuation procedure for the binomial lattice covered earlier, except that only a random sample of paths is used in the simulation valuations.

In practice it is usually assumed that one period interest rates have either a normal or a lognormal distribution. The lognormal model has the advantage of automatically excluding negative one period interest rates.

Exchange-traded interest rate options

Interest rate derivatives are available in both the over-the-counter market and on futures and options exchanges around the world. In Australia the major exchange-traded interest rate option contracts are those on the Sydney Futures Exchange (SFE). These contracts are options on the interest rate futures contracts on the SFE. Options are available on the 90 day BAB, the 3 year Treasury bond and the 10 year Treasury bond futures contracts. Because the option contracts expire at practically the same time as the underlying futures contract, they are equivalent to an option on the forward value of the underlying asset. The options are quoted in points of premium. The actual dollar premium is determined by calculating the value of a basis point for the underlying futures contract at the strike yield and multiplying this by the points of premium. The price value of a basis point is determined by calculating the value of the futures contract at the exercise yield and then the value for an increase in the exercise yield of 1 basis point (0.01%). The exercise yield is (100-exercise price) since SFE interest rate futures are quoted as (100-yield). SFE options on futures are settled using a futures-style margining system where the value of the option contract is marked to market each day. Under this system the option premium is effectively paid on the expiration date of the contract.

Example 9.5

A 3 year bond option contract on the SFE has an exercise price of 91.60 and is quoted at a premium of 0.25. Calculate the premium in dollars.

Solution

The value of the futures contract at the exercise price is:

$$6000a_{\overline{6}|} + 100\,000v^6 \text{ at } (100 - 91.60)/2 \text{ or } 4.2\%$$

$$= 109\,374.7182$$

Increasing the p.a. exercise yield by 0.01% to 8.41% is equivalent to decreasing the quoted price by 0.01 to 91.59 and this gives a futures contract value of:

$$6000a_{\overline{6}|} + 100\,000v^6 \text{ at } (100 - 91.59)/2 \text{ or } 4.205\%$$

$$= 109\,347.1611$$

The value of a basis point is the difference of 27.5571 so that the premium in dollars will be 25 points of premium times the value of a basis point:

$$25 \times 27.5571 = \$688.93$$

Options on futures contracts are on the forward value of the underlying asset and are settled using the futures margining system on the expiry date. Futures contracts provide no income during the option life, unlike physical assets. The value of the SFE futures option contracts can be calculated with a modified Black–Scholes formula allowing for these factors. For a call option the formula is:

■ *Equation 9.3*

$$c = FN(d_1) - XN(d_2)$$

where:

- $d_1 = \dfrac{\ln\left(\dfrac{F}{X}\right) + \dfrac{\sigma^2}{2}T}{\sigma\sqrt{T}},$
- $d_2 = d_1 - \sigma\sqrt{T},$
- F is the value of the futures contract at the current futures price,
- X is the exercise value of the futures contract at the exercise price,
- T is the time to maturity in years, and
- σ is the volatility of the futures value.

Note that this formula assumes that the futures price has a lognormal distribution.

Example 9.6

Calculate the premium for a 3 month 10 year SFE futures bond option with exercise price of 91.00. The current futures price is 91.50. Use a volatility of 5% for the futures price.

Solution

The exercise value of the 10 year futures bond option is:

$$6000a_{\overline{20}|} + 100\,000v^{20} \text{ at } (100 - 91)/2\% \text{ or } 4.5\%$$

$$= 119\,511.90$$

The current value of the 10 year futures contract is:

$$6000a_{\overline{20}|} + 100\,000v^{20} \text{ at } (100 - 91.50)/2\% \text{ or } 4.25\%$$

$$= 123\,265.14$$

$$d_1 = \frac{\ln(119\,511.90/112\,462.21) + \dfrac{1}{2}(0.05)^2\dfrac{3}{12}}{0.05\sqrt{\dfrac{3}{12}}} = 2.4444$$

$$d_2 = d_1 - 0.05\sqrt{\frac{3}{12}} = 2.4194$$

$$N(d_1) = 0.99275$$

$$N(d_2) = 0.99223$$

$$c = 123\,265.14 \times 0.99275 - 119\,511.90 \times 0.99223 = 3789.07$$

The price value of a basis point of premium at the exercise price of 91.00 is $119\,511.90 - 119\,438.44 = 73.46$ so that the premium is $3789.07/73.46 = 51.6$ points of premium or 0.516.

Bond options and swaptions

A bond option has a payoff equal to $(B - X)^+$ for a call option and $(X - B)^+$ for a put option where B is the bond value on the exercise date and X is the value of the bond at the exercise yield to maturity. Over-the-counter bond options are contracts on actual physical bonds. These contracts are different from options on SFE futures, since the underlying bond pays coupons during the life of the option. They are also not settled using a futures-style margining system. The Black–Scholes formula is often used in practice to value these options with an adjustment for the coupon payments during the life of the option. These options can also be valued using the binomial lattice method set out in this chapter. One of the problems with using the Black–Scholes formula, despite its common use for bond options, is that the formula assumes that interest rates are known and constant. If this were the case then bond prices would not change and there would be no need for bond options. This means that there is an inconsistency in using the Black–Scholes formula for these options. The Black–Scholes formula also assumes that the bond price has a lognormal distribution which is only an approximation for bond prices.

A swaption is an option on a swap contract. The exercise yield in the swaption is the swap rate that will apply to the fixed rate in the swap. Because a swap is equivalent to swapping a fixed rate bond with a coupon rate equal to the swap rate for a floating rate bond with present value equal to the notional principal of the swap, a swaption is identical to a bond option.

Example 9.7

Calculate the value of a 6 month European put option with a strike yield to maturity of 8.0% p.a. (semi-annual compounding) on a $100 000 face value 10% p.a. semi-annual coupon 6.25 year maturity bond, assuming that a coupon is due in 3 months. Three and 6 month interest rates are 6.5% and 6.75% p.a. (simple), respectively, the bond has a current market yield to maturity of 8.5% p.a. and the proportionate bond price volatility is assumed to be 10% p.a.

Solution

The value of the put option using the Black–Scholes formula will be:

$$p = X \frac{1}{\left(1 + \frac{6}{12} \times 0.0675\right)} N(-d_2) - B^* N(-d_1)$$

where the current bond price is reduced by the value of the coupon due before the expiration date to get:

$$B^* = (1.0425)^{-3/6} [5000 (1 + a_{\overline{12}|}) + 100\,000 v^{12} \text{ at } 4.25\%]$$

$$-5000 \frac{1}{(1 + \frac{3}{12} \times 0.065)} = 109\,632.35 - 4920.05$$

$$= 104\,712.30$$

$$X = (1.04)^{-3/6} [5000 (1 + a_{\overline{11}|}) + 100\,000 v^{11} \text{ at } 4.0\%]$$

$$= 111\,551.33 \text{ using the strike yield}$$

$$X \frac{1}{(1 + \frac{6}{12} \times 0.0675)} = 107\,909.38$$

$$d_1 = \frac{\ln(104\,712.30/107\,909.38) + \frac{1}{2}(0.1)^2 \frac{6}{12}}{0.1 \sqrt{\frac{6}{12}}} = -0.38997$$

$$d_2 = d_1 - 0.1 \sqrt{\frac{6}{12}} = -0.46068$$

$$N(-d_2) = 0.6774$$

$$N(-d_1) = 0.6517$$

so the value of the bond put option is:

$$p = 107\,909.38 \times 0.6774 - 104\,712.30 \times 0.6517 = \$4856.81$$

Caps and floors

Caps are agreements that place an upper limit on the floating interest rate paid during the term of the cap. Floors place lower limits on the floating interest rate that applies during the term of the floor. Caps and floors are options on interest rates. In practice, caps and floors are valued using the Black–Scholes option pricing formula adapted to forward interest rates. This formula assumes that interest rates have a lognormal distribution. It is important to determine the volatility for these caps and floors in a manner consistent with bond price and other interest rate volatility. Caps and floors can be readily valued using the binomial method covered in this chapter.

Callable and puttable bonds
(optional redemption dates)

Some bonds on issue in the international bond markets allow the borrower
to redeem the bond early. These bonds are callable at the borrower's
option. The borrower will pay an amount more than the face value to
redeem the bonds. If this amount is X, then it will pay to redeem the
bonds if the value of the bonds denoted by B is greater than X. The value
of the bonds, B, must reflect the value of the option for the investor to
redeem the bond on future dates as well as the value of the coupon and
maturity payments.

There are also bonds that allow the investor, or the lender, to redeem
the bond early at their option. These bonds are puttable bonds. In this case
the lender will put the bond to the borrower if the value of the bonds, B,
is less than the amount received if the bonds are redeemed.

Because of these call and put features these bonds have optional
redemption dates. The yield on these bonds is often quoted as the yield
to early redemption if it would pay to redeem the bond early, assuming
current conditions hold to the redemption date, or the yield to maturity
for the case where it does not pay to redeem early.

The option to redeem the bond must be valued allowing for the early
redemption options. This can be readily allowed for using a binomial
lattice for interest rates. The bond value can be calculated for future values
of interest rates on the lattice and these values are used to determine if it
is worth putting or calling the bond. The values of the bond allowing for
when it will pay to put or call the bond are calculated by taking expected
values and discounting backward down the lattice. Such a valuation
approach is readily programmed using a binomial model on a computer.

Glossary of securities

Glossary terms are in chapter order.

Short-term securities

Australian Treasury note a note issued by the Australian Government with 13 and 26 weeks to maturity at issue. They pay the face value on the maturity date with no separate interest or coupon payment. The difference between the price paid and the maturity value is the return on the security. Securities which pay only the face value on the maturity date are often referred to as discount securities. In the US, Treasury notes are long-term coupon-paying securities with maturities at issue of up to 10 years. The short-term US Treasury security equivalent to the Australian Treasury note is the US Treasury bill

bill of exchange a security that evidences a company or a bank promise to pay the face value of the bill on maturity. The company or bank giving the promise is called the acceptor of the bill. Bills of exchange are typically issued for 90 and 180 day maturities. On the sale of the security the seller endorses the back of the bill. They are also referred to as either commercial bills, which do not have a bank as acceptor or endorser, or bank bills, which do have a bank as an acceptor or endorser. If a bank is the acceptor then they are also referred to as Bankers' Acceptances. Bank Accepted Bills of Exchange are sometimes referred to as BABs in the Australian market

certificate of deposit a certificate evidencing a deposit at a bank which can be negotiable. The certificate specifies that the bank will pay the face value of the CD on maturity. Some CDs are interest bearing and pay the face value plus interest on the face value at a fixed rate on the maturity date. The face value and the interest rate (when the security is interest bearing) are specified on the certificate. Most Australian CDs pay only the face value on maturity and are discount securities. Most US CDs pay the face value plus a fixed interest payment

promissory note a note issued by a semigovernment organisation or large company for maturity of less than 1 year at issue. They pay the face value on maturity as for the Australian Treasury note. Also called 'one-name' paper since the seller does not endorse the back of the security when it is sold and hence only 1 name appears on the security (the issuer). Referred to as Commercial paper in the US market where these securities usually have less than 270 days to maturity at issue

Long-term securities

Australian Treasury bond a long-term security with a maturity at issue of more than 1 year (and generally up to 10 to 15 years). They pay half-yearly interest payments, called coupon payments, equal to the annual coupon (or interest) rate times the face value divided by 2. The face value is paid on the maturity date along with the final coupon. Coupons are paid on the fifteenth of the month on which interest falls due and the maturity payment is also paid on the fifteenth of the maturity month (in the year of maturity). Treasury bonds go 'ex-interest' 7 days prior to the interest payment, which means that the owner on that date receives the next coupon even if the security is sold to another investor. The buyer of an 'ex-interest' security does not receive the next coupon then due. These securities are priced using compound interest except when they have less than 6 months to maturity, when simple interest is used. US Treasury bonds are interest-bearing securities with 10 years or more to maturity at issue

Australian Treasury Indexed Bonds indexed bonds of the Australian Government are issued in capital-indexed and interest-indexed forms with maturities of between 10 and 20 years. Capital-indexed bonds pay the face value increased by the quarterly rates of change in the Consumer Price Index (CPI) on the maturity date. Interest is paid quarterly at a low fixed coupon rate (around 4% p.a.) times the indexed face value. Interest-indexed bonds pay a fixed face value on maturity and pay quarterly coupons equal to the quarterly rate of change in the CPI plus a fixed real interest rate. The quarterly rate of change in the CPI is determined as half the change in the CPI for the 6 months preceding the quarter for which the CPI change is being determined

Debentures and notes interest-bearing securities which pay fixed coupon payments at regular intervals and the face value on the maturity date. They are issued by companies. There are no standard frequencies and dates for interest payments which vary from security to security

Eurobonds interest-bearing securities paying regular interest payments (quarterly, semi-annually and annually) and the face value on maturity. They are issued in the Euromarkets which are markets dealing in foreign currencies, particularly the US dollar, outside the country of the currency in which the transaction is denominated

Floating Rate Notes securities that pay variable interest or coupon payments equal to a fixed margin over a specified floating rate, such as LIBOR (London Inter-Bank Offer Rate) or the bank bill rate. Interest payments are typically quarterly, semi-annually or annually. They pay the face value of the security on the maturity date. Interest-indexed securities are equivalent to a floating rate security with the rate of change in the CPI as the floating rate

indexed annuities securities that pay a stream of indexed payments as an annuity. The payment amount, which includes principal and interest, is indexed to an inflation index such as the CPI or AWE (average weekly earnings).

semigovernment bonds bonds issued by government-owned authorities. Many of these issues are currently made by Central Borrowing authorities such as the NSW Treasury Corporation. Most of these securities pay half-yearly interest (or coupons), usually on the first of the month in which interest is due. The face value is paid on the maturity date. Some of these securities pay interest quarterly and some are indexed bonds

zero coupon bonds the long-term equivalent of a discount security paying only the face value on the maturity date. The coupon payments are zero and hence the name. They are usually priced using compound interest

Futures and forwards

forward contract an agreement to buy, or to sell, a specific commodity, currency or financial instrument (the underlying asset) for a predetermined price (the forward price) on a fixed future date (the settlement date). The party who is the buyer in the forward contract is said to have a 'long' position and the party who is the seller is said to have a 'short' position. The net effective settlement payment (on the fixed future date) under a forward contract is the difference between the market value on the settlement date and the forward price for the underlying asset

forward rate agreement a standard agreement where 2 counterparties agree to compensate each other for the difference between a fixed interest rate and the then current market interest rate for a specified future period on a specified future date. One party is referred to as the borrower and the other as the lender. If the fixed interest rate exceeds the market rate then the borrower pays the lender and vice versa

futures contract a contract similar to a forward contract in that it is the standardised futures exchange equivalent of a forward contract. The main difference is that a futures contract is settled on a daily basis as the market value of the underlying asset changes by daily settlement payments, referred to as margin calls. This daily settlement practice is referred to as 'marking-to-market'

Swaps

bill swap a transaction whose cash flows are equivalent to those of a zero coupon security that is generated using a strip of futures contracts at varying future dates. They are usually priced using compound interest although they can also be priced using simple interest

cross currency swap an agreement between 2 counterparties to exchange prespecified principal and interest payments in 2 different currencies on prespecified dates

deposit or foreign exchange swap the simultaneous purchase and sale of a foreign currency with settlement for the purchase and the sale on different dates

interest rate swap an agreement between 2 counterparties to exchange interest payments in the same currency on specified dates based on specified interest rates. If 1 party pays a fixed interest rate and the other pays a floating or variable interest rate then the swap is referred to as a 'coupon swap'. If both parties pay a floating interest rate then the swap is referred to as a 'basis swap'

Options

American option a contract that gives the holder the right to buy (a call option) or sell (a put option) an underlying asset (a share, commodity, financial instrument, currency or futures contract) for a prespecified price (the strike or exercise price) on or before a prespecified future date (the expiration date)

call option a contract that gives the holder the right, but not the obligation, to buy an underlying asset for a prespecified price. The seller or writer of the contract must sell the underlying asset at the prespecified price if the holder exercises the option. Net effective payments under a call option, from the seller to the buyer, will be zero if the market price of the underlying asset on the exercise date is less than or equal to the exercise price or the difference between the market price and the exercise price if the market price is greater than the exercise price

convertible bond or note a bond or note with a fixed maturity, generally between 5 and 10 years, paying interest and principal with an option feature. The option feature allows the holder to convert the bond into a fixed number of ordinary shares (the conversion ratio) effectively at a fixed exercise price (the conversion price). Because of the option feature, convertible bond and note market yields can be 2% to 3% below non-convertible bond or note yields

European option a contract that gives the holder the right to buy (a call option) or sell (a put option) an underlying asset for a prespecified price which can only be exercised on the expiration date

exotic option a non-standard option. These include: Asian options, which are options on the average asset price, exchange rate or interest rate; Chooser options, which are options that allow the holder to select if they are put or call options; Lookback options, which have a payoff based on the maximum or minimum asset price or interest rate during the life of the option; and Barrier options, which can expire or come into effect if a specified price barrier is reached

put option a contract that gives the holder the right, but not the obligation, to sell an underlying asset for a prespecified price. The seller or writer of the contract must buy the underlying asset at the prespecified price if the holder exercises the option. Net effective payments under a put option, from the seller of the option to the holder of the option, will be zero if the market price of the underlying asset on the exercise date is greater than or equal to the exercise price or the difference between the exercise price and the market price if the market price is less than the exercise price

warrant a document that gives the owner the right, but not the obligation, to buy shares in a specific company for a fixed price on or before specific dates. These are often issued as detachable warrants with bonds. They are also referred to as company options. They differ from options in that options are written on existing shares and do not change the total shares on issue when exercised. Exercising warrants or company options results in a dilution effect

Interest rate derivatives

bond option an option to buy (a call) or sell (a put) a physical bond on a future date at a fixed exercise yield to maturity

cap agreement an agreement to compensate the holder whenever a floating rate of interest for a prespecified term exceeds a prespecified level during the life of the cap. The compensation is equal to the difference between the floating and fixed interest rates times the notional principal, provided this is positive

floor agreement an agreement to compensate the holder whenever a floating rate of interest for a prespecified term falls below a prespecified level during the life of the floor

interest rate futures option an option on an interest rate futures contract. In Australia these contracts are the 90 day BAB, 3 year bond and 10 year bond futures options. On the SFE these contracts have the same delivery months as the underlying futures contract and are equivalent to an option on the underlying instrument. The SFE contracts are settled using a futures-style margining system

swaption an option on a swap agreement that gives the holder the right to enter into an interest rate swap on the expiry date of the option at a fixed prespecified interest rate

Bibliography and further references

Anderson, T. J. (1987). *Currency and Interest Rate Hedging.* New York Institute of Finance, Prentice Hall.

Bierwag, G. O. (1987). *Duration Analysis: Managing Interest Rate Risk.* Cambridge, Massachusetts: Ballinger Publishing Company.

Bookstaber, Richard M. (1981). *Option Pricing and Strategies in Investing.* Reading, Massachusetts: Addison-Wesley.

Bookstaber, Richard M. (1985). *The Complete Investment Book.* Glenview, Illinois: Scott-Foresman & Company.

Cox, John C., Rubinstein, Mark (1985). *Options Markets.* Englewood Cliffs, New Jersey: Prentice Hall.

Daugaard, Dan, Valentine, Tom (1995). *Financial Risk Management.* HarperEducational (Australia).

Fabozzi, Frank J. (1988). *Fixed Income Mathematics.* Chicago, Illinois: Probus Publishing Company.

Fink, R. E., Feduniak, R. B. (1988). *Futures Trading: Concepts and Strategies.* New York Institute of Finance, Prentice Hall.

Hull, John (1993). *Options, Futures and Other Derivative Securities.* Prentice Hall International.

McCutcheon, J. J., Scott, W. F. (1986). *An Introduction to the Mathematics of Finance.* London: William Heinemann Ltd.

Manuell, Guy (1986). *Floating Down Under: Foreign Exchange in Australia.* Sydney: The Law Book Company.

Marshall, John (1989). *Money Equals Maths.* Sydney: Allen & Unwin.

Platt, R. B. (1986). *Controlling Interest Rate Risk.* New York: John Wiley & Sons.

Ritchken, Peter (1987). *Options: Theory, Strategy and Applications.* Glenview, Illinois: Scott Foresman & Company.

Stigum, Marcia (1983). *The Money Market.* Homewood, Illinois: Dow Jones-Irwin.

Walmsley, Julian (1988). *The New Financial Instruments.* New York: John Wiley & Sons.

Wilmott, Paul, Howison, Sam, Dewynne, Jeff (1995). *The Mathematics of Financial Derivatives: A Student Introduction.* Cambridge: Cambridge University Press.

Index

For Product Safety Concerns and Information please contact our EU
representative GPSR@taylorandfrancis.com
Taylor & Francis Verlag GmbH, Kaufingerstraße 24, 80331 München, Germany

www.ingramcontent.com/pod-product-compliance
Ingram Content Group UK Ltd.
Pitfield, Milton Keynes, MK11 3LW, UK
UKHW020958180425
457613UK00019B/738